Acting Out

ACTING OUT

Coping with Big City Schools

Roland W. Betts

With an Introduction by John Holt

Little, Brown and Company BOSTON TORONTO

FIRST EDITION
T 06/78

Library of Congress Cataloging in Publication Data

Betts, Roland W
    Acting out.

    1. Public schools — United States. 2. Students —
United States. I. Title.
LA217.B47   371'.01'0973   78-4131
ISBN 0-316-09232-0

Design by Chris Benders

*Published simultaneously in Canada
by Little, Brown & Company (Canada) Limited*

PRINTED IN THE UNITED STATES OF AMERICA

Acknowledgments

The author is grateful to Dodd, Mead and Company, publishers of *The Complete Poems of Paul Lawrence Dunbar*, for permission to quote from Paul Lawrence Dunbar's "The Party," and to Mr. Roy Blount for permission to use his lyrics, which appear on page 166.

To Lois, my wife
Mags and Jessie, my daughters
and Roy, my friend

Introduction

THIS IS A VERY FUNNY, sad, unsparing, compassionate, and frightening account of the lives of people, both students and adults, in the
public schools of one of our great cities.

It may well be that when the book appears school people all over
the country will say, "Oh, that's just New York; hell, what did you
expect, the rest of us aren't like that." We should take all such
remarks with a great deal of salt. People who have worked in other
school systems or been students in them tell us, and the figures
back them up, that the New York City schools are no worse than,
and not much different from, the systems of most other big cities,
and are indeed better than some. We may therefore take this book
as a very accurate description of urban mass education and mass
schooling in the United States — a failure and a disaster.

It may seem odd or mistaken to call compassionate such a damn-
ing and devastating book. But Mr. Betts does not divide the people
he describes into heroes and villains. Only one of them, the head

custodian who confiscated, stole, and sold the rug that one teacher had bought with his own money and put in his classroom to make it slightly more comfortable and welcoming to the students, comes across to me as wholly unlikable, without any redeeming virtues at all. The others may be foolish, irritating if not maddening, and absurd; but not hateful. At least from the safe distance of the reader, it is hard not to feel for many of them a wry and amused affection. It seems very possible that many or even most of them, when they first came into the schools to work, in whatever capacity, wanted (in Mr. Betts's words) "to do good." If instead, and usually very quickly, they have learned to do bad, it is because of the institution they work in. It is clear that in the schools Mr. Betts describes, no one, whether teacher, custodian, counselor, secretary, or principal, can do good work, the work he is supposed to do, is paid to do, and (at least at first) wanted to do. Anyone trying to do good work will soon be driven crazy by endless obstacles and distractions. The best people can do, and what almost all of them do, is to fall back on strategies of personal survival, that is, to ask — "How do I keep from going nuts in this place?" But a building full of people who spend most of their time trying to keep from going crazy, itself becomes crazy, like something invented by Kafka. The schools are caught in a vicious downward cycle. They can't be reformed from the top, as the short career of Chancellor Harvey Scribner, a determined, resourceful, and tough-minded administrator, makes clear. And they certainly can't be reformed from the bottom. Note that Mr. Betts points out that the Open Corridor movement in New York's elementary schools, into which a great many teachers put much time and effort, and which I myself strongly supported, was by 1976 "out of fashion and out of sight." In such places, all such reforms have short lives.

It is also clear from this account that the schools of New York City have not been made better, and are not likely to be made better, by the device of "community control," at least, not as now defined by the laws of New York State. In the first place, the idea that a school (or anything else) *can* be responsive to and democratically controlled by a "community" of twenty thousand or more persons is an absurdity. For a few dozen families to run democratically a school of less than a hundred kids is an extraordinarily difficult and demanding job, and takes just about all the time, energy, and ability they have. Community control of large school systems, as Mr. Betts makes plain, means that the schools will be run by the loudest shouters and the cleverest schemers, the ones who learn best how to manipulate the machinery of control. Beyond that, just as the regulatory agencies of the federal government were quickly taken over by the industries they were supposed to regulate, because no one else was willing to give them so much time and serious attention, so the community school boards in New York City were quickly taken over, at least wherever it seemed worth making the effort, by the very teachers' union whose power they were supposed to counterbalance.

In the same way, the idea that parents could make better schools by going down to the school building and raising hell any time the school did something they did not like has completely backfired. The parents who went down to raise hell were in many, or perhaps even most, cases not those with the most legitimate grievances, but simply people who liked to raise hell, or had nothing else to do but raise hell, and whose children were more often than not among those raising the most hell in school. The schools responded as they had to, and as anyone could have guessed they would: they simply set up more and more elaborate screens, most amusingly described by Mr. Betts, to hide and protect the teachers or administrators from the parents. These assure that no people, even those with wholly legitimate requests or grievances, can reach the school, and so make the schools even more remote, unresponsive, and irresponsible than ever. And so another vicious circle winds steadily downward.

Of all the people Mr. Betts describes, the children, for all their faults and problems, and whatever their reading scores may say, come across very strongly as the most lively, intelligent, and resourceful (dear Heaven, how resourceful!) people in the building. But I am unhappily reminded that when James Herndon described some years ago, in his book *The Way It Spozed to Be*, his own earlier teaching in a ghetto junior high school on the West Coast, he was able to make clear at the start that, though his readers might be disappointed, they were not going to hear about any violence — after all, as he said, these people he was writing about were *children*. But children have changed; many of even the youngest elementary school children in affluent suburbs are far more frequently and dangerously violent than they used to be. In the inner city the problem is far worse. Our big city schools are largely populated, and will be increasingly populated, by the children of the nonwhite poor, the youngest members and victims of a sick subculture of a sick society, obsessed by violence and the media-inspired worship of dominance, luxury, and power. This culture, or more accurately, anticulture, has done more harm to its members and victims, has fragmented, degraded, and corrupted them more than centuries of slavery and the most brutal repression were able to do. Every day this anticulture, in the person of the children, invades the schools. If the schools had a true and humane culture of their own, which they really understood, believed in, cared about, and lived by, as did the First Street School some years ago (of which more later), they might put up a stiff resistance, might even win some of the children over. But since the culture of the school is only a pale and somewhat more timid and genteel version of the culture of the street outside, and since in any case the adults are nowhere near as united in dealing with the children as the children are in resisting and fighting them, nothing changes. Far from being able to woo the children away from greed, envy, and violence, the schools cannot even protect them against each other.

Why would anyone want to go to such places? Perhaps more to the point, why should anyone have to go? I have a private reason for asking. Unlike most people, and as far as I know, unlike Mr. Betts, I do not believe in education, that is, in compulsory learning, in any form, in or out of school, nor in the part-time jailing of children to "make them learn." I would like to see compulsory school-attendance laws done away with. For some time now, individual parents, here and there in different parts of the country, have tried to take their children out of school on the grounds that they were not learning there, and with the help of their parents would learn more at home. Sometimes the courts have allowed this, more often not. Where they have not, it has usually been on the grounds that, however skillful the parents might be at teaching school subjects, and however high the test scores of their children might be, the parents could not in the nature of things provide the necessary socializing, civilizing, democratizing experience of going to school with large numbers of other children. Having read Mr. Betts, I cannot but wonder, on what grounds could any reasonable judge *compel* children to attend the kind of schools here described. Indeed, I hope his book may be one piece of ammunition, among others, for parents to use who are trying to get their children out of schools.

Another piece of ammunition might be *School Violence and Vandalism*, the report of the Subcommittee to Investigate Juvenile Delinquency of the Committee on the Judiciary of the United States Senate, Ninety-fourth Congress (copies of the report may be obtained from the office of Senator Birch Bayh, the chairman). It is in two parts. The first part, 599 pages, mostly closely printed, describes the extent of the problem, while the second part, 1074 pages, suggests possible ways of dealing with it. When we consider these ways against the background of the schools Mr. Betts describes, most of these proposals seem laughable. They would require a number of things the schools don't have and are not likely to get: much more money, a wide range of supporting social services, and above all, and most unlikely of all, a faculty and administration which was itself unified in spirit, organized, determined, efficient, and *competent*. Even then, any measures they might think up could and probably would be easily defeated as the students became more angry, better equipped (armed), and more resourceful.

Is there any hope, any remedy? Setting aside for the moment my strong conviction that all compulsory learning and compulsory schooling are by their very nature bad, and trying to see them through the eyes of the majority of people who believe in them, I think the answer is Yes, there is a slight hope. That is, I think there are some things that might be done, even within the framework of compulsory schooling, that might make these schools substantially less bad, less destructive for all the people in them, than they are now. Even Mr. Betts's grim account points toward remedies. He says that the children were at their best when they went *out* of the school, on trips into the city — it made very little difference where — or when making preparations for a party, that is, when doing real work, toward an objective they supported and understood. The party was real, and it was theirs, so they worked hard and sensibly to make it a good one. And their parents, though poor, cooked food for the party which was vastly better than anything the school served from its expensive kitchens.

To see more clearly what might be done, we must look to the experience of the First Street School, described by George Dennison in *The Lives of Children*. This was a very small, privately supported, free elementary school. Its twenty-three students were about evenly divided among white, Hispanic, and black. Most were poor. Many had come (from public schools) with long histories (considering their age) of learning problems, "acting out," trouble, and violence. At the First Street School they all got better, grew, and learned, most of them at a rate two or three times as fast as that of even good students in the public schools. And all this at a cost per pupil no greater than that spent by the public schools themselves. Why did this school work so much better? For many reasons, but this above all others: it was small.

Since early in this century, almost all the people who have run our schools have acted on the belief that the army, or the large industrial corporation, was the ideal model of the way to get things done. They thought that size, centralized management, specialized function, and clear lines of authority made for efficiency, and so they made and are still making our schools into giant educational factories. *Acting Out* describes for us the terminal illness, the death throes, of one of these factories, and by extension, of all of them. While they keep their present forms, these institutions cannot be saved, cannot be made kindly, or interesting, or responsive, or even minimally competent. The weight of their own past is too heavy on them. The people in them, from the top to the bottom, must spend too much of their time and energy protecting themselves against the enduring consequences of their own and other people's mistakes. If people insist — as they do — on compulsory schooling for their children, they must put these schools in new places, and organize them on the principle that even though all other things must remain the same, if the schools are made smaller they will become better.

Without any proof or possibility of proof, I assert that if all the adults *who now work* in the New York City (or in any other) public schools — administrators, secretaries, teachers, custodians, bus drivers, everyone — had their names put in a pool; and if names were drawn from that pool *at random* in groups of six; and if each of these groups of six randomly selected people were assigned a group of not more than one hundred children, of different ages, and were given some space to work in (preferably not in the present school buildings), and were told, "Okay, you're a school, work it out any way you can," 95 percent of these schools, and maybe all of them, would be better than almost any of the schools that now exist. This would be true even in their first year of wild confusion, and much more so later; for in these small schools, where everyone would know everyone else, where people would come together as people and not as the holders of jobs and players of roles and defenders of prerogatives, where everyone's work would have a purpose and all could see the purpose, where none could be shielded or hidden from the consequences of their acts, *people would learn from their experience and would get better at their work.* Most such minischools would not be as good as the First Street School, nor obtain such astonishing results, because only a fairly small minority of the people now working in the public schools are as intelligent, perceptive, compassionate, resourceful, strong, and patient as the people who worked at First Street. But the minischools would get steadily better. And those who could not learn to like or trust or deal with or teach children would either quit, or if they dared not quit, would get themselves (or be pushed) out of the way of the people doing the real teaching. More and more of the parents themselves would begin to enter a serious and fruitful partnership with the schools. They could see what the school was doing. If they didn't like it, they could argue for a while with the teachers responsible. If that didn't change anything, they could find another small school that suited them better — for there would surely be a wide variety.

How might we begin to create in our large cities a growing number of small schools that could be genuinely responsive and responsible to the children and parents they serve? Perhaps the best way might be through so-called voucher plans. In these, whatever money the city and state are ready to spend on each school-age child is given to the parents of that child, to pay to whatever existing school, public or private, they may wish to send their child to, or if they like none of them, to use with other people in starting a school of their own. But so far there does not seem to be much public interest in such plans. Most parents, as the experience of "community control" shows, are not willing, for one reason or another, to use much of their time to take part in the overseeing or running of schools. Where voucher plans have been instituted, most parents seem to pick whatever school is closest; few do the kind of comparing and choosing which the plan is supposed to make possible.

Beyond that, there are other difficulties. Any plan to give parents a wide choice of schools, or the option of making schools of their own, might well be overturned by the courts, at least in those areas where the courts are trying to reduce interracial prejudice and tension by mixing children of different races in all the schools. Even if large numbers of parents wanted a voucher-supported choice in schools for their children, and even if the courts would allow this, there would, in New York at least, be another serious obstacle: the teachers' union, that is, Albert Shanker. The battle over community control made clear that nothing can be done in the New York City schools without Mr. Shanker's approval; at least, nothing that might affect in any way the pay or job security or seniority privileges of teachers. It seems as sure as anything can be that he would not approve any measure that might make it possible for tax-supported schools to hire teachers from outside the existing public schools, or under any conditions except those set forth in the present union contract. But there is a chance, if there were enough public demand for some sort of voucher plan, that Mr. Shanker would approve it, provided it said that any school receiving voucher-plan money had to hire all its teachers from the existing pool of teachers' union members and under the existing union contract. This would not help the administrators; in the kind of small schools I am talking about, there would be no administrators. Everyone would be a teacher, and whatever work of administration there might be (which in small schools is very little) would be shared among these teachers as they thought best.

None of this is going to happen soon, say, within the next five or ten years, and it may not happen at all. Still, the only hope I can see lies in this direction. Meanwhile, the schools will go on as they are, trying desperately now this, now that, open classrooms one year, guard dogs the next, all the while sending out cheery, Vietnam-style bulletins from time to time about the worst of the crisis having passed and there being light at the end of the tunnel, but for the most part remaining exactly as Mr. Betts has described them here. Though he offers us no message of hope, we should at least be grateful to him for making clear to us what really goes on.

John Holt

Contents

Acting Out

The Title

THE FIRST TIME that I can remember hearing the expression "acting out" was in the spring of 1971. I was talking with Bill Holtzman, principal of P.S. 702 in Manhattan, in his office. He had had a very difficult year. Most of the teaching staff had "turned over" during the first seven months of the year. The fourth-, fifth-, and sixth-grade students had been rampaging through the halls since October. The student population had experienced 100 percent turnover from the previous year. That is, all the students were new — not one had been in the school the previous year. Thirty-one of the teachers had been robbed on the block between the door to the school and the entrance to the subway. The assistant principal had been jumped on the platform of the subway station by a gang of graduates of the school.

Bill Holtzman was skimming through a proposal from the district office and shaking his head. When he came to the last page, he tossed the proposal in my direction, slammed both fists down on his

3

desk, and said, "It'll never work! It'll never work in this school! There are just too damn many *acting-out* children in this school!"

In the most literal sense, "acting out" has emerged as the latest label in the lexicon of educational jargon, and is applied to children whose behavior leaves something to be desired. "Acting out" appears as a verb — "Samson Sorruellas is forever acting out!"; as a noun — "Samson Sorruellas's acting-out is about to drive me up a wall!"; and as an adjective — "Samson Sorruellas is in a class loaded with acting-out children." Acting-out children spend their days outacting other acting-out children.

But in a broader, more universal sense, "acting out" seems to me to be an appropriate description of most of the antics of most school people most of the time.

I have been around nothing but New York City school people for the past decade. I have been a teacher and I have trained teachers. I have been an administrator and I have trained administrators. I have been a substitute teacher and I have trained substitute teachers. I have been in and out of schools in New York, Washington, Philadelphia, Atlanta, and North Carolina.

I have consulted and I have been consulted. I have been forced to sit through boring workshops and seminars, and I have forced others to sit through mine. I have helped open new schools and helped close down others. I have taught undergraduate education courses to parents in search of a B.A. degree; I have taught graduate education courses to teachers in search of master's and doctor's degrees. I have organized parents and paraprofessionals. I have provoked confrontations. I have worked in the most ordinary schools and in the most controversial ones. I have worked in all-black schools, all-white schools, integrated schools, open-classroom schools, traditional schools, free schools, and schools without walls. I have worked for exorbitant sums of money and I have worked for free.

I have been given standing ovations and I have been booed away from the microphone. I have fallen in love with some children and come close to strangling others. I have worshiped some teachers and fired others. I have honored children for their accomplishments and suspended them for their foolishness. I have seen schools rise up

out of the mire and watched others fall down around me. I have
worked with spiteful principals. I have worked with charismatic principals. I have witnessed acts of rare beauty and grace, and lived
through moments of violence and terror.

At different times I have approached education with idealism,
optimism, skepticism, pessimism, and cynicism. I have been a
catalyst and a critic.

I have done my share of acting out.

I sat in the Teachers' Room in I.S. 201 one afternoon in the spring
of 1969. The teacher on the couch across from me was reading the
last few pages of Jonathan Kozol's *Death at an Early Age*. As she
finished the last page, she closed the book and brought it down
easily into her lap. "That's a great book," she said. "Everybody says
it's a great book and it is. But, shit, when is somebody going to write
a book about what life is *really* like in the public schools!"

Now, eight years later, I have tried to write such a book. When I
renovated the basement of our house two years ago, my wife used to
come down to the hot, dusty work area, and say, "Are you crazy?
Are you out of your mind? Why do you insist on working down
here?" But since I first sat down to put this book together, she has
offered me nothing but support. Perhaps I'm finally on the right
track.

Acting Out is a compilation of hundreds of anecdotes, character
sketches, and vignettes, which together convey a sense of what life
in the public schools is indeed like. It is written for people who
know nothing about the schools. It invites them in and shows them
around. It encourages educators to stand back a step from themselves and their work, to laugh at their idiosyncrasies, and to reflect
on their universe. *Acting Out* seeks neither to commend nor con-
demn. It is about a school system that comprises 1.1 million pupils,
1,200 buildings, close to 100,000 employees, and that costs the taxpayers $2,800,000 a year. It is about School People and
School Life.

SCHOOL PEOPLE

The Lord of
the Manor

EVERYTHING IN NEW YORK is locked. Doors and windows, gates and closets, apartments and automobiles, telephones and motorcycles, bicycles and baby carriages; even some locks are locked. A bicycle shop on the West Side wagers with bike buyers (after the money has changed hands) that their bikes will be stolen within a year. A different bike shop in a different section of the city sells chain with links that a small child might be able to squeeze through. The dealer unravels the desired length and effortlessly snips the chain with a gargantuan pair of shears. He also sells the shears and confesses that shear sales about parallel bike sales.

It is not uncommon in New York to pass apartment doors adorned with locks the length of the jamb. Women's handbags are weighted down with coils of keys that defy exaggeration. Many New Yorkers for years carry keys that they no longer can locate a lock for but are afraid to throw away. Losing one's keys is as disastrous as eviction. But having great rings of keys connotes ownership, wealth, power, and right. Substantial key rings transcend leases and loans, exciting in the mind of the bearer grandiose illusions of Carnegies, Mellons, and Morgenthaus. No matter that a two-bedroom apartment soaks up six thousand non-tax-deductible dollars a year, an impressive set of keys conveys magnificence far beyond such a pittance. The highest honor the mayor of New York confers upon his worthy guests is, of course, a key. The great city, once open and beckoning across the ocean to victims of potato famines and political purges, is locked up tight.

Schools are no exception. Every orifice in every building is double- and triple-locked. Fire doors are locked and chained during school hours. Books, typewriters, pencils, finger paints, and chalk are sealed in closets whose meager handles serve as belt loops for enormous lengths of chain. Windows are shut and locked, girded on the outside by heavy wire-mesh cages, which are themselves locked and chained so as to repel bricks, bottles, and people. A quiet little war is waged nightly in the city of New York. School buildings in every neighborhood attest to the relentless assaults on their seams. The booty is minimal: typewriters, adding machines, lunch money, library fines, and sometimes, in elementary schools, toys. An Upper West Side bartender, whose customers are often tempted by inventory rivaling that of Brooks Brothers on Labor Day, claims that he has no patience with "hot toy" salesmen.

Principals have keys to their offices, a skeleton key to the classrooms, and a half-dozen other keys to a half-dozen other places. Assistant principals usually have a key or two less. Teachers have keys that open everything in their respective classrooms and nowhere else, which virtually ensures that they will be in their respective classrooms and nowhere else. Substitute teachers have no keys. They find themselves trapped in halls they would rather not be in and unable to enter any of the locked classrooms: locked out and thereby locked in. Their lack of keys serves as a form of castration. A teacher who suffers the misfortune of losing her keys becomes an object of derision, singled out by her principal at faculty meetings, ostracized by her peers, unable to collect her final paycheck of the school year, an object of contempt to her assistant principal, who must constantly be available to lock and unlock her door, a highly paid wet nurse. All classroom doors are kept locked whether a teacher is inside or not. An empty classroom invites "pocketbook fishermen"; a full room draws thrill seekers from the streets, mostly graduates who have since dropped out of high school and who mysteriously find their way to the third floor. Lost keys sometimes take a full year to replace. One teaching veteran distinguishes her eighth year from the other seventeen: "Oh yes, that was the worst group of children I ever had; that was the year I lost my keys."

Only one man has all the keys to all the locks. He is the Head Custodian (sometimes called the Custodial Engineer). His potency is unrivaled. He swaggers where others only walk. Principals crawl obsequiously to his door seeking the key to the boys' room. He is the Lord of the Manor, a member of the landed gentry in a city where there is no land. The school is his fiefdom and his castle. He tolerates education and the inconveniences it causes him. He often rivals the robber barons and the pimps in his love of fine clothes, fast women (including an occasional teacher), and faster cars. He is accountable only to the BPOM (Bureau of Plant Operations and Management), an entity so remote that he is convinced he is accountable to no man, and an entity with an annual budget in excess of $120 million, of which close to $100 million goes toward custodians' salaries. After all, he, and only he, is the Keeper of the Keys.

Although by day he will often imitate the dress of his hands-and-knees serfs, the custodians, he rarely ruffles the starch in his collar or violates the crease in his trousers or the shine on his shoes. He appears never to have been on all fours. His position seems to have been inherited, perhaps through a loophole in a trust or a compact with an anonymous philanthropist.

The students are never permitted a look at the Head Custodian, but they are aware of his existence because their teachers, who are unwillingly entwined in his web, make contemptuous, teeth-clenched references to him. Many teachers never see the Head Custodian either. He grants few audiences and countenances even fewer favors. Teachers are mere guests in his school, his stronghold, and are welcome by day only.

In the half-light of dawn the Head Custodian travels to the school to fire up his boilers (flick a switch) and warm the farthest reaches of his fiefdom. Then he vanishes into his office, the size and lavishness of which remain a matter of conjecture among the teaching staff. The sole decoration on his steel door is a cold slit for messages and prayers from paralyzed teachers. Communications with teachers can go only in one direction, which is the only way the Head Custodian will have it. In contrast, the Head Custodian is benign toward his own troops of common custodians, but he cares only marginally for the condition of the building he dominates. He tolerates negligence and carelessness, but not interference.

The Head Custodian's great door swings open when the day people have vanished. He struts about his real estate with an unparalleled arrogance. One West Side Head Custodian sports loud bow ties, a handlebar moustache, and a TR–6 that appears to be waxed on the half-hour. His keys hang in silvery opulence from his belt as he surveys the day's damage, entering nooks and crannies that only he knows exist; he views with an expressionless immunity the fresh graffiti that tarnish *his* walls and the scuffs that distort the reflection from *his* floors. Because after-school programs were cut back drastically in Washington (he must manipulate an awesome lobby) and his exorbitant hourly rental rate has discouraged community groups from meeting in the building, his empire is once again undefiled — the Barbarians have been pushed back. By six the ticking of the clocks is the only sound the Head Custodian hears. All is as it should be.

Some Head Custodians, deluded by the apparent power that consorts with apparent ownership, have taken to bearing arms. In 1969, an article in the New York *Post* entitled "School Board Disarms Its Custodians" read:

> The Board of Education has disarmed its pistol-packing Head Custodians. It ordered them to turn in their guns after parents, a Principal and a local school board on the West Side protested the sight of a Head

Custodian walking around a school on Election Day with jacket off and holster showing.

An official of local school board #5 said he was told several custodians carried weapons. . . . Police at the West 68th Street station said Thomas J. Mason, custodian at P.S. 87, surrendered his gun November 28. Mr. Mason could not be reached for comment.

The sight of an armed custodian prompted local school board #5 to introduce this motion to be voted on at the next meeting:

"All Board of Education personnel are prohibited from carrying or storing guns or other lethal weapons on school premises."

A coup narrowly averted.

Ironically, in the New York City schools, a Head Custodian is uniquely capable of uniting (if briefly) principal, teachers, and students in a common purpose: a tenant rebellion. Such is the effectiveness of the union that the Head Custodian does his utmost to prevent open warfare during the day, when the opposing forces are all on the spot. The odds against him are too great then, as the following incident illustrates:

A teacher in an uptown intermediate school brought a second-hand rug into his classroom, attempting to mitigate some of the sterile atmosphere that schools exude. (Although such homey trappings are common in elementary schools, where the open-classroom ethos is tolerated, if not genuinely accepted, they are virtually unknown in junior high schools.) The carpet was accompanied by a carpet sweeper (an implement) and several carpet sweepers (children) who took turns ensuring that it was left clean each afternoon. On the evening of the third day it disappeared.

The teacher checked with the custodian of the floor and learned that the Head Custodian had ordered the carpet removed. The teacher inundated the slot in the Head Custodian's door with notes and invectives, knocked and beat on the door daily for more than a week, but was unable to arouse the giant. One afternoon the teacher lingered in his classroom, patiently awaiting the predictable rounds. The Head Custodian darkened the door at 6:45 P.M.

"James tells me that you had my rug taken up," the teacher challenged.

"That is correct."

"Why?"

"Because it makes work for my men. I will not have them cleaning rugs."

"Baloney! That rug is spotless. I've seen that it's cleaned daily. Put the rug back!"

"The rug will not be returned."

"Your stole that rug. You have no right to it and I'll haul you into court if it's not returned by tomorrow."

"The rug will not be returned. This is not your building."

The rug was not returned the following day, so the teacher took up the matter with his assistant principal, who shuttled him over to the principal. Surprisingly, the principal was sympathetic, even a touch angry, and instructed the teacher to leave the matter in his hands, assuring him overconfidently that the rug would be back "tomorrow." The rug did not reappear overnight and now the principal lost his cool. Enraged by the defiance, he beat on the Head Custodian's door. A healthy crowd of teachers and kids had gathered. The door swung slowly open.

"I thought I told you to put that rug back in this man's classroom by this morning!" the principal blasted.

"The rug is gone."

"What do you mean the rug is gone?"

"The rug is gone."

"Where the hell did it go?"

"I don't know and if I did know I wouldn't put it back anyway. I will not have rugs in *my* school."

"*Your* school! You son of a bitch! You drag your milk-white ass up here from Georgia [that much was pure speculation on the black principal's part] to jet-black Harlem and you've got the nerve to tell me this is *your* goddamn school!"

The onlooking kids were in seventh heaven. The Head Custodian stood stock-still for what seemed like an hour, obviously infuriated at himself for committing the cardinal sin of public exposure. Then slowly, and seemingly without moving his feet, he turned and disappeared into his office. The door appeared to close on its own. John D. Rockefeller could have done no better.

An underling custodian confirmed that the rug was in fact gone. A bill was tendered to the Head Custodian by the principal. An unsigned check was offered as compensation. The unsigned check was returned through the slot in the door. A signed check was offered to the teacher through the principal. That check bounced. The rug is now in a bar under the elevated railroad tracks on upper Park Avenue. The bar owner, and now rug owner, insists that he bought it but refuses to say where.

Common custodians bear no resemblance to their masters. They bear all the marks of men treated cruelly by life. Their mouths are dotted with crooked teeth. Their uniforms are filthy and worn. They work *hard* for a living. There are as few as two in some schools and as many as eight in others. They are humble and kind to children who will tolerate them; objects of scorn and undeserved hatred from the bullies and wisecrackers, who may someday be custodians themselves. One custodian complained of a boy who came by nightly to taunt and spit on him while he attempted to complete his rounds. He was too old to catch his nemesis and too weak not to cry. When custodians are women they are called matrons. Their province is the girls' bathroom. Unclogging drains, toilets, and hand dryers — all are regularly stuffed with Kotexes — is the end-all of their life's labors. They don't report smoking and pushing in some of the worst bathrooms in some of the worst junior high schools because they have learned to be afraid. Life is hard enough as it is. They have all measured the depth and breadth of children's cruelty and find it easier to look the other way.

Many custodians are sick and dying. Many drink. Many have livers that are as temporary as common light bulbs. One custodian passed out at the wheel of his car on the way to the hospital with double pneumonia. He destroyed a parked car, snapped off the tips of all his teeth and broke a half-dozen ribs. He was arrested for drunken driving, misdiagnosed at the emergency room of the hospital, sued, jailed, and put out of work for two years. Custodians are a defenseless lot doing a job no others would wish to do, too proud not to work.

Mr. Caldwell told of the "Mad Crapper" who once mysteriously plagued his school. As if the daily wear and tear on the school building was not enough, someone began defecating at unlikely places around the building. One deposit appeared in a urinal in the boys' bathroom. Mr. Caldwell took it out. Another was nestled in the corner behind a little-used stairwell. Call Mr. Caldwell. Another was tucked in a sewing teacher's desk drawer. She opened the drawer, gagged, threw up, and passed out. Mr. Caldwell cleaned up both messes. The next appeared on the assistant principal's desk, bracketed by big U.S. Keds footprints and a Magic Marker inscription that read "The Unknown." Mr. Caldwell wiped the desk clean. In recollecting the ordeal he smiled and told me, "We finally caught that little crapper one night. She was crapping in an ashtray in the Teachers' Room. Caught her red-handed, I guess you could say. It was that fat girl in the eighth grade, Mary Dennison."

Another school is tormented by a bathroom off the principal's office that occasionally regurgitates sewage from the bowels of the entire building. The building empties its innards generously into the principal's domain in an ankle-deep flow that spreads quickly into the main office and out into the hallway. Secretaries have been stranded atop their desks for hours, like Honduran hurricane victims; an aggrieved mother, come to vent her spleen at the school's administration, was marooned on an office couch and became doubly incensed; twice the principal has jumped from his first-floor office window, and on one occasion he elected to close the school early. The odor in this school is unrelenting, pervasive, uniquely nauseating. It is a conglomerate of all the worst smells buried so carefully in the city's sewers.

When a hysterical secretary's voice bursts through the public-address system, "Mr. Peters, please come to the main office immediately," the custodian, Mr. Peters, recognizes the nature of the emergency. He arrives armed with plumber's helper, "snake," mops, shovels, pails, sponges, and his hands, aware that the rest of the day will be spent in sewage up over his socks. He has never once complained to anyone and no one has ever made an effort to exorcize the evil spirit possessing that bathroom. Mr. Peter theorizes that when the cafeteria serves spaghetti and ends up disposing of great quantities of it down the sink on the second floor, the toilet on the first floor responds in anger. He confesses that his stomach churns each time spaghetti is served and that he loads up his emergency plumbing "just in case."

More than one custodian has lost his job from drinking. Mr. Silver ended his career sitting in the front lobby of a junior high school slouched over a desk he had dragged from the library. His drunken impersonation of the school's administrators drew mixed reviews.

"Come 'ere, sweetheart," he cried. "Lemme see your pass. Okay, okay, get your buns out of the halls! Okay, get in class. Clear these goddamn halls! Clear the halls! The bell's rung! Get outta the damn halls!"

By his attempt at humor, Mr. Silver had brought embarrassment to the Head Custodian and was dismissed by the following Monday.

The Head Custodian generally tolerates all but the most extreme excesses of poor work, slovenliness, or no work at all. He seems to resent deeply the presence of the children and the disrespect they show toward his building. He tolerates laxity among his men, appearing content to have the children live in at least part of their own filth. New York City schools are neither very clean nor very dirty. The general mediocrity that New Yorkers have grown accustomed to applies also to the maintenance of their public schools.

One custodian plays basketball much of the day, regardless of whether or not a class is scheduled to use the gym. A teacher complained to the principal that her class's gym period had been unfairly canceled because "the custodian and a bunch of his buddies from the Sanitation Department" had a full-court game in progress.

But many custodians are often the unsung heroes of a child's school life. Custodians are without the pretense and distance that teachers and administrators so intently cultivate. They are real to children: loving and compassionate. They offer what is so often missing in a teacher: a warmth; an unavoidable humanness. Children see custodians laugh, smile, get angry, and rant and rave like themselves. One little girl told me in strict confidence that she had even seen a custodian cry. She added that it was the only time she had ever seen a man cry. Because of it, she said, he was her favorite "teacher."

One junior high school sets aside one morning a year when students change places with adults. The most popular exchanges every year are with the matrons and the custodians. There is an annual waiting list that the teachers envy but are at a loss to explain.

A frail little eleven-year-old girl named Paula, who had had a minor heart attack at the age of nine, fell in love with a custodian. She seemed always to be with him, able to find him in the few moments between classes. She held his hand at every opportunity, making him feel proud and bright. She eventually persuaded her parents to let him move into a room they had decided to rent for extra money. He walked her to school every day. One April morning, without warning of any sort, he died in his sleep.

Where Head Custodians come from remains a mystery. I met one ordinary custodian who seemed better kept, wealthier, than the rest. Perhaps he was an heir apparent in his building. I asked him if he had designs on a head-custodianship.

"No. Not me," he replied, apparently puzzled that I had asked.

"Well," I continued hesitantly," how is it, that, well, you have a new car and seem, well, to live a little higher than the rest?" I amazed myself with my impudence and daring.

He chuckled from his substantial belly, apparently at my cowardly approach; then looking closely down both ends of the hall to ensure that we were alone he whispered, "Well, let's just say that on one of my lucky days I stumbled on a couple people fuckin' who shouldn't 'a been fuckin', at least not in the nurse's office. And they've been very generous to me ever since."

A Hard, Calloused Hand

THE TRAGICOMIC REALITY of the New York public schools is that most of them have become alienated from the communities they purport to serve. The distrust that probably half (a conservative estimate) of the community residents feel toward those who work in the schools, and the reciprocal apprehension with which at least half of the school people approach their "clients," have reached genuinely absurd proportions.

The emergence of two all-but-armed camps virtually guarantees that children will not learn. Thought too young and therefore too innocent to notice, children are exposed to both drawing rooms of criticism. Many children, despite the fact that they may not have mastered what the school has taught, have learned to play skillfully one party off against the other. Their primary tool is guilt. Parents are stung by their daughter's sudden outburst: "My teacher was right about you!" They are not only green with curiosity about what the teacher *did* say about them, but also annoyed that the teacher is

19

influencing their child. Consequently, they momentarily change their ways, which is precisely why the child makes the remark in the first place.

The converse is also true. A third grader innocently raises her hand and says, "My mother says you was all wrong about what you was tellin' us about the moon and the stars yesterday and she says you don't know nothin'." All the children sense the tension that exists between home and school, and that type of remark can generate enough skepticism to undercut any credibility the teacher might have, at least regarding astronomy. She shifts gears to a different subject, which is again precisely why the child made her remark in the first place.

For the most part, the "turf rights" of the rival forces are respected. Teachers (who rarely live within walking distance of their schools) make their incursions into the host community on neutral buses and subways, and walk no more than a block or two to the security of *their* building. Parents, on the other hand, stick to the surrounding streets, seldom going much closer than a block from the building, often traveling out of their way to cut a wide berth around the school. Teachers who visited parents in their homes during their early years recall with intensity the anxiety that came over them as they rang strange doorbells in strange buildings and entered strange apartments. They remember becoming withdrawn and defensive, aware that they were out of their element, plagued by a sense of being behind enemy lines. Many parents offer similar accounts of their "visits" to the schools. The wrath that burned so mightily in the comfort and familiarity of the streets is dissipated with the first step into the fortress that belongs to "them." A smell or vibration the building gives off warns parents that they have entered a world they will be unable to cope with. There seems to be no common place where the client and the teacher (or the taxpayer and his employee, depending upon your perspective) can do battle as equals in strength and confidence. The nature of their skirmishes is such that one is always at a disadvantage vis-à-vis the other.

The occasions of head-to-head combat are few. These encounters begin under anything but pleasant circumstances. There are two standard scenarios, with only slight variations in trim and in degree that such clashes tend to follow: either (a) the school gets in touch with the parents and says that the child is out of order and that one of the parents must come in immediately; or (b) the parents get in touch with the school and say that the teacher is out of order and that one of them is coming in immediately. Little is demanded of the reader's imagination to envision the mood of the parley.

Regardless of scenario, there is a single point of tangency between the parent and the school. That point is the main office and it is often manned by a hearty collection of shock troops. These are the school secretaries and their first responsibility is the maintenance of the 38th Parallel. In 1975 there were 2,254 of them in the city's elementary and junior high schools.

Main offices, which vary little in design in the more than nine hundred schools the city supports, are ideal for the purposes of the secretaries. Each office is divided roughly in half by a long wooden counter that separates the secretaries from the public. The configuration of tables and desks which the secretaries agree upon on their side of the counter varies with their individual whims (Malcolm X and the Godfather both refused to sit in a seat that did not face the door and they have many imitators in the secretarial ranks; others prefer to show their backs) and roles in projected times of crisis. Small swinging doors at either end of the counter are used only by the secretaries as they enter and leave the building for lunch. The public sector rarely offers anything more comfortable than a long shallow wooden bench and usually offers nothing at all, thereby forcing parents to stand or pace. The offices of the principal and the assistant principal are set off from the secretaries' half of the main office, and are therefore out of the immediate reach.

The secretaries are the hand offered by the schools to the public. And it is a hard, calloused hand indeed. Women of the most even-tempered disposition are soon hardened by the constant pressure and interference their job entails. Many afford a perfect buffer for their bosses, keeping parents and the public at bay with cover-up lies, offhand insulting barbs, or absolute indifference. Secretaries have several "tools" at their disposal that take years of practice and modification to perfect.

A school secretary can "play dumb" better than the best Broadway actor. She can know nothing about nothing at any given moment. She can look a parent square in the face, cloud her eyes with a glaze of ignorance, drop her lower lip until it is perfectly limp, shake her head slowly so that the lip waggles ever so slightly, and mutter, "No, I don't know anything about that. I'm afraid I don't know what you are talking about."

A school secretary can work the "hold" button on her telephone as well as Herbie Mann can play his flute. She will put the most irate and roundly feared parent on "hold" for a minute while she alerts the rest of the "girls" that she's got a "hot one" on the line, then interject unexpectedly that another call has come in, opening the line just long enough to speak her phrase, never allowing the disgruntled parent to sneak in a word. Then suddenly she plays a chord on the buttons with her right hand. The little lights flash quickly off and the line goes dead. A pregnant moment passes while the infuriated parent redials the number. This time a different secretary will answer, feign ignorance, and work the same game as her colleague all but competing for showmanship. On other occasions the caller will be shuttled to "hold" and forced to remain there until he grows hungry or can no longer afford the cost of silence. Finally, a secretary will promise to have her superior return a call "the minute he's free," but fails to take down either the number or the name of the aggrieved.

Many a secretary has the gift of "selective deafness." She sharpens her acts of omission on teachers and students throughout the day and is at her tournament best with angry parents. Ignoring a parent totally, another worthy weapon in any good secretary's arsenal, is less convincing and less devastating than an ear that hears some things and is unable to pick up others. Lucinda Pershing is an accomplished master of this "slight of ear." Lucinda hears calls to lunch, idle chatter about what's on sale where, and gossip about whether Mr. Gresham has "gotten into the new math teacher's drawers as yet." But Lucinda is unable to hear the telephone; she is deaf to teachers' requests for supplies, to administrators in search of attendance figures, to visitors who ask nothing more than to sign the guest register. During a time of crisis her act is so convincing that an incensed mother will temper her anger out of pity for the poor woman, who she fears is growing prematurely deaf. When the crisis has passed, Lucinda smiles and chuckles aloud at her own cunning and prowess.

Another of the secretary's skills is the ability to cover for her boss under the most trying circumstances. I have seen Joan Mason hold mock conversations with Principal Schwartz, who she knows is either out to lunch, late to work, or isn't coming in at all, on his private wire under the hawkish glare of a flustered, but militant, mother. With Mrs. Platte hanging over her shoulder one morning, claiming that her son John was punched in the nose by his metal-shop teacher, Joan calmly buzzes Mr. Schwartz's empty office. She cups her hand over the receiver and confides to Mrs. Platte that she is using his "emergency line."

"Mr. Schwartz, Mrs. Platte is here and very upset. She would like to see you immediately." She hesitates. "Hold on a minute, I'll ask her." She turns to Mrs. Platte, again covering the dead receiver with her right hand. "Mr. Schwartz says he has a meeting with Dr. Wilson [the community superintendent] and that he's already fifteen minutes late. Could you possibly be in at ten tomorrow morning?" Mrs. Platte nods reluctantly. Joan confirms the appointment through the receiver, says goodby, and hangs up. Mrs. Platte turns and leaves the office. "Deaf" Lucinda Pershing turns respectfully to Joan Mason and says. "You done good. I couldn't have done it any better myself."

The ultimate measure the school secretaries have at their disposal is an all-out overt attack that converts a main office into a cacophony of jungle-bird shrieks. They prefer to avoid this strategy as a rule, but occasionally are forced to use it — when their nerves have been shattered or exposed by a constant stream of troubled children sent either on errands by their wary teachers or evicted from their classrooms and told to "go sit in the office." A salesman wandering in at one of those times runs the risk of instantaneous devastation by the collective wrath of some of the hardest and coldest women in the city. One entered the office of an intermediate school saying inauspiciously that he was from McGraw-Hill and that he wanted to see whoever was in charge of curriculum. They hit him like a ton of bricks. His tragic mistake was his inopportune timing.

The first began the assault. "I'm sick and tired of these damn salesmen coming in and expecting the world to stop turning for them."

From behind another desk (the woman did not even raise her eyes): "Don't you jerks know when lunch is around here? I bet you don't. I bet you're so interested in making all that money off your crummy books that you never bother to eat. I bet you haven't eaten lunch this month."

"And those books certainly are lousy. If your books weren't so lousy, these kids wouldn't be running all over the halls as I'm sure you noticed on your way in here. When are you coming in here with some decent books anyway?"

The barrage continues relentlessly even after the salesman has turned tail and fled.

A sideshow not to be missed takes place in one Brooklyn junior high school the first of every month when the exterminator arrives for his regular tour. Secretaries Frieda and Ellen go to work:

Frieda: Hey, Ellen, look out the window and see who's comin'. It's that fat little man who can't kill no roaches.

Ellen: I don't know why he bothers.

Exterminator: Good morning, girls. Exterminator.

Frieda: Girls! Who do you think you're callin' girls? These are *ladies*, my fat friend, and I really don't know why you're here in the first place. That shit you spray just attracts the roaches. I was hopin' that maybe you'd miss a month 'cause the bugs were just startin' to disappear. Ain't much point in you sprayin' nothin' if you're just gonna track a whole bunch in with you.

Ellen: Hey, Frieda, I bet his house is covered with roaches, what do you think?

Frieda: I bet he's married to a big old fat roach. What do you say,
   mister? Are you married to a roach? Is that why you come in here,
   feedin' 'em and just pretendin' to kill 'em?
Exterminator: Girls, I wish you would let a man at work alone
   once in a while. Finished, see you in a month.
Frieda: Here he comes with that "girls" shit again.

The exterminator turns and leaves, aware that the same scene will
be played out again in full in a month's time. Only a few secretaries
openly assault visitors to the school regardless of the mission. They
look on such outbursts as prostitutions of their art. They regret, after
the fact, an explosion that could have been avoided or was aggravated by unrelated circumstances.

The work of a school secretary is usually frightfully dull and unre-
warding, and interrupted constantly by students and visitors. Her
role as public relations anti-agent far overshadows the trivia of re-
porting daily attendance, recording numbers from rolls of lunch
tickets, writing passes to the nurse's office, typing an occasional
inane memo, and answering the telephone. Because she gives prior-
ity to cultivating, even though subconsciously, a front of rudeness
and ice-coldness, the quality of the work she produces, however
trivial, suffers accordingly. Some secretaries appear to enjoy having
to do the same job twice. They grunt and groan as their principal
points out the innumerable careless errors in completing an
Elementary and Secondary Education Act report, but they make
those same mistakes time and time again in essentially identical
assignments. The face they project to the public, that of an insensitive, inefficient bureaucrat unwilling to extend herself an inch beyond the work specified in her contract, seems to be the face they
have chosen to project.

Not infrequently a secretary becomes a surrogate parent. An
erring child is ordinarily sent by his angry teacher to the principal
for discipline. While he waits to see the great man, one of the
secretaries may coax him into doing a routine job, such as stuffing
leaflets into teachers' mailboxes. The two strike up an acquaintance

that can ripen into real friendship, one that provides both parties with a respite from the goings-on in their respective corners of the school.

In every school in New York one of the secretaries is designated the payroll secretary and given the responsibility of distributing the paychecks to the teachers. A wise first-year teacher will devote as much time to the cultivation of the payroll secretary's friendship as to the preparation of her lessons. Teachers who fall from grace in the eyes of the payroll secretary are grateful to get paid at all. Their checks often mysteriously arrive a day or two late from the district office or in the most acute cases are "lost" and take months to be stopped and reissued.

The final day of each school year can be termed the payroll secretary's Coronation Day. She reigns supreme, knowing that no paycheck is to be issued until each teacher has presented a list of completed errands, each initialed by the appropriate administrator or guidance counselor. The entire process of completing and turning in records, accurately updating and summarizing roll books (these are public legal documents), disposing of keys properly, mailing report cards, returning books, and straightening rooms can take an experienced veteran the better part of a six-hour day. To the first-year teacher it is a nightmare. But only after that labyrinth has been run and appropriate initials placed in appropriate boxes, is the teacher "allowed" to get in line for his money. The power that increases in the hands of the payroll secretary often distorts her image of herself. She feels she is doing a teacher a great favor by presenting him with compensation for work he has already performed.

In one noteworthy and harsh episode, Payroll Secretary Shirley Goodson spotted a black teacher, Terri Regan, trying to jump a few places ahead in line. Terri was engaged to a white teacher on the staff and the wedding was less than a week away.

Shirley tore into her: "Hey, bitch! Don't be thinkin' you can be cuttin' into my line just because you're gonna be sleepin' with all that pink meat." When Terri reached the head of the line, Shirley was unable to locate her check (the matter was actually complicated by the fact that Shirley had not been invited to the wedding), but she agreed to drop it in the mail when it "showed up."

After five years of administering a teacher-training program and a junior high school, I decided that I needed to gain perspective on what the life of a substitute teacher was like. I devoted a full day to visiting twenty schools scattered about the city for the purpose of entering my name in the substitute pools. My mission was ostensibly simple: I sought only to add my name to a list of others whose interests were similar to my own. My contact with school personnel during this nomadic day was limited almost exclusively to the secretaries and the door guards. In virtually every school I entered I was ignored for as long as twenty minutes, an apparent measurement of my interest and stamina. Once the purpose of my mission was revealed, the matter took on some complexities and began to vary according to the vibrations and dynamics of the individual school. In some schools I was asked to complete prepared forms inquiring after my formal education, the type of teaching license I held, my teaching experience, my available days, my interests, and my allergies. In others I was asked to put pertinent information on a file card, and in one, a secretary whose hair color and eyebrows didn't come close to matching shoved a piece of paper under my nose and mumbled, "Here, write what you want."

In another school I was told that I would have to see Mr. Blintze, who turned out to be the principal. After a marginal interview, in which I apparently made a favorable impression on Mr. Blintze (would they dare call him "Cheese"?), I was told that I was going to be placed on the "Action List." When I inquired what exactly being on the Action List meant, I was informed that he felt I was "combat-ready." And this was an East Side Manhattan school with a posh address.

As a prospective substitute I believe I encountered what must have been the reigning guru in the office of an intermediate school on the East Side of Manhattan. I made my interests known as I had at other schools during the day. But this particular secretary (she must have at least had payroll-secretary status if not consideration as the Imperial Wizard of her clan), known to her colleagues as Rosey (an unlikely name if there ever was one), threw what amounted to little less than an epileptic fit.

"I can't stand it! I can't stand it! I can't stand it!" she bellowed, at once baffling and embarrassing me. "I can't stand all these subs! These subs are driving me crazy! I bet he doesn't even have his papers! I bet he's got no papers! He probably doesn't even have a pen! [I had no idea what my "papers" even were, and I *did* have a pen.] Get these subs out of here! I can't stand them! I've got more important things to do! What's the matter with these subs!" At this point an assistant principal, who had heard the commotion from the hallway, came breathlessly to my rescue. He spirited me into his office, slamming the door on Rosey's continued bellowing.

"She's a fucking bitch, isn't she?" His only words.

The one moment of pathos during the day's travels occurred in an exchange with a secretary in an elementary school. After all the information had been collected, she snapped at me, "Have you had much experience?"

"Yes, a great deal," I replied.

Her countenance dropped momentarily. A wave of sympathy came over her face. "It's rough out there, isn't it?" she offered softly.

The Big Bad Wolf

"Your attention please! All teachers please look in the hallway. Emily Dickinson is missing!"
— Loudspeaker announcement by the principal of P.S. 75, who had lost his cat

I SPENT AN OCTOBER WEEKEND in 1974 in the Adirondacks wilderness: fishing, hiking through the rapidly changing fall foliage, and living close to the land. For four days, my two companions and I moved from one primitive hut to another along lakes with names like Honnedoga, Panther, Little Moose, and Minnewaga, seeing no one but ourselves. Phoebe, a small dog rescued from the jaws of the gas chamber in the New York City Pound several years before, chased squirrels and chipmunks, flushed pheasants, frightened deer, and rode high in a rowboat as we trolled and flew flies across the many still pools in the Moose River. Phoebe often found herself submerged in the near-freezing waters, once narrowly escaping drowning, in an effort to stay close to her human companions. On another occasion her zeal to remain close to her master netted her a hook in her underbelly.

We feasted on the trout we were able to catch, and drank the plentiful spring water, a fifth of bourbon, and a fifth of scotch. The

29

most taxing decisions we were forced to make revolved around whether a Muddler Minnow or a Royal Coachman was the appropriate fly for the day's conditions. We had no responsibilities to anyone but ourselves. Our only restrictions were those imposed by the weather. We lost track of time and the date and on our return attacked the New York *Times* in a way that suggested we had been away for years, not days. We had been briefly suspended from time and commitment in an unspeakably beautiful corner of the world. There had been no strings attached.

Exactly one year before the trip I had been an administrator in a city school. No two situations could be more dissimilar. The endless freedom that living in the woods allows is not part of the experience of a public school administrator. By contrast his is a life of constant pressure.

The public school principal is under the greatest pressure and scrutiny from parents, who all but move into his office with complaints and requests for special favors for their children. They bulldog him for the job his teachers are not doing, for the homework assignments their children do not receive, for the notice of a Parents Association meeting they failed to see, for the way he dresses or does not dress, for an appearance he failed to make at a community school board meeting. Parents rant and rave about a grade their child received in sewing, about the quality of the school lunches, about the extortion of a nickel that took place in the boys' bathroom, about a substitute who failed to gain control of her class, about a bus that was supposed to pick up their child but never arrived. Parents want their children moved from one shop class to another, from morning gym to afternoon gym, out of one poorly reputed teacher's clutches and into another's fabled arms. They want their children in and out of bilingual classes, in and out of Open Corridor* programs, and in and out of structured, traditional classrooms. They want certain teachers censured or fired; they want certain paraprofessionals denied employment; they want alcoholic custodians removed.

*A name given to programs that use the space in the corridors as an additional room. A teacher is posted in the hall with a variety of materials which children are free to come and work with at their leisure.

They want school open when it snows twelve inches and they want it closed on Black Solidarity Day and Sal Mineo's birthday. They want all-black classes, all-white classes, and a perfectly integrated school. They insist that the halls be polished, that the bathrooms be spotless, that light bulbs and fixtures be replaced. They want other parents' children out of classes that their children are in; they want each other's children tossed out of school. And most importantly, whatever it is that parents decide they want from a principal, they want it immediately.

Parents expect a principal to do their bidding and do it fast. They evaluate him according to his willingness to satisfy their wishes. They will leave their own jobs to interfere with his. They argue that since they experienced public school themselves, they are capable of doing his job. They crowd the office waiting room for an opportunity to bend his ear; they compete with each other for a percentage of his time, of his life. No matter how often he has his unlisted telephone number changed, they are able to discover it in a matter of hours. They are unabashed about waking his wife and children in the wee hours of the morning. They want him at all places at all times; they expect him to be able to transcend conflicts of time and place and be where they want him to be when they want him to be there. They are not satisfied with anything less than all of his time. They wrench him from his family (in at least one case, they caused the breakup of his marriage of many years). They stop at nothing short of dominating his entire life.

Custodians want a piece of the principal's time also. They want to squeal on teachers whose windows are left open and whose children desecrate the classrooms in the course of each and every day. They complain that mops and dustpans have not been provided. They despair about unerasable graffiti and about broken lockers which they don't have the tools to repair. Custodians level their sights on substitutes who sit idly by as children break into art cabinets, pulling the locks clean out of the woodwork and freely distributing the booty. They want filthy bathrooms locked, chained, and monitored; they want hordes of children pushed from the hallways. They want fire extinguishers refilled and fire alarms turned off. Those on the day shift want to be switched to the night; and those who work at night prefer the day. They want soda, cigarette and coffee machines in the supply room. They insist on their cut of the principal's time.

Teachers place greater demands on their principal than he has time to place on them. They want the books they ordered but have never received, they want more chalk, more cardboard, more staples and erasers, more of whatever they have tasted. Teachers want unlimited access to Xerox machines, ditto duplicators, and typewriters. They want quieter, cleaner places in which to prepare their lessons. They don't want to share a room with Mr. Allison because he leaves it in such disarray; they want to move off one corridor and on to another. If they teach fifth grade they want to be switched to first; if they are assigned to eighth-grade math, they want sixth-grade social studies. If they are in a school that leans toward open classrooms, they want a traditional arrangement.

Teachers want discipline problems handled by the principal with a terrible swift sword. When they drag a screaming, kicking child to the office, they expect miracles. They barge past lineups of parents and other people from the community and storm into the principal's office demanding action. They want slow, disruptive children transferred out of their classes, and brighter, more cooperative ones substituted. They want to work with teachers other than those assigned to their departments or corridors or programs. They want order and peace to reign in the hallways. They want to be able to strut around the building in the fashion of kings and queens.

Teachers are forever begging small favors of the principal. They want to be excused from faculty meetings to get to Korvettes ahead of the rush; they want to leave early every Thursday for a series of root-canal appointments; they want extraordinary tales explaining latenesses to be believed; and they want extra "sick days" when they have no more. They want days off without loss of pay for funerals of second cousins and step-grandmothers in California. They want a share of the good life and they feel it is the principal's to give. When unsatisfied or neglected they turn cruel and nasty and go to great lengths to double and triple the unbearable nature of his job.

Secretaries, too, place demands on the principal's ear. Each has a clear breaking point, beyond which she cannot tolerate the noise and confusion in the main office, and each one turns to the principal when that point has been reached. They cry and curse in his office; they threaten and scorn him momentarily and then melt into a chair by his desk in a flood of tears. They tell him how they hate their jobs, their marriages, and their lives. They demand compassion and understanding in return. Once composed and on the verge of returning to the fray, they confide their differences with their fellow secretaries. They mimic each other's incompetencies for the principal's benefit. Some turn ugly behind closed doors, criticizing him for his handling of certain situations, chastising him for his treatment of certain parents. Those who live nearby, and particularly those who have children enrolled in the school, serve him by acting as grapevines and weathervanes. They keep him abreast of what the community thinks of him. IIe burns to know in what direction community opinion is blowing.

School nurses are known to burst in on the principal for their own particular emergencies. On rare occasions they bring him up to date on serious accidents that have befallen his charges; on normal regular visits they demand more control over the ebb and flow of hypochondriacs and test evaders that pass through their offices. They tell him who they think might be pregnant or who might have a loathsome disease. They want certain teachers who constantly send them children denied the right to do so regardless of circumstance. They want guidelines and policies clearly defined and enforced. They want new systems of passes developed to curtail forgery. They dump their own caseloads in the principal's lap.

Lunchroom people have their axes to grind as well, and willingly leave their posts to pound on the principal's door to have their matters attended to. They want lunch tickets distributed differently; they want lunch lines straighter and language cleaner; they want the stronger aides to modify their strength in controlling the masses, while they want fires lit under the weaker, milder aides. They want children who speak with anything less than effervescence about the menu to be forced to miss lunch. They want swindlers and chocolate-milk thieves barred from the cafeteria forever. They want children, aides, and teachers quartered on one side of the steam table and themselves on the other. Those who work in the lunchroom where the children actually eat want cleaner, sturdier tables, less confusion and noise, and more garbage in the garbage cans than on the floor. They want violators severely dealt with and are willing to leave a lunchroom of five hundred and ninety-nine students to drag one to the principal's office for instant gratification. They want bigger, louder microphones and more people assigned to assist them in the cafeteria. If their lunchtime beat is the exits, they want identification cards, stamps with invisible ink, and more bodies to wage the daily wars that rage from twelve to one o'clock. They want the principal himself in the lunchroom or by the doors as a show of strength and support. For one hour in the middle of every day they place enormous demands on the man at the top.

Guidance counselors often constitute the gravest threat to the principal's distribution of his own time and to his sanity. Not burdened by classroom assignments, they have too much time on their own hands and expend it badgering him with petty requests and favors. They want less paperwork and fewer forms to fill out if they enjoy seeing children who are in need of help; but some want to lower their caseloads in order to make time for the clerical work. They want quieter, more remote offices with fewer interruptions from teachers and telephones. They want better secretaries. They want students who create great problems removed from their responsibility, and others, whose anomalies are shyness and introversion, assigned. They develop personality conflicts with parents and want the children of these parents transferred to a different counselor. They want differences that have developed over provinces of responsibility with social workers and school psychologists ironed out. They want wood-shop classes enlarged and moved from period two to period three; they want teachers who have always taught eighth grade switched to sixth. They want teachers who can't abide each other's presence scheduled to work together because it suits their own convenience. They want the principal to leave his office and come cope with irate parents on the telephone. If conferences they are running grow hot and boil over, they send student messengers to the principal's office with instructions for him to report immediately. They request permission to attend conferences in Utah. If they are white, they sometimes push for an all-white clientele; if they are black, they fight for black counselees; if they are women they want all girls; and if they box they want prospective boxers. They want the principal's time and they expect it when they need it.

Students place considerable demands upon the principal. They see him as the point of last call, as the ultimate arbitrator, as the Chief Judge of the Court of Appeals. Even in the most rebellious of schools in the city they still regard him and the office he holds with some fear, with reserve. They will run from him in the hallway regardless of his temperament or his physical attributes. But they turn to him in times of crisis. They want him there when their quarters have been stolen, or when they are on the threshold of a fight they fear they cannot win. They pit him against every member of his staff. They blame teachers for low grades on tests and papers and they want him to investigate their claims and change their grades. They want him to all but annihilate teachers who hit or threaten to hit them. They want action, and when they don't get it from him, they bring their parents to school in the morning to act in their behalf. They blackmail their principal. They complain to him about teachers who make them sit in the back of the room, about lunchroom people who snatch and tear up their tickets, about assistant principals who refuse them bus passes, about guidance counselors who are always too busy to see them, about aides who push them around going in and out of the building for lunch, and about paraprofessionals who play favorites. They are great consumers of human attention and they don't shortchange their principal.

Community representatives in their various and sundry manifestations also consume much of the principal's time and energy. Firemen want him to crack down on students who have pulled fire alarms; police want fewer dropouts on the streets and more homework demanded to keep the vagrants indoors in the evening. Politicians want favors of all sizes and shapes. Civic groups want speeches and expert opinion. Pastors and reverends want principals up in pulpits preaching the gospel of education to their dissident flocks. The Urban League wants surveys conducted and data evaluated. School-board members want Utopia realized and expect it to be done overnight.

Race transcends caste and profession, and exacts its enormous toll on the city's principals. Black principals are suspect and under keen surveillance by white parents and teachers. Black principals are often resented by other blacks and community leaders for their successes and accomplishments. Puerto Ricans distrust black administrators. White principals must prove themselves to all the races in their constituencies. Their actions are blameworthy to one group and praiseworthy to another. They are damned if they do and damned if they don't. Puerto Rican and Chinese principals, just because they are so few, are under the closest scrutiny of all. Every move a principal makes is evaluated in terms of its effect on the various racial and ethnic constituencies, rarely on its educational merit. Principals are constantly confronted with novel interpretations of their actions and decisions, interpretations they may have never considered when the incident or problem arose. Preparation and track records have no bearing on matters such as these. Most principals discover that they have the greatest difficulty convincing "their own."

Superintendents, too, place demands on their front-line lieutenants. A common practice is to pull the principals out of their schools for all-day, districtwide meetings every Monday, leaving assistant principals in charge. Another is to confront the principals with mountains of complaints from parents who have taken advantage of leverage they have with the superintendent or who have gone over the principal's head. They want principals to get state reports in on time, to cut back on the use of the telephone, to improve the quality of evaluation of their staffs, to stiffen in matters of discipline and decorum, to pay closer attention to districtwide circulars, and to start showing up at meetings on time. One principal, tired of abuse from his superior, arrived at a meeting wearing a cat on his head.

Fishing in the Adirondacks and being principal of a New York City public school represent perfect polar opposites. One presupposes freedom and peace while the other is characterized by relentless churning anxiety. Few callings are more demanding. A principal's preparation and training are by nature theoretical and hypothetical. Although the more successful principal is able to anticipate the existence of multiple conflicting constituencies, he has no way of predicting the character, disposition, and relative strengths both within and between the interest groups. The more successful principals are not those whose educational approach is either unique or effectively implemented, but those who have the political acumen to manipulate the interplay of existing forces. Drowning principals find themselves manipulated by the interest groups they seek to control, and caught in cross fires they are unable to avoid. Principals either develop the art of compromise or are consumed by their jobs.

The methods used in selecting principals changed substantially in the late sixties and early seventies, as did the kind of men and women whom the job has attracted. Formerly, candidates were placed on Board of Examiners seniority lists after completing the necessary paperwork. There they waited patiently, sometimes for as long as three years, for their names to float to the surface. The job proffered might well be in some far-off borough which the prospective principal knew nothing about. He had no alternative but to accept. Refusal shuttled him back to the tail end of the list. The advent of community control in 1968 and decentralization in 1970 changed the rules by giving representative screening committees an opportunity to voice their opinions on candidates for neighborhood schools. The final appointment of a principal now rests unclearly between the superintendent and the community school board.

Luis Mercado's accession to power in a largely white West Side elementary school was typical of the new pattern. When the former principal announced that she would be leaving in June 1970, the school elected parents and teachers to a screening committee. Luis Mercado, a vocal Lower East Side Puerto Rican, emerged as the people's choice. The committee felt that they had found a man who would fight for their interests as well as his own. The fact that he was Puerto Rican necessarily complicated the issue. Their anticipated struggle with the Board of Examiners became ethnic as well as political.

There followed several demonstrations (community actings-out) complete with pictures, posters, chants of "We want Luis!" and "No Mercado, no school!" They were all duly acknowledged in the press. The fact that the faces doing the chanting and creating the hoopla were white added yet another wrinkle to the matter. At the time the newly elected community school board appointed Mr. Mercado principal, it also appointed two other persons to principalships in the district. Predictably, the Board of Education threatened to take the matter to court. Mercado (and two others similarly situated) beat the Board to the punch. They sued on the grounds that the Board of Examiners' practices were discriminatory. In 1972 they won the suit and became legitimate principals of New York City public schools without showing the Board of Examiners much more than the seats of their pants, thereby establishing a new procedure for the selection of school principals.

Whether or not the change in the selection process ensures better principals is open to debate. Although the attitude of the new incumbents toward the community may have been improved, the spectrum of interest groups still remains. The kid-glove treatment that community-screened principals enjoy does not seem to last beyond the first few months of the school year. Business goes on as usual.

The New York City principal, man or woman, has been stereotyped as insensitive and gray-haired, addicted to fleeing to New Jersey or Long Island at the stroke of three (actually, in 1977 most principals found it impossible to leave much before five and many frequented their buildings on weekends). He is uninterested in parents and hides behind his office door all day to avoid them. He is unconcerned about the unending chaos and the deluge of problems that constantly threaten to engulf the school. He is also seen as an incompetent relic, who was tenured in the days when tenure was easy to come by and is now threatened by the advent of decentralization.

Unfortunately, the stereotype has proved to be all too true too often. It has become entrenched in the minds of parents, teachers, students, and community residents, so much so that principals of the new breed have made little headway in changing it. Said a new young principal to his students and staff on opening day of his first year on the job: "I am the Man! I am the Big Bad Wolf!"

One reason for the persistence of the stereotype is that many of the new principals have assumed the attributes of their ignoble predecessors. The task seems to be bigger than the person. The task seems to grab hold of even the strongest and most optimistic, tugging and wrenching them into unrecognizable configurations. The task suggests that the "old" principals, now so crusted and bureaucratic, were once idealistic, vigorous, and hopeful. The task consumes the strong with the weak. The task transforms reformers and political militants into the mold they once vociferously denounced. In one highly controversial Bronx junior high school, Principal David Dudley took the helm five years ago with promises to develop a model for an all-black, all-poor ghetto school. He offered new staffing patterns, new curriculum materials, new teaching techniques, and a vigorous campaign to clear the standing-room-only hallways. By the end of his third year he was no longer calling staff meetings, he rarely appeared at his own faculty meetings, and he was absent from the building as often as three days a week. He barricaded himself in his office with strict instructions to his secretary that no one short of Abe Beame was to get through.

In 1972, in another school, a talent hunt for a new principal went on for seven months. The search finally turned up a tough, intelligent woman with many years of experience in the South Bronx. She was offered the job and she accepted. At her first faculty meeting during the late-August faculty orientation, she promised the teachers and the community that a New Order was on the way. Her reputation as a mover of mountains in the South Bronx (kids growing up in Harlem are afraid to walk in the South Bronx) added credibility to her projections. Within four months she had been consumed by the task. She began leaving school early to beat the traffic back to Queens. She accepted part-time consultant work that took her out of the building two afternoons a week. Her behavior was noted at the public meetings of the Board of Education. She responded with a score sheet of the number of meetings she had attended, the number of conferences she had held, the number of parents she had met, and the number of students she had taken the time to see. The seemingly endless list looked like a column of New York Stock Exchange closing prices and was about as relevant.

Teachers and community people were indignant at her audacity. Copies of a second list mysteriously appeared in the staff's mailboxes and were distributed to a public meeting of the Board. The new anonymous list included the number of times she had insulted teachers, the number of conferences with parents she had failed to attend, the number of times she had been seen leaving school early, the number of times she was absent without explanation, and a new calculation of what her annual wage should be, based on the hours she had actually worked and the dollars she had actually earned. In April the community school board cast a 7–0 vote not to renew her contract. A succession of one-year principals, by 1976 numbering four, has followed.

Whereas tenure for teachers has become a routine, almost biological, process, principals are fully aware that they will be engaged in a public, highly political, and emotionally charged "happening" in the spring of their third year. (Tenure laws governing administrators were changed frequently during the early seventies, varying tenure from three years to five years to none.) Principals who survive the unavoidable ordeal do so because they have mastered the art of creating delicate alliances between interest groups and holding those alliances together long enough to corral four votes from the seven-person Board of Education. They need know little about education, they need not have improved the school over the three years; but they must be maverick politicians capable of estimating accurately the relative strengths and weaknesses of the various lobbies well before the final vote is cast. Ironically, if they should devote inordinate amounts of time to improving their schools, at the expense of scratching the appropriate backs, in all likelihood they will find themselves on the short end of a 4–3 decision.

Tenure issues are decided behind closed doors. The public vote, which legalizes the clandestine vote, rarely differs from it. The public is invited to speak at the open meetings and does so in great numbers and with great fanfare that occasionally turns violent. But these harangues, which may push the actual tenure vote back into the wee hours of the morning, rarely affect the outcome. This is the community's hour to act out. The meetings are pure theater. They attract enormous hell-bent-for-action crowds, providing a forum similar to that of the Orators' Corner in Hyde Park.

Two memorable tenure debates are worthy of mention. One revolved around a woman, Mrs. Abigail Daly, who had served as principal of a New York elementary school for three years. Although the school attracted a largely middle- to upper-middle-class clientele, it was characterized by the chaos and confusion associated with schools situated significantly farther uptown. Mrs. Daly, a woman in her mid-forties, had a raspy voice, which her adversaries claimed complemented her personality. Many parents distrusted her greatly, and as her tenure year drew to a close, they grew increasingly open in their contempt for her. Morale in the school was low; a parent observed that if one stood outside the school at the end of the day and watched teachers sprint through the parking lot for their cars and the suburbs, one would have thought that the building was in flames.

Throughout her third year, Mrs. Daly noted that the number of parents infuriated by her habit of closeting herself in her office had increased and that they had begun organizing to remove her. Integrated groups of parents, always a danger sign, began meeting and listing their grievances. The parents made several vain attempts to meet with Mrs. Daly but were regularly informed that she was busy. They took their case to the community superintendent. The only information, he said, that would influence either his decision to retain Mrs. Daly or the recommendation he would make to the community school board would be well-documented, clearly presented, hard cold facts. Not realizing that the superintendent had installed Abigail Daly in the first place and that he was committed to her defense, the parents set to work compiling specific grievances. They interviewed numerous fellow parents and recorded the information in a collective log. Eventually, they typed their efforts into a single-spaced, fifty-two-page document whose embarrassing contents indicted Abigail Daly. Included was a tale of a little boy who allegedly came to the main office in tears begging to see Mrs. Daly. She was busy. He yelled through the door that a bigger boy "peed on me in the hallway"; the secretaries pinched their noses, wrinkled their upper lips, and confirmed his accusation to Mrs. Daly. She allegedly yelled back through the door that she was in conference and instructed the secretary to send him back to class.

The parents sent copies of their document to each member of the community school board, to the superintendent, and to Mrs. Daly. They awaited responses. Certain that the report would arouse much controversy and that the authenticity of many of the more bizarre charges would be challenged, the parents were baffled by an ominous silence. They notified the recipients that they would be more than willing to meet at any given place and time, and that they were committed to doing whatever was necessary to ensure that their children were in the hands of a different principal come September. Still they drew no response. They grew angry. They began extensive door-to-door canvassing of parents to attract a large crowd for the public meeting.

What the parents failed to understand was that, although Mrs. Daly was a questionable school administrator, she knew where her bread was buttered. Quietly, and well behind the scenes, she kept in close touch with the superintendent and the four board members whom she regarded as allies. She notified them of every move the parents made and carefully eroded any confidence the board members may have placed in the report that the parents had filed. Mrs. Daly chipped away at her adversaries' credibility while building her political base. By the time the board met publicly, she knew that the vote taken in closed session had been 4 to 3 in her favor. She attended the meeting only to study the faces of the four heads she was counting, and to keep a wary eye peeled for any symptoms indicating a change of heart.

The decorum at the meeting, or lack of it, was predictable a month in advance. More than five hundred people shoehorned into the auditorium. The agenda included but one item. Within thirty minutes the circus was under way. Few people spoke in defense of Mrs. Daly and those who did were rudely shouted down. A throng of people lined up to speak against her tenure. By midnight much of the fifty-two-page report had been read to the public. Mrs. Daly surveyed the faithful from her vantage point in the rear of the room. Finally the superintendent seized the microphone and ordered further debate suspended, claiming that the attacks had become too personal.

The crowd erupted. They were not going to be denied the opportunity to act out. People came up out of their seats and moved toward the front of the room, where they were able to shout nose to nose with the board members. The one gargantuan bouncer assigned the responsibility of maintaining order was cut off from his clients. Two board members, both sympathetic to Mrs. Daly's cause, recalled a similar donnybrook the year before, when the entire school board had been locked in a closet until four o'clock in the morning; they broke for the exits behind the stage. One, wearing a charcoal suit and Converse All-Star sneakers, seemed to have anticipated the turn of events and dressed accordingly. A stout Puerto Rican wrenched the microphone from the superintendent's grasp, leaped on top of the table, and rabble-roused his followers in bawdy Spanish. Order was eventually restored, the showmen exhausted by their own performances, and again the superintendent urged the chairman to call for a vote. The votes were cast one by one, as groups of angry parents slowly overturned the tables in the front of the room. Mrs. Daly slipped unnoticed out the back door as her tenure became law by a 4–3 vote.

David Frazier's case included many of the same variables and a similarly spectacular public finale. He was a young, vigorous, and well-respected black man rooted in the integrated community he served as principal. For three years he was greatly praised for the job he had done in improving his intermediate school, which was beset with typical secondary-school woes. At the close of his second year his tenure seemed a foregone conclusion, both to the staff and to the community. Being young, attuned to the interests of young people and an active resident of the community, David Frazier enjoyed a relationship with his students that few administrators even dream possible. The students not only tolerated him, but imitated his walk and his mannerisms. Passengers riding home in his car felt as if they were in a ticker-tape parade.

But at the beginning of his tenure year a new superintendent was hired and David Frazier got off to a poor start with him. Both were headstrong, and Frazier showed little patience for an outsider who knew nothing of his school but seemed intent upon telling him how to run it. They had several flare-ups at districtwide meetings and the superintendent began granting audiences to a hard core of fifteen white parents who had strongly opposed Frazier's appointment three years earlier. Over the next few months the superintendent met with these parents on numerous separate occasions and began to mistake their view for the view of the community at large. Few people, Frazier included, were aware of the ground swell that was being created.

By March, when the tenure issue was to be decided, the superintendent had assumed that the protestations in his ear represented the tip of an iceberg. He recommended to the board that Frazier not be granted tenure. The superintendent worked closely with the four board members who had confirmed his own appointment, arguing that this represented his first major decision since taking office and that the character of his superintendency would be determined by its outcome. He prevailed upon them to support his position and he came away from the meeting with a 4–3 vote against Frazier. The vote would have to be confirmed in public the following Monday, but so few people saw Frazier's tenure as even being in doubt, that a light turnout was expected.

The one variable not anticipated was that a board member would reveal the outcome of the secret vote to the press. The splashy headlines that followed outraged the community. The day it was released the entire student body of nine hundred marched to the superintendent's office and demanded an audience. At the close of school that same afternoon the faculty assembled briefly in the library and then followed the identical route to the superintendent's door. Parents besieged him for three days. He began to realize that he had badly misjudged the appraisal of the community and, with the die clearly cast, he saw no way to avoid a showdown. He got in touch with the four board members influenced by his vote and exhorted them to remain solid. He was concerned about the commitment of at least two of them — they seemed to feel that they had been misled by the bill of goods he had sold them. Furthermore, they raised very real fears of community violence.

On the designated Monday the meeting site was shifted from the small board room to the school auditorium. Seven hundred parents, teachers, and students attended. Surveying the crowd, the superintendent realized that he could not count more than a scattered handful in his camp. The anxiety on the faces of the board members well before the meeting was called to order reflected their fears about what lay ahead.

The evening resembled that of the Daly case, with spokesmen from all sectors tearing into the board's decision and raising questions about what part the new superintendent had played in it. Publicly he had claimed that he was so new on the job that he had left the decision entirely in the board's hands. The longer the meeting dragged on, the more unruly and ugly the crowd became and the more adamant its defense of David Frazier. Finally, at nearly 1 A.M. the vote was taken and his tenure was granted. Although it appeared to all those assembled that their protest had turned the tide, and had changed the mind of one newly appointed board member, the fact was that some of the more experienced of Frazier's followers had quietly been applying pressure and had collected a sure vote by Monday morning.

Although few tenure decisions are rendered with such public fanfare, all principals are aware that the decisions will always be made behind closed doors. They are aware of the forces that are at work. They are aware that if they are to ensure their own security, they must devote considerable effort to weighing and measuring the forces at hand and manipulating them to their own advantage. One New Jersey principal was hired by a school board to "raise hell" and shake up a school already in a sorry state. His first bombastic ma-

neuvers were met head on by the teachers' union in a host of grievances. He took the matter to the board in private, arguing that if
they really wanted him to clean house, he needed from them a show
of muscle that would intimidate teacher uprisings and be a lesson to
all potentially insubordinate onlookers. Within eight months of his
appointment, he had maneuvered himself into a position of domi-
nant strength and leverage, and had succeeded in acquiring tenure.
He had been able to do so less because of any overriding educational
philosophy, than because of his political cunning.

The tragedy of the principal's position is that most of his power is
in actuality no more than an illusion. Rigid budgetary constraints,
powerful teacher contracts, erratic superintendents, and conflicting
interest groups yearning to have favors granted them severely limit
the potency which the general public assumes rests in his hands.
Most principals end up devoting eighty to ninety percent of their
time to hearing complaints and requests from their various constituencies and allocating the remainder of the time to the politicking necessary to keep their jobs.

After a few months in the job, the principal discovers that he is
the educational leader of the building in name only. His rather
amorphous responsibility of "running the school" has evolved into a
purely defensive posture of reacting to emergencies.

The drains on his time and energy make his contacts with parents,
students, and staff necessarily formal, infrequent, and rarely posi-
tive. The relations between him and the spokesmen of the many
groups making demands upon his time grow strained and uncomfortable. In trying to satisfy all by evenly distributing his time, he
satisfies none. He is often the object of derision and ridicule in the
Teachers' Room, in children's homes, in places where parents
gather. He is able to deliver so little of what is expected that he is
foredoomed to failure.

His life becomes one of endless dilemmas and frustrations, measured in soporific PTA meetings and midnight telephone calls. Like
a shark he must keep swimming to keep breathing.

All principals would do well to take an occasional week in the
woods.

Bein' Abuuuused

"I don't know how much longer I'm going to be able to run down children in the hallways. My hips and my ankles seem to be giving out."

— Donald Kelsey, assistant principal, aged thirty

IN 1976 THERE WERE 1,351 assistant principals in the New York elementary and junior high schools, a number reduced by ten percent from 1975. Assistant principals are more assistants than principals. All assistant principals are teachers and many at some point become principals. As assistant principals they are passing through a stage of their careers that is regrettably unavoidable. Their movement through the ranks has no correlation with their abilities either as teachers or prospective principals. That passage is related exclusively to ambition. Other than physical jobsite, the three positions have little in common. As already pointed out, principals are stereotyped as hard, insensitive persons who are no longer moved by the interests and concerns of either their students or their teachers. They acquired these traits when they were assistant principals.

Good, compassionate teachers are often totally unsuccessful as assistant principals. The understanding they are accustomed to

47

showing toward the children with whom they work closely the year round loses effectiveness when they are dealing infrequently with large numbers of children. Conversely, unsuccessful teachers often become effective junior administrators.

The most depressing aspect of the assistant principal's job is that whatever hopes he may have entertained about completing his assigned duties of teacher training, setting up model learning laboratories, making classroom observations, overseeing a floor or a corridor, exercising leadership over a corps of teachers, or improving the quality of life in the school, he soon discovers that he is overwhelmed by petty disciplinary problems. What he had hoped would be a life spent in close touch with teachers and students turns out to be one in which he must constantly respond to emergencies. By definition the assistant principal deals with teachers who have in some way been infuriated by their children, or parents who have been infuriated by just about anything.

The assistant principal is a disciplinarian because of the forces of history. Graduate schools of education drill into prospective teachers that "when a disciplinary problem arises, call for the assistant principal, that's what he's there for." If the assistant principal should neglect discipline in order to run training sessions for teachers, those same teachers regard him as shirking his duties. During five years in the position, the assistant principal may never meet a child who does not get into fights, or curse his teacher, or fail a subject, or cut classes. He may never have occasion to speak to a teacher about something novel and exciting she had tried in her classroom. He may never encounter a parent who is not seething at something the school has done. His experiences in the job often leave him a changed and bitter man, suspect of all who work with him, down on children, and skeptical of the true interests of parents. At this point he is supposedly prepared to assume a principalship. Actually, he is ready to live up to the worst aspects of the stereotype: he has been well schooled in the practice of dealing with people at their very worst.

Disciplinary matters have certain characteristics in common. They are unexpected; they involve a highly distraught student or a

highly distraught teacher, or both; they arise at the most inconve-
nient moments; they are based on pettiness; they require many
hours and much paperwork before they are settled; and they further
strain already-strained relationships.

Assistant Principal Covington has been conferring with a salesman from Random House for less than five minutes, when in storms
a disheveled, red-faced Mr. Payson dragging a screaming Donald by
one arm and one leg.

Mr. Payson: This kid tried to cut in line in the cafeteria and I won't
  have it! I won't have . . .
Donald: The motherfucker hit me! The motherfucker hit me! My
  father's gonna kill you, motherfucker!
Mr. Payson: If this kid is not suspended I'm filing a grievance
  against you! I want his mother in immediately!

Twenty minutes later Mr. Payson regains his self-control and
returns to the cafeteria. Donald sulks quietly in the corner as Mr.
Covington telephones his mother and sets up a conference for the
following morning. The door to his office remains open, and the
meeting with the Random House emissary is resumed.

Less than a minute passes before Mr. Lang, a math teacher who is
sixty-four years old, bald-headed, and slow-talking, appears at the
door. "Are you busy right now?" he inquires, knowing full well that
Mr. Covington is busy.

"Yes, I am, Mr. Lang," Covington replies. "Is this a matter that
can wait twenty minutes?"

Mr. Lang turns ugly and sarcastic. "Why, yes it is. It doesn't
matter to me if they're abuuuusin' me! No, I guess I kind of like
bein' abuuuuused! I wish my wife would start calling me an 'old
bald-head motherfucker.' No bother. Next time I guess I'll just turn
my back like all the other teachers do when they see you boys
abuuuusin' them!"

Mr. Covington again excuses himself from his guest and speaks
with Mr. Lang in the hallway outside his office. The name of the
culprit is revealed, and he is marched to the office and made to sit

catty-corner to Donald. His mother is also called but she is neither at home nor at work. A letter will have to be written and in the attendance officer's hands by three o'clock, informing the mother of the "abuuuusin' " her child was guilty of.

The conference is again resumed with sympathetic comments from the salesman on the assistant principal's plight. Almost at that instant, Mr. Prince, a gym teacher on hall duty during the lunch period, drags "Chunky" and "Sweet Pea" into the office by the scruffs of their necks and explains that he caught them fighting and cussing outside the cafeteria. He deposits both in Mr. Covington's office, where they continue a vicious round of the "Dozens" (a ritual of exchanging insults, with a premium on imaginativeness) for another few minutes. A telephone call or a letter will have to go out to the parents of both before three o'clock and it is now close to one-thirty.

Before Mr. Covington has even made a pretense of resuming the conference, Michelle comes strolling through the open door with all of her books under one arm. She produces a note from Mrs. Gordon:

Mr. Covington,
Michelle refuses to sit in her assigned seat. She also refuses to place her gum in the trash can, as I have requested six times already this period. It is a Herculean task to try to get order in this class. I must see her mother before she is readmitted to my room. If I am unable to, I am liable to lose face with the class.

[Unsigned]

Michelle adds, "I can't stand that old Mary Poppins lady."

In walks Ms. Davidson, the hefty teacher from the Girls Physical Education Department. She surveys the crowd of five plus the salesman, who is packing up his wares and leaving a card, and says, "Good crowd you got here today. Look, I came up to tell you that Robin was not in gym again today and that somebody had better let her mother know, because you remember how she was the last time she found out. I just thought I had better let somebody know. Hey, by the way, how'd you like those Giants yesterday? Mendenhall and Gregory were out of sight, eh?" The salesman drops his card on the desk and asks Mr. Covington to call him when he gets a free moment.

The parade is by no means over. Mrs. Redley will drag in a hysterical little girl whom she accuses of stealing a bobbin from one of the school sewing machines. Mr. Marshall will march five young men all the way from the gymnasium at the other end of the school building, boys who come to gym without gym clothes five days a week. Mrs. Michael will escort in a little girl who, she says, threw her lunch across the cafeteria. Mr. Reed, the attendance officer, will usher in four hooky players whom he found in a candy store six blocks away and a fifth boy, who, he alleges, was standing waist-deep in the Harlem meer, stoned, playing the bongos. Ms. Salton, a "rookie," will come in crying because of an incident that took place in her classroom, but it is one she "would rather not talk about."

Each episode requires hours to unravel. Conferences with the teachers involved will have to be scheduled so as not to conflict with their teaching assignments. In the more severe cases parents will be summoned to the school to help resolve the matter. These parent conferences are rarely pleasant. To attend, parents have to miss half a day's work and therefore half a day's pay, and they take out their resentment for that fact on the school's representative, the assistant principal. Parents who are summoned to the school with great regularity occasionally lose their jobs.

In one of these conferences, the parent enters with the intention of fighting the teacher. In another the parent levels her sights on the balding assistant principal, saying as she turns to go, "The next time you call me off my job, I'm gonna make the hair start growing on your head again." At another conference, two parents, called to school because their children had been in a fight during science class, end up rolling around on the floor themselves.

Parents come to the school to see the assistant principal because he has summoned them to straighten out a matter that erupted there, or they come to school to "investigate" a matter their children have reported to them. If the latter, they come in irate. Typical are instances in which a child has been robbed, extorted of his lunch money, punched by another student, wrongly accused of something, made to buy "insurance" (premiums paid by small students to large students to prevent physical abuse), or hit, grabbed, or molested by a teacher.

Mrs. Feathers breaks down crying (clearly an instance of parental acting-out) in the assistant principal's office as she hears her son Dennis describe how Mr. Spock took Dennis's arm and twisted it behind his back. Mr. Spock does not deny any part of the story but reminds Mrs. Feathers that Dennis had called him a "black motherfucker" in front of the fourth-period class.

Mrs. Tennyson glares at Mr. Madison, whom her son John accuses of having punched him in the back. Under intense cross-examination by both Mr. Madison and the assistant principal, John decides that "maybe it wasn't Mr. Madison, maybe it was that other teacher who looks kinda like him."

Mr. and Mrs. Foxx sit uneasily as their son Anthony describes how Mr. Tessio threw him across the auto-mechanics shop. Mr. Tessio, a Lithuanian refugee who has great difficulty with the English language but who knows a frameup when he sees one, eventually explains that Anthony neglected to mention that he had been in a fistfight with another boy at the time the incident took place.

Mrs. Chambers points an accusing finger at a Mr. Andrews for shoving her son out of the street, even after he explains that a car was coming. The assistant principal dismisses the case. Mrs. Chambers is not satisfied, so she files assault and battery charges against the teacher and takes him to court. Three months later the judge dismisses the case as cavalierly as had the assistant principal on the grounds that Mr. Andrews was acting in the child's best interest.

Reverend Dellwood sits quietly as his daughter explains to the assistant principal how Señor Ramírez made passes at her during the lunch period. She accuses him of asking her if she had ever gone steady with anyone and if she loved him. Twice he had put his hand on her leg and whispered that his wife and his three children were all the way down in Venezuela and would never know if he had a little girlfriend in the United States. (Ramírez's defense of his actions was shaky to say the least. The minister's daughter was removed from his class and Señor Ramírez was persuaded to retire in June.

Mr. Trent listens uncomfortably as one of his young students accuses him of "teacher brutality" during graphic-shop class. He confesses to the incident, apologizes, and thereby keeps his job.

Mrs. Rodríguez accuses Mr. Longstreth of slapping her son Carlos hard on the back of the head. The teacher acknowledges the act and is warned that a recurrence will cost him his job.

Mrs. Taylor comes for her twentieth conference of the year, this one about Sharon's accusation that her science teacher threw away her test paper and cursed at her. Mrs. Taylor is a former heroin addict, and before the conference begins, she tells everyone present that her methadone clinic was closed this morning and that she will have to return in the afternoon to receive her dosage. Not ten minutes after the conference has begun, as Sharon's teacher begins his defense of his actions, Mrs. Taylor's chin drops to her chest and she begins snoring loudly. The assistant principal tries in vain to wake her, but ends up walking the semicomatose woman to his car, and driving both her and Sharon home for the day.

Mr. Elton, an avowed nonviolent Muslim, enters the office with a large stick, intent on annihilating the assistant principal for failing to settle an argument that had erupted into a fight several hours after school and left his daughter hospitalized.

The beat goes on.

One assistant principal, Sam Wilson, tried to be patient and understanding with each child brought to his office door. By eleven o'clock every morning he had accumulated a crowd at least twenty strong. By two o'clock he had to move his charges into the school auditorium because their numbers had swelled beyond the capacity of his office.

Eighty to ninety percent of an assistant principal's time is devoted to matters of discipline; the rest is generally consumed by trivia. One assistant principal kept a detailed list on a yellow, legal-size pad of every single nondisciplinary item he was supposed to see to over an entire school year. Favors that teachers asked him to do and forgettable requests they made of him as he passed them in the hallway or peeked into a classroom were also included. By June the items numbered 1,419. A modest selection from the list provides an unparalleled view of an assistant principal's life:

1. Have Mr. Williams clean blinds in Benson's room.
3. Call Ann Dreisson re contract ext. 253.
4. Put outlets in Title VII reading room.
5. Move blackboard from 204 to 126.
10. See Mr. Cook re dirty windows.
15. Distribute Curriculum Conference notices (memo).
18. Talk to LT re L'il Abner.
37. See Bench about ditto machine in science stockroom.
43. Write and distribute intramural athletic contracts.
72. Remind counselors to put 10 eighth graders and 11 seventh graders in Stevenson's class.
91. Write team leaders agenda and meeting notices.
120. Make afternoon PA announcement re lateness.
141. See Mrs. Trainer about Pedro Santiago and period 1 art.
154. Write letter to LT to keep John Holiday on sixth grade cluster.
174. Check to Xerox for $105.32.
191. Type up minutes of clusters meeting.
206. Suspend Kevin for 'm-fing' Mrs. Stevenson.
233. Call Claudia for raincheck.
235. Conference with Mrs. Gibson re Sheila's abortion 3 p.m. — postponed.
241. 10/10 call Words-in-Color lady re new pointer and chalk.
252. Outdoor Ed. planning meeting in library 3:00 p.m.
253. Get three parents for Malone to serve on Title VII Advis. Comm., Urban League.
256. Write Back-to-School-Night schedules.
282. See pain-in-the-ass Mrs. Arlow 10:00 a.m. Tues. Oct. 23.
311. Get memo to all teachers for Nov. 9 Jazz assembly.
321. 8:30 Mon Dr. Spady re Andy D. tell B. Wash. to join meeting.
327. Distribute notices for Social studies meeting.

390. Per 3 DANAC.
400. Announcement re students in Teachers' Room.
412. Grades for related arts? Yes or no? First cycle? see LT.
415. 12:00 Meet with God awful Mrs. Brady.
446. Change Ann Tew's algebra grade, post parent conference.
477. Mon a.m. check with Bonney on Hauser's progress.
509. Draft D&R for Administrative Assistants.
517. See B. Washington re Pop.
523. Write postponement memo re Public Speaking Contest.
551. Call Saveno re Unified Science I&II.
611. See LT re mess-up in aides Dec payment.
623. McNeil!!
655. Letter to probation officer Collon bros.
690. 9:45 Mr. Johnson vs. Mrs. Setavian my office.
730. Change lunch hours for matrons.
742. Meeting with LT re memo for extended homeroom 2/4/74.
761. Per 7, Team V vs. Administration in Main Office.
770. Set up meeting with Reasoner and Mrs. H 3:30 Thurs.
793. Suspend Marvelous Marvin.
798. Tell Betty Josephs to bring home DeDe O'Connell's report card.
818. Man Cafeteria ticket line per 5a and 5b.
843. Add Rita Rose to Sub list.
917. Leave note on Ms. Sanchez door.
985. Return ice cream 25¢ for Gwen.
1,018. 9:30 conference with Mrs. Sylen and Simone re slugging.
1,020. Write and distribute report card memo.
1,028. Collect Sci. Behavioral objectives from Mary Klein.
1,041. Announce resignation at faculty meeting (brief and straight).
1,046. Per 7 Curriculum Conf. with Neilson.
1,051. Settle lovers quarrel with Dresson/Sessler 4/18/74.
1,080. Observe Morgan and write his sup. report.
1,085. Call state office of Educ 518 474-3901 12:45-3:30.
1,098. 8:00 a.m. conference with Mrs. Alou and Arturo. (NO SHOW)

1,113.   Students here from H.S. to distribute questionnaire.

1,126.   Move Naomi Hentoff to First Honor Roll.

1,164.   Per 7, spelling Team 1 vs. Team 4, left side of caf.

1,177.   Change Kerry Sludge's class (stop the wars).

1,248.   Turn over letter and paper to Ann.

1,261.   Mr. and Mrs. Adams vs. Mr. Santelli.

1,273.   Arrange for a sub. in 123 per 7&8.

1,281.   Balance Speech and Drama account (if possible).

1,321.   Memo to all teachers re awards Assembly.

1,325.   File accident report on Alexander's punched jaw.

1,367.   Gregory, HR 313b, accused of stealing lunch tickets.

1,395.   Memo for Thurs graduation rehearsal to all staff.

1,419.   Say goodbye to all my pals.

Obscured at number 1,041 was his decision to resign. It was given no more fanfare than a reminder to have the custodians refill the Kotex dispenser in the girls' room.

The unfortunate aspect of becoming a principal in a New York City public school is that one first has to serve time as an assistant principal. The job that an assistant principal performs in no way prepares him for a principalship. Cops or housebroken gorillas could do the job as well. Then perhaps men and women unscarred by years of dealing only with the grimmer side of humanity would not find themselves running schools.

Teachers: Rookies

"When the time comes for Teacher Recognition Day, don't nobody call me to bake no cake or nothin'."

— Mrs. Simpson, parent, at a community school board meeting during the 1968 teachers' strike

IN 1976 NEW YORK was employing more than 50,000 teachers, 35,178 of them in its nine hundred elementary and junior high schools, a comedown from 41,766 in 1975. The elementary teachers cost the city over $600,000,000 in salaries, pensions and social security payments; the teachers in the junior high schools (grades 7, 8, and 9) and intermediate schools (grades 6, 7, and 8) cost the city about $300,000,000.* Beginning teachers are paid $9,800, while senior veterans make $20,350, based on a pay scale so steep that the maximum pay is reached in seven years. In twenty years a teacher is eligible for retirement — at a pay scale higher than his highest salaried year but not collectible until age sixty-five.

*Several years ago, the powers that be sought to convert all junior high schools to intermediate schools. Like so many things in the school system, the changeover was never completed. Both kinds of schools now exist side by side.

Beginning to teach is like coming into puberty a second time. The opening day of school leaves the most stable new teachers, men and women alike, completely disoriented and distraught. They take crosstown buses to go uptown. They get off subways at stops they have never heard of, in boroughs they don't live in. They take the IRT when they want the IND. Some eat constantly and lose weight; others stop eating altogether and get fat. They call their wives by their mothers' names. They wear wool suits in early September and leave their pocketbooks in cabs. They tip the lady at the supermarket checkout counter. They forget their telephone numbers and get hopelessly lost going to the corner for a newspaper. They walk down "up" escalators. They swallow chewing gum and light the wrong end of their cigarettes. The kids call them "rookies."

For a new teacher the first day of school marks the exact moment in his life when he ceases to be a dependent being. There is no equivalent moment in any other profession. New teachers have spent their lives leaning on their parents, their friends, their schools, their colleges, and their graduate schools. They have fulfilled the threshold requirements of the trade: college, education courses, Board of Examiners licensing exams, and they have been assigned a file number. They have succeeded in life thus far, always in a position to take and to receive. They have developed the art of criticism, but have yet to be judged themselves. Some are accomplished cynics, complacent through their success in school, confident that they are, in the words of Henry Adams, "men of the world fit for any emergency."

But the first day of school abruptly pitches the new teacher into adulthood. It compresses into a fraction of a second a process nature allots years to accomplish.

Every teacher can recall the exact details of the first hour, the first sixty minutes that he stood before a group of thirty strange children — alone. He can remember the clothes he wore, the thoughts that passed so rapidly through his mind, the feelings he felt. Beginning to teach in New York City is an unsettling experience for which no amount of preparation can be perfectly adequate.

The moment is immensely personal. One young man spoke uncertainly from the front of the classroom with his eyes glued to his feet for forty-five minutes. He recalls wishing that his mother were seated in the back of the room when he finally mustered the courage to raise his eyes.

New teachers are enigmas to their students. They are beings without form or shape or substance. They are stared at as if they are unable to talk, as if they are inanimate. They need definition, personality, character. Children see it as their inherent responsibility to *define* teachers. They must push them and poke them and see just how far they will bend or stretch before they will finally snap, becoming exactly like the others they have known as "teachers." Children feel a compulsion to get on with the determination of that definition immediately. They may grant a new teacher as much as half an hour's grace, but after that, their curiosity consumes them. Is this to be a year when they can throw clay and crayons and pull hair at will, or will they be intimidated into keeping their seats, set in perfect geometric rows, molding cows, dogs, and frogs on sections of the Sunday New York *Times?* They must know. Where will this teacher draw the line?

The children define a new teacher not by what he permits them to do, but by what he does not permit them to do. He is by definition the sum total of all the specific limits he sets. When the children sense that they have pushed a new teacher to within a hair's breadth of his breaking point, they push some more. He throws his hands high above his head, appearing for an instant to be some creature they have never encountered before (King Kong?), and several children in the back of the room plug their fingers in their ears in anticipation of what they know is coming. Suddenly the new teacher screams, "NOOOOOO!" in a voice that sounds as if it could not possibly be his. But the ordeal is not ended; it is just beginning. They push again to see if he really *means* no. He says it even louder this time, but the kids know that they have to push him one more time to see if he is *consistent.* They do and he is. He has begun to take shape for them and for himself. The new teacher has done the very things he thought he would never do. He has reached inside himself and discovered something he never knew or thought or dreamed was there. For an instant he is not sure that he is still he.

One teacher described coming into class on the first day of school armed with one hundred copies of a diagnostic math quiz and one hundred copies of spelling words he had prepared the previous evening. (Most of the materials used in New York classrooms are drafted by the teachers and distributed in rexograph or mimeograph form.) About half an hour before lunch, after having his fourth graders fill out pink, yellow, blue, and white IBM cards for the main office to misplace, he decided that the time had finally arrived to begin his first lesson, to say things to his class in his own words, to become somebody in their eyes, to do what they expected him to do: to teach.

"This little piece of paper that I am going to pass out [he held it up nervously] is not a test. It's just a kind of little game I am going to ask you to help me with so I can tell what kind of math you had last year and figure out what kind we will start with this year. So when I give you the paper, you may begin. There are addition and subtraction problems on the back. Don't worry about this, just do the best you can."

The children sat expressionlessly, following his eyes, as he walked slowly down the left aisle, carefully placing a paper on each child's desk, smiling weakly as he progressed. When he was about halfway through, a little boy with curly blond hair, who was sitting near the front of the room, balled his paper up and dropped it on the floor. The new teacher hesitated (fatal), debated reprimanding the boy, but decided to complete his tour first. Seeing that there had been no repercussions, a little girl did the same thing with her paper. The teacher contemplated screaming at both of them, but gave each a new paper and picked up the two on the floor. The little boy balled his second paper up as he had the first. A girl with no front teeth sitting in the back of the classroom laughed out loud and did the same thing to her paper. Gradually the whole class began balling up their papers and laughing and tossing them on the floor.

The teacher replaced the papers as fast as the children balled them up. He thinks in retrospect that there was a great deal of noise in the room but he is not certain. He claims that he heard his heart pounding and some of the kids did too. He kept repeating to himself, "Don't run!" He distributed the hundred math quizzes and when they had all been deposited on the floor, he started distributing the spelling sheets. But the palace revolt continued unchecked. When the bell rang for lunch, his class disappeared as if filet mignon were on the menu. He was left standing knee-deep in crumpled paper, sweating from head to toe, with only three sheets of paper left in his hand and no idea what he would have done had the bell not bailed him out.

"Jesus Christ," he said out loud. A weak smile crossed his face as he realized that he could speak.

Children have certain specific expectations of what a teacher is, and a new teacher who fails to conform to those expectations is quickly in troubled waters.

"We are going to begin at the beginning," Ms. Rookie told her fifth graders. "Now, what do we call this?" Her index finger went up as if hailing a cab.

"That's your finger, lady," came the response from several quarters.

"Good. Does anyone else know another name for a finger?"

Silence. Some of the children began to squirm (coping with ambiguity is a major problem in New York's schools). They all were perplexed.

"Well, another name is a digit, d-i-g-i-t." She wrote it on the blackboard. "The digit is the basic unit of counting and our hands were the first tools our ancestors used to count with."

Perplexity turned to confusion and then to anger. They began to break rank.

"Hey, you ain't talkin' 'bout my mother is you?"*

*In a similar misunderstanding I once said to eleven-year-old Mike Adams, who was six feet tall and weighed 170 pounds: "You sure are a big boy, Mike; I bet your father is big too." To which he replied, "What you say about my father?"

"Wait a minute, this ain't no math!"

"Give us some 'times.' I don't want to know about no 'dig-its'!"

"You ain't no teacher!"

"We want a *real* teacher!"

I used to train new teachers for a living, and I grew accustomed to holding their hands and changing their bedpans through those first few traumatic weeks in September. One young woman attributed her failures of the first two days to the excessive length of each activity she had planned. She theorized that the attention spans of third graders were so brief that her salvation lay in planning many more, and much shorter, activities — as many as she needed to fill the day. By the end of her second week of teaching, she was changing activities every ten minutes and had lost eleven pounds. She had calculated that she needed thirty-six, separate, ten-minute lessons a day to make it safely to three o'clock. She had not slept more than three hours a night since the day school had opened.

Another young woman was given a 5–1 class. Since this is the most advanced fifth-grade class in the school, the parents believed that all their children would go to Harvard and become neurosurgeons. They besieged her in and out of the classroom from her second day to her tenth, which was her last. The principal mercifully persuaded her to retire. It seems that several children had gone home on day one and reported to their parents that they had "a pretty new teacher in a yellow dress who talked very softly and was scared to death."

The one event that a new teacher neither anticipates nor relishes on the first day of teaching is a fight. More than anything else, a new teacher wants to be able to stand by the time clock at 3 P.M. with a smile on his face, secure in the knowledge that his first day went without a catastrophic incident. He reasons that if he can make it to the bus before crumbling to little pieces or vomiting or whatever, the day will be deemed a success.

I was not so fortunate. There were only forty-five minutes remaining in what had been a tolerable opening day. Belinda Davis came up to my desk to ask me if she could use the bathroom. Someone was already out of the room, so I asked her to please hold on for a moment and I would make certain that she was the next to go. The rest of the sixth grade was working reasonably quietly on a puzzle I had borrowed in desperation from a veteran across the hall. Belinda turned and went back to her seat. I moved about the room helping those who needed help with the puzzle and trying to match names and faces. Learning a child's name can eliminate a great deal of the anxiety of the first week. There is a world of difference between "Cut that out!" and "Cut that out, Jimmy!" The anonymity that children sense in the presence of a stranger becomes their leverage to mischief.

Marguerite Mason came back from the girls' room and brought the pass to me in the rear of the room. I had learned her name the previous Friday because she had just moved to Manhattan from the Bronx and I had met her and her mother in school during registration the previous week. (The week preceding the opening of school is Orientation Week for all new teachers; most of them agree that it is uniformly worthless.) She was as captivating as an eleven-year-old can be. She returned to her seat and I motioned to Belinda, who was watching my every move, to come get the pass. On her way to me, K. B. Wilson stuck out his foot and tripped her. She stumbled, caught her balance, and wheeled around to face him. He bolted from his seat and stood trembling in anticipation, nose to nose with Belinda. They were breathing each other's breath. No one moved.

Establishing a clear order of dominance is an inevitability at the beginning of each school year in every public school homeroom. The pecking order is as clear-cut as a challenge ladder at an exclusive tennis club. Each child knows exactly who sits a notch below and a notch above everyone else. Determinations of dominance in the sixth grade are almost entirely physical. Children who move into new neighborhoods have to be properly placed on the ladder. Children who grow eight inches or gain fifty pounds over the summer return to school prepared to update their rankings. Dominance does not discriminate according to height, weight, or sex. Children new to a school live in anxiety until the first blows have been struck and the first fight has been had. One second-grade class was having recess outside on a jungle gym when a little boy, new to the school and the neighborhood, who had been sitting off by himself, arose and yelled to his classmates to come off the jungle gym and gather around him. They did. "My name is Stanley," he began tersely. "I'm new around here but I want all of you to know that I don't take no bullshit." He waited a second and then concluded, "You can go back and play now."

Belinda Davis hit K. B. Wilson with a right cross to the mouth that was reminiscent of the blow Ingemar Johansson pinned on Floyd Patterson in the fifties. "Tunder and Lightning." Everyone in the class knew it was coming, but no one really saw the punch. K. B. went backwards over his chair, bleeding heavily from the corner of his mouth. He came up throwing: lefts, rights, books, chairs, even a desk. I finally got control of his arms and crammed him out the door after a monumental struggle. He was slight but wiry, quick, and ferocious. I slammed the door in his tear-stained face, knowing that it was locked from the outside. A few girls began to rearrange the furniture as I began to restore some semblance of order. All I could think of was going home.

Belinda stood stock-still in the front of the classroom, staring through me and the blackboard behind me. Suddenly the back door burst open (one of my little traitors had apparently opened it from the inside), and K. B. Wilson charged in with a chair held high in the air. In an instant he was behind Belinda and was bringing it down on her head. Somehow I managed to get both my forearms between Belinda Davis's head and that chair. I can't remember being hit so hard or hurting so much in my entire life. My arms began swelling immediately. I had tears in my eyes. I couldn't pick up a piece of chalk or my books or put on my jacket. I soaked my arms in the tub that night until the wee hours of the morning. I called K. B. Wilson's home and learned that he had gotten four stitches in his lip and a beating with an "ironing cord" from his mother. I wish Belinda Davis had knocked him stiff. It was a while before I headed the dominance order in K. B. Wilson's class.

Arthur Block's first year of teaching was typical of young teachers who eventually succeed. Many do not. Arthur was an intelligent young man of twenty-two, fresh out of college, sensitive, an idealist set on making a contribution to improving education in New York, at least in some small measure. He was imaginative, quick-witted, and innovative, confident that by the end of his first year he would prevail. His was a trial by fire in and out of the classroom. One afternoon during his second week, he was trudging down a relatively deserted cross street and staring at the ground as he tried to unravel the day's happenings, to separate out its few successes from its many failures. First-year teachers have a characteristic walk that makes them noticeable anywhere in the city. Their vision seems entirely inward; their eyes are all but rolled back in their heads; they seem to struggle with a piece of history that is exclusively their own. There are eight million people in New York but not one who can help a new teacher out of his personal quandary. Art Block all of a sudden found himself on his back on the sidewalk looking up at the sky, the buildings, and the three men who were taking his watch, his wallet, and his change. They left him a subway token. He continued home more distracted by the experiences in his classroom than by the robbery.

As a teacher-trainer with a nonprofit corporation, The Teachers, Inc., I agreed to meet Arthur Block one afternoon after school in his classroom to assist him with some ideas he had for carpentry. I arrived at the school at about ten minutes to three. I could hear Art's fourth-grade, fourth-floor class from the main lobby. The noise grew louder as I climbed the stairs, deafening by the time I reached the fourth-floor landing. Art Block had his back to the glass in the door. The sweat from his back and neck had clouded the upper two panes. I knocked. No response. I yelled to be heard over the din. He turned around: pale-faced, exhausted, his glasses hooked only on his left ear. He managed a weak smile and squeezed the door open ever so slightly to allow me to enter. All the windows in the room were closed and most were fogged. The temperature outdoors was in the high eighties, with typically high New York humidity, but it seemed comfortable compared to Art Block's classroom. I thought for a moment that I was in a stable. All the kids were soaking wet with sweat and not one of them was standing still. There seemed to be two or three classes in Art Block's room. I noticed a wall cabinet that had several paintbrushes and rulers crammed in its handles and was rhythmically pulsating. I waded through the debris created by all the activity to the back of the room and removed the rulers and brushes, unlocking the cabinet doors. Four kids fell out. Art Block knew they were in there but had been too afraid to leave his post by the door. He had decided on a policy of containment until help arrived. But all new teachers know or should know that in most schools help does not arrive.

Art Block explained later that he had been trying to line up his children since eleven-thirty, first to go to lunch, then to gym, and finally to go home. Having been called on the carpet by his principal on more than one occasion for his class's poor demeanor in moving through the halls, he had insisted on straight, orderly lines. His class never left the room.

On another occasion when I was observing Art Block's progress more than a month later, his every move was being perfectly mimicked — to Art's annoyance and the delight of the class — by an odd-looking little boy named Pierre. As a last resort he began mimicking Pierre mimicking him, which hardly got him off the hook.

Even the most seemingly reliable elements of school life betray new teachers. A film guaranteed to captivate the attention of even the most restless children stops abruptly and unexpectedly in the middle of the first reel. The image on the screen freezes like a stop-action television football play, then a brilliant beam of light emerges in its center and spreads quickly to its edges. The heat from the bulb has neatly cut the film in half. The film is rewound, the projector rethreaded, and the show begins anew. Next, the projector mysteriously stops, never to start again. Ditto machines that crank out copies flawlessly for hours on end falter when the new teacher stands up to take his turn. Like the children themselves, the machines twist the screw one notch tighter; they too seem to want to test the neophyte's constitution. They measure his stamina and resiliency, his adaptation to pressure and anxiety, his essence. Most rookies become paranoid about such occurrences, which they contend bear the unmistakable mark of conspiracy.

Richie Segura, new to New York from the University of San Juan, a new teacher in a fifth-grade class, pounded his fist against the blackboard seeking a momentary stay against the surrounding confusion. His fist went clean through the blackboard and created a hole a foot in diameter. The hole remained unrepaired throughout the remainder of the year. Screams of "Mira! Mira!" rang down the hallways of the old tired building. Gradually he learned to write around the hole, to incorporate it into his maps and diagrams. The hole became the Pacific Ocean.

Christine Paulson was enjoying the finest morning of her first week of teaching. The thirty-minute units she had laboriously planned for her classes were working flawlessly. Just as her students tired of one pursuit, she ladled out another — different, refreshing, intriguing, and curiosity-provoking. She sensed that the time had come to shift gears again. She turned to the ammunition stacked neatly on her desk. Nothing. The desk was empty. A large flat barren piece of wood. She panicked, noticed the open window and hurried to it, fearing the worst. There, four stories below, her papers dotted the street. A few that were caught in updrafts floated lazily to the ground. Some had landed on the lower roofs. The serenity of the street suggested that a parade had passed leaving a trail of confetti; perhaps a wedding.

Mrs. Paulson gets a grip on herself, spins, and explodes. "If I can't keep these goddamn windows open without having all my papers thrown out on the street, I won't! I don't care how hot it gets or how uncomfortable you are!"

She raises both hands to the top of the sash and with a great grunt slams the window shut. The entire piece of glass tumbles outward onto the street.

Most new teachers bear up under apparently insurmountable odds and gradually metamorphose into old teachers. But some do not. Some are battered and broken and driven from the profession by early October. I went to one school to check on Melanie Day, one of my trainees who was floundering mercilessly. Her classroom was empty. I cornered the principal, who told me of her sudden, tearful resignation. I hurried to her apartment. Her feet were surrounded by a half-dozen empty beer cans; she was slugging away at one in her hand; her face was swollen from crying. "I never thought teaching would be quite like that," she said.

There are those new teachers who give meaning to the word *charisma*. They walk into their classrooms in September and fall in love and are fallen in love with. They make the rest of the teachers, old and new, mad by their success. The time and money that has been expended in trying to isolate the "one thing" that such teachers possess has not paid great dividends. As one principal stated summarily after a massive three-year retraining and retooling period with his whole staff, "Some got it, some don't." The number in any given school of teachers who "got it" are too small — 10 percent, 20 percent (25 percent at most).

If what they had could be bottled, New York would be a better place. But they are rare birds indeed, and even those schools fortunate enough to have them have difficulty convincing them to stay and keep up the pace — year after year after year.

Teachers: Veterans

Kevin Anderson (aged thirteen) to Mr. Schneider, a veteran teacher:
"Do you like Ray Charles?"
Mr. Schneider: "Whose class is he in?"
       — Heard in an intermediate school hallway

THE AGE OF INNOCENCE that characterizes a teacher's apprentice-
ship in the New York City public school system comes to a formal
conclusion after three full years of teaching. A legal state of being,
known as tenure, "happens" to a teacher at the conclusion of the
prescribed time span (over the past decade the particular length of
time has vacillated between three and five years according to the
whim of the state legislature), in the same way that little girls have
to start shaving their legs and men go bald. Tenure is supposed to
confer excellence, create job security, and strengthen the school
system. The law states that tenure is to be granted only after the
candidate's performance in the classroom has been carefully "observed" by his immediate supervisor. In addition, the supervisor is
legally required to hold a conference with the candidate both before
and after the observation, and to submit his conclusions clearly, in
writing, with copies for all concerned parties and for posterity. Tenure is formally granted in the public forum of an open meeting of the

69

community school board; names up for consideration are listed in alphabetical order on the public agenda; the general public is even encouraged to make comments and to challenge the award of tenure to a prospective recipient.

But the actual conferring of tenure rarely follows the legal prescription. Administrators, too mired down by petty disciplinary matters, may never enter a teacher's classroom. In perusing a teacher's file a school board may discover that she has never been properly observed, but may grant her tenure anyway, out of fear of legal reprisal under the omnibus "due process" aegis. One woman stood up at a Manhattan school board meeting and challenged her own tenure. She stated that she had never been observed or offered assistance, that her supervisor of the past two years had not been seen on her floor, much less in her classroom, and that she doubted whether he knew her name. She concluded by saying that she was not satisfied with her work and described herself as a "shit teacher." She was granted tenure by a unanimous vote.

If tenure is no more than a physiological process and all teachers who choose to stick it out for three years automatically are granted it, how then does the school system go about weeding out its ranks? In a word, it doesn't. The single most incredible attribute of the largest system of public education in the world is that a teacher cannot be fired.

In the fall of 1968 the teachers went on strike twice, the second time for six weeks. Parents and other interested people in the community will tell you that the teachers union struck to avoid losing power to the movement for community control that was bubbling at I.S. 201 (Harlem), Two Bridges (Lower East Side), and Oceanhill–Brownsville (Brooklyn). Albert Shanker and UFT sympathizers claim that the issue was the lack of "due process" when Rhody McCoy tried to "fire" large numbers of teachers.

McCoy and his Oceanhill–Brownsville entourage were blamed by the press and by the UFT for precipitating the Great Strike of 1968 by apparently attempting to fire more than one hundred teachers. McCoy recognized the absurdity of that charge and tried vainly to get the press to understand that a teacher may be transferred to another district but never fired. He did, in fact, order wholesale teacher transfers, a political strategy that in retrospect proved too bold for the moment. Had he had the power to fire, he might well have used it, but neither he nor anyone else in the city has the power to fire a teacher. The current tenure practice, as opposed to structure, and the wide range of "due process" requirements that are part of the determination of a tenure issue, are a quiet legacy to the immense presence of Albert Shanker.

A teacher who has "gone through" tenure has a blanket immunity against every conceivable mandate for removal. One principal contends that "short of a first-degree murder conviction, I doubt that I could remove a teacher and have it hold up in court." He implies by that statement that second-degree murder, although grounds for a sharp reprimand and perhaps a letter in the teacher's file, would be tenuous grounds for negotiating a dismissal. I know of only two instances in which teachers were forced to resign. One was the incident of Señor Ramírez and the minister's daughter, described previously. The other involved a man who had already come into tenure. His apartment was raided one evening by the police on the suspicion that he possessed drugs. In addition to substantial quantities of marijuana and cocaine, the police found stacks of eight-by-ten glossies of the teacher in question involved in a host of unnatural acts with several students whom he was fond of taking on camping trips. Anything shy of this sort of atrocity makes it a waste of time for an administrator to try to cleanse his Augean stables.

The 1968 teachers' strike that was on again off again for three months opened schisms within schools and their faculties and between schools and their communities, schisms which in 1978 still show up clearly. The seeds of division had been sown gradually through the practices of the Board of Examiners and the demographics of hopscotching neighborhoods (in a few schools, *all* the children are "new" *every* year). A catastrophic blowout, a release of the tensions that had been welling up, seemed inevitable. The sparks from the community-control struggle set off the conflagration. The Board of Examiners had molded a staff of teachers some sixty thousand strong that was largely white, Jewish, middle-class, middle-aged, and female. Most did not live in the neighborhoods they worked in. Many lived in relative luxury outside the city limits. As time passed, more and more of their students came from minority groups: blacks, Puerto Ricans, Haitians, Dominicans, and Chinese. But more importantly they were poor, and because they were poor they lived in poor houses on crowded streets, sometimes with one parent, sometimes with none. By 1968 they had become a population reared less by their families than by the streets of the city.

The breach that developed in the sixties between the teachers and their students was more cultural than ethnic in its origins. The set of values the teachers attempted to impose upon their students and the set the streets endorsed became mutually exclusive. To please a teacher a child had to come to school on time; he had to bathe and brush his teeth; he had to come with his hair combed and his homework done; his clothes had to be clean and his shoes tied; he came to school to cooperate with the teacher, to work, to study, to learn; he had to get good grades and aspire to go to college; he had to have good manners, be polite, and help his family as they had helped him.

But the streets were whispering other messages into a young boy's ear. To live within the ethos of the streets, a boy had to be able to make lay-ups with either hand; he had to be willing to miss a few days of school now and then; he had to cut a few classes here and there; he had to steal unchained bicycles from the school yard and sodas from the grocery store; he had to be comfortable rapping to the girls on the corner; he had to know how to throw dice and be willing to smoke "reefer" and perhaps sell a little now and again; he had to wear tailor-made pants ("TM's"), a *real* leather jacket, and Converse All-Star sneakers; he had to keep more than a few dollars in his pocket, curse like a sailor, and wear his "apple" tilted rakishly to one side. The street wanted kids in all neighborhoods in all colors. The street taught them that, by definition, whatever the school supported they were to avoid. The street became for too many children a source of guidance and direction: a family.

I have only encountered one child who functioned in both

spheres and was able to rise to a position of leadership in each. James Thompson read voraciously. By the end of his sixth-grade year he was reading at a college level. He was a leader of those in the school culture. He was president of his class year after year after year. He won contests for poetry readings and starred in school plays. He never misbehaved. He had his homework done and handed it in before it was due. He was consistently on the Honor Roll. James Thompson worked hard.

But when James Thompson hit the streets he was a transformed child. He could talk to bad little girls about bad little things. He smoked pot openly on busy street corners. And he make a basketball jump and dance in his hands. He was offered as a model, as a standard of excellence, by his teachers and by the junkies and pimps on the corner. At fifteen he told me he had two ambitions in life: "to go to Harvard Law School and to knock off Chicken Delight."

Few children even bother to seek success in both worlds. One streetwise twelve-year-old, Pedro Dabón, ambled into math class one morning for the first time in a month and discovered that many of his classmates had strings of little gold stars by their names on a wall chart. Pedro returned at lunchtime and threatened his teacher with a glistening switchblade. She willingly put a healthy dose of stars by his name.

The 1968 strike exposed all the best-kept secrets of public education in New York. Parents for the first time noticed teachers in their schools that they didn't like and didn't want teaching their children. Teachers in 1968 either supported a strike against their clients or they did not. There was no middle ground, no safe base, as in a game of tag.

The 1968 strike created two strata of veteran teachers, where there had formerly been but one. The teachers who had earned their tenure by 1968 (by that time they had already taught five, ten, fifteen, or even twenty years) are a separate caste from the post-strike veterans, most of whom were in their probationary years in 1968.

Many of the older veterans are men and women who appear to have been scarred by the trauma of their first few months of teaching. That abrupt passage from one plane of being to another transformed many of them into people they would rather not have been. The passage was too fast, too startling; it broke them apart and reconstructed them in a moment's time. Many appear externally the same, but inside they know themselves to be different. They met the challenge of the first moments of teaching not with compassion but with fear. Now they appear afraid to show compassion. They live in fear: fear of being laid wide open by the probing questions of their students. David Spencer, chairman of the I. S. 201 community control board, once warned a congregation of new teachers that the children would " 'why' them to death." Their struggle is one to save face, never to let a child gain the upper hand, to use the resources for discipline which the school makes available, never to turn their backs. They attempt to run their classes in an orderly and rigidly controlled fashion. They seek to have their children sit in straight rows and speak only when spoken to. They live in fear of exposure because such is likely to reveal an image of themselves that they would prefer not to unearth. Younger veterans quip of those with twenty years in the trade that "they have had one year of experience twenty times."

The most hardened veterans, probably a quarter of any given school's faculty, fight learning and growth. They have become anti-intellectual in an intellectual trade. They resist anything new and provocative; they squirm through mandatory training sessions and cautiously avoid their younger colleagues. They check their watches continuously and walk out at 3 P.M. They know nothing of the new ideas and new materials that are changing the content and pedagogy of public education. They prefer the "old way." They are the old way. They insist upon learning and studying for their students and fight it for themselves. They live in self-imposed isolation. They have great difficulty communicating with their students and their classes. They lay the blame for the resultant chaos on the children and their families. They can afford to be themselves only for the few minutes in every day when they are in the haven of the Teachers' Room, surrounded by their diminishing colleagues. Commiseration becomes the order of the day. They have learned how not to learn.

Jeffrey Atherton was a boy caught between the culture of the streets and the culture of the school. He proved too awkward, too clumsy, too rough for the world of the streets, that demanded that things be "cool and smooth." Nor was Jeffrey Atherton successful in school. He was too loud and mischievous and he had not yet learned how to read. Jeffrey was reared by his grandmother, who was called to school so often during his sixth-grade year that the office secretaries once ceremoniously presented her with a time card. Jeffrey knew that he could not read and knew that he was unsuccessful in school because of this shortcoming. He told his veteran teacher, "The only reason you don't like me is because I can't read." He appealed to all his teachers year after year to assist him in learning how to read but his pleas were never acknowledged. He wanted to be liked and he wanted desperately to learn to read. One October morning out of a clear blue sky, he reported matter-of-factly that he had developed a scheme whereby he was going to learn how to read by himself. He planned to cut pictures out of the sports sections of the daily papers and out of *Sports Illustrated,* paste them in a scrapbook, and recopy the captions below. In that way, he reasoned, he would learn how to read.

Jeffrey Atherton worked religiously on his private project, which he wisely refused to bring to school. On more than one occasion, after his grandmother had left for work, he doubled back to his apartment to put in a full day's work on his masterpiece. Rumors about Jeffrey Atherton's book gradually began circulating, first around the class and eventually the school. Jeffrey invited selected friends back to his apartment for sneak previews, peeks at his manuscript. The reviewers always returned to school with favorable reports. In late June of that year, with less than a week of school remaining, Jeffrey brought in his chef d'oeuvre. It was truly magnificent. The work was 651 pages in length and stood a good five inches above the desk. He had separate chapters on baseball, boxing, football, hockey, and karate. He had complete rosters of every professional team in sports, over one hundred pages of neatly printed names, numbers, and positions. Each of over one thousand photographs was captioned in handwriting that could belong only to

Jeffrey Atherton. The book bore his mark throughout. Jeffrey boasted that he could read every word in it. He flipped to page 309 and started, "Darryl Lamonica recovers his own fumble in a game against Kansas City . . . ," to prove his point. Many of Jeffrey's skeptical classmates stood in respectful silence. They were awed by the clumsy kid whose grandmother seemed to live in the principal's office.

Later that same afternoon Jeffrey's Spanish teacher, a veteran of eighteen years, appeared hysterically at the principal's door. She wanted Jeffrey Atherton thrown out of school; she wanted him jailed or sent away. When the principal was finally able to calm her down and ask why, she screamed that he had slashed all four tires on her Volkswagen and had thrown a brick through the windshield. When the principal was again able to cut through her hysteria and ask "why" a second time, she replied that the only thing that could have possibly annoyed him was a little incident that had taken place during her class in the afternoon. She reported that the class had refused to settle down because of a "scrapbook" Jeffrey was passing around and that she had confiscated it. When the class had protested further, she said, she had torn the "scrapbook" up and had thrown it in the trash.

Many veteran teachers whose authority is constantly being challenged spend their days calling for principals, assistant principals, deans, and guidance counselors, and telling tales on little children. "He refuses to take his assigned seat!" "She keeps chewing her gum and won't spit it out!" "He told me he wasn't going to do his work!" "She refuses to get dressed for gym!" "He has lost the same book three times this year!" "I'm sick and tired of her smart little mouth!" "I want to see his mother!" "I want you to call her father!" "I want him suspended!" "I want her expelled!"

When a veteran teacher is not yelling for help, he is dragging some screaming, kicking child to the office. Invariably he is being told what Father or Big Brother is going to do to him. The principal is usually tied up with some other similar matter in his office and the secretaries don't exactly relish having a hysterical child on their hands. The whole show is an embarrassment for the principal, the teacher, the child, and the school, and is almost always unnecessary.

Some veteran teachers seem to feel that they are the heirs to all things petty. Most battles with students begin with something as inconsequential as a piece of gum. One strong male veteran, who turned his classroom into a weight room at 3 P.M. daily, got himself involved in a wrestling match with a twelve-year-old girl because she was going to her locker just after lunch instead of just before. He had placed a padlock on her locker to break her habit and she had seen him putting it on.

But a new breed of veterans is emerging. The city's teachers who came on board in the mid-sixties, who have now been teaching for five to ten years, have a different angle on the same profession. Now, ten years later, amid rigorous budgetary cutbacks, they are struggling to leave their mark. Many came to skirt the draft and Vietnam. Most sympathized with the community-control struggle. Their weaning appears to have been different. They can take an occasional kick in the teeth. They are not too afraid to admit to their students that there are many things that they don't know and that there are many times when they are wrong. They genuinely like their students. They are willing to show compassion.

They flock to new programs and embrace new ideas. They change the look of their classrooms and their styles of teaching each year. They are open and willing to learn and to grow. Many of them have learned the hard way; they regard compassion as a show of strength not weakness. They are as healthy for the children as the children are for them. A few schools are blessed with whole staffs composed of young veterans — at least one such was held up as a national model on the cover of the *New York Times Magazine*. The majority of schools have a healthy chunk of this group, but too many, often in the direst neighborhoods where high turnover is a fact of life, have a mere sprinkling.

They make many of the same mistakes as the senior veterans. They too become entwined in pettiness, blinded by trivia, trapped by bad habit. But they manage to get out. Their lives are closer to those of the children they teach, not so much because they really are, but because they want them to be. They show a tolerance for ambiguity. Many live where they teach and invest far more than eight hours a day in their communities.

They have become a source of inspiration for their senior colleagues and for the city's schools. They have many converts. They sense that they are part of a movement, a struggle that somehow must be won. Winning to them means with the kids, not against them. They understand partnership and teamwork in the best sense. Their sights are set on tomorrow, not yesterday. They waste no idle hours lamenting the great growing pains New York is experiencing. They recognize that real quality will take time to restore and they seem willing to commit that time.

The Contract

"Is Albert Shanker any relation to Ravi Shanker?"
"No, but I bet if he want to be he could find a way."
— Conversation overheard in the Teachers'
Room of P.S. 76

DESPITE ALL THE MENTAL anguish and physical abuse that teachers suffer, they hold their chins up high, defend their profession to the hilt, and strut around the building and the streets of New York with a characteristic pomp that was spawned by the UFT Contract. That their arrogant pride flourishes under the most adverse conditions is testimony to the wallop Albert Shanker packs. The Contract Strut evokes a sense of security that few occupations in New York rival. The teachers are the Eliot Nesses of the 1970's, as "untouchable" in their own right as he was in his.

Roughly 89 percent of the teachers are white; 33 percent of the children are white. Roughly 9 percent of the teachers are black; 36 percent of the children are black. Roughly 3 percent of the teachers are Hispanic; 27 percent of the children are Hispanic.

Membership in the unique club known as the United Federation of Teachers does not come easily. Like gaining admission to Harvard Law School, getting into the UFT is far more of an accomplishment

79

than staying in. Although the advent of community control and decentralization has forced a relaxation in the admissions procedure and opened access routes through state machinery previously off limits, most teachers still gain admission through the archbureaucrats at the Board of Examiners. A look at the obstacle course the teachers must run leads to a better understanding of their coming-of-age.

Patience, more than brilliance or valor, is the commodity rewarded. All applicants have to present a minimum of twelve education credits to apply for even the most basic rank: Common Branches Day Elementary Temporary Per Diem Substitute License. Once the credits have been amassed, the prospective teacher takes a written exam in his respective field. The catch is that the individual exams are offered as infrequently as once every three years. After the extensive wait, the exam itself is anticlimactic for even the most poorly prepared of applicants. The exams are then corrected and the results mailed to the examinees, a process that somehow takes eight weeks. Assuming that a passing grade is achieved (I have never known anyone who falters at this stage of the game, although I'm certain that the Board of Examiners could disprove this), a date is established when the prospective teacher meets on a designated evening with two representatives of the vast bureaucracy and is interrogated before a tape recorder. The interrogation is as innocuous or as vitriolic as the bureaucrats whom the individual happens to draw. Although the experience of most is that the questions are bland and routine, several recall heated arguments, which they claim were generated by sarcastic remarks made by the examiner. David Leventhal, when asked what would be the first thing he would do with a fifth-grade math class, suggested that he would consult the children's fourth-grade teachers and from the information he collected he would draft a diagnostic exam. The heavily jowled examiner turned to his colleague and said, "You hear that, Sal? Diagnostic tests. We heard that one before, haven't we, pal!"

In the early sixties the most important aspect of the interview was giving the Board of Examiners a chance to examine the applicant's pigmentation. He would then be passed or failed depending on whether any teachers from his particular minority group were needed at the time. In fact, after being criticized in the press for this practice, the Board of Examiners began withholding the scores on the written part of the exam until the oral part had also been completed. In that way candidates who turned out to be black or who spoke with a Spanish accent in their interviews were often sent letters saying that they had failed the written portion. The results of the oral portion took several weeks to reach the candidate. If he was patient enough to wait and if he passed, he was advanced to the next phase: the physical exam.

Texas beef cattle on the road to slaughter are afforded more personal respect and dignity than New York City teachers-to-be during the physical. The process takes the better part of a day, most of which is spent waiting nude or seminude for something to happen. No one fails the physical. The system is constructed so that the worst, most communicable diseases could be passed on to the waiting masses.

The end result of the entire process is a postcard informing the applicant that he has met the Board of Examiners' many requirements and that his license and file number will be forwarded to him shortly. What the postcard fails to mention is that, although the recipient may now go out and find a job, he will receive no monetary compensation until his all-important file number has been assigned. Just as the Board of Education insists on naming its buildings after famous numbers, so does it extend the same impersonal hand to its employees in assigning each a permanent six-figure file number, which for all practical purposes replaces the necessity of a name. It's a wonder that children don't run home after their first day at P.S. 156, yelling to their mothers that their "new teacher's name is 408531, and she's real nice."

One new teacher, Tad Champion, desperate for his first paycheck after six weeks of work, was told confidentially by his principal to take a full day off and go down to the Board of Examiners in Brooklyn and "walk your papers through." Mr. Champion accepted his advice and soon found himself in a large room at 65 Court Street with forty-eight desks in eight tidy rows of six, each jockeyed by a male or female bureaucrat. After several vain attempts, Mr. Champion enlisted one of the forty-eight in his cause and heeled by his side like an obedient poodle as his papers were taken from floor to floor and decorated with a rainbow of different stamps. When the two-hour ordeal had ended, and Mr. Champion had been honored with a six-digit number all his own, he asked the helpful gentleman for his name, with an eye toward expressing his gratitude with flowers or a bottle of wine. The bureaucrat responded meekly, "My name? Oh, I don't have a — It really doesn't matter." Mr. Champion sent the flowers anyway with a note that read, "To the kind gentleman in Room 2601 who sits four rows back and three seats over."

But once this treacherous course has been run, the teacher is all but guaranteed a career in the teaching profession, and one that carries the most lucrative salary for teaching anywhere on earth. Tenure lies but three short years down the road and under current practices is virtually automatic. Membership includes access to all the rights and privileges of one of the most encompassing contracts in the history of the labor movement. The UFT Contract, directly related to the stick-to-it-iveness of Albert Shanker, leaves to arbitration very little of the affairs of administering a school.

The Contract specifies the number of periods a teacher may teach, the number of students in each classroom, the number of minutes per period, and the nature of the teacher-pupil contact. The Contract establishes medical and dental plans for teachers and grants them a variety of sick days and professional days, on which they are excused from their regular classes. The Contract protects them against having to work in the student cafeteria, from having to patrol the halls, from having to fill out certain attendance records, and from having to collect money for any reason. The Contract establishes strict grievance procedures, complex legal handcuffs on the principal's latitude, with neatly articulated steps and specified lengths of time allotted for each phase. And the Contract includes one of the most lucrative pension plans ever devised.

The Contract has changed the nature of administration of both individual schools and school districts. No principal is ever too far from his copy of the Contract. He keeps it at center stage on his desk or carries it in his inside coat pocket. Most principals live in dread of its contents. They claim that it has drastically altered the nature of their trade. The Contract has become a straitjacket. Administrators argue that they are now unwilling to take risks in innovative planning, aware that the terms of the Contract are too restrictive to accommodate change.

The Contract has contributed to a considerable exodus of talent from the schools. Those who leave are aware that the revamping which the public schools so desperately need is an impossibility under the current conditions. In addition to rendering administrators impotent, the biannual negotiations for the Contract open wounds between teachers and administrators, teachers and the community, teachers and taxpayers, that take years to heal. Schools with strong union chapters elect strong chapter chairmen, who are often more respected by the staff than the principal.

A newcomer to the administrative hierarchy who takes the Contract lightly seals his doom before he is too far out of the starting blocks. Dr. Harvey Scribner of Montpelier, Vermont, once accepted the chancellorship of the New York City public schools. On the eve of his departure for New York to assume his duties, he confessed to Jason Latham, president of The Teachers, Inc., "No, I really haven't had a chance to read that contract just yet." Latham left Scribner's office in a daze.

To Guide and to Counsel

TO GUIDE AND to counsel. It would be difficult to imagine a loftier, more noble-sounding pursuit. The men and women whom public schools employ for such honorable labor must represent the public's morality and good conscience. Those called to the task must be men and women gifted with patience, rare good judgment, understanding, and a willingness to improve the lot of their fellowman.

Not surprisingly, the gulf that has opened between the idyllic role that a guidance counselor might have played, and the role he or she actually does play, has brought the metaphysicians back down to earth. Counselors are responsible for programming and scheduling their children, providing for their smooth transit from one grade to the next and from one school to the next, updating their cumulative records, and seeing their charges with enough frequency to handle any problems that may arise in their adjustment to school. A counselor's caseload is well beyond the limitations of feasibility. There were in 1976 only 559 positions remaining in the elementary and

84

junior high schools, a loss of 304 from the previous year. A single counselor in an intermediate school typically has five hundred children assigned to him, altogether too many of whom are in need of help in regular massive dosages. School guidance counselors are saddled with tomorrow's unemployed, tomorrow's jailed, tomorrow's downtrodden. Their assigned clientele and its many-faceted hardships and abnormalities would boggle the mind of the most confidant psychiatrist.

Elementary schools rarely have more than one counselor. Intermediate and junior high schools, before 1975, had anywhere from three to six. The 1976 budget squeeze rerouted many counselors back into the classroom, thereby shoving younger teachers out into the streets and turning the counselor's office into a supply closet.

At their very best counselors create an impression of omnipresence. They dart in and out of classrooms, hold regular "rap sessions" with groups of children, meet children individually, keep in close touch with armies of parents, and stay until seven or eight o'clock in the evening trying to catch up on the paperwork they have had to postpone because of the presence of children. They are aware that they are only scratching the surface. Their likes are difficult to find in a system that serves large numbers of veteran teachers as a steppingstone to administration. Good counselors compensate for bad teaching. They provide lonely, confused children with a toehold on understanding the rest of the world. Good guidance counselors actually guide and actually counsel. Few schools have witnessed more than one.

Poor counselors, the majority of the ranks by a considerable percentage, often create as many snares in the human dynamics of a public school as they succeed in smoothing out. Too many counselors devote too much of their time to inventing diversions to keep them busily away from the children. Unlike the teachers, who are locked into their positions by a yellow three-by-five schedule card, counselors are granted the luxury of budgeting their own time. Sadly, the results of their independence suggest that freedom and hard work are more polar than magnetic.

David Bromwell, whom the children refer to as The Phantom,

chooses to busy himself in preparing and duplicating endless copies of trivial forms, applications, and memos. Most of his counselees claim that they know neither his face nor the sound of his voice. Although always busy updating Anecdotal Records (with anything but anecdotes), men and women like David Bromwell rarely budget a free moment for dealing with children face to face.

Sam Jamison, a boxing coach for years, uses the opportunity his position affords to generate new recruits. His counselees contend that unless they are on an active "weight program" and are built like Mean Joe Greene, Mr. Jamison is too busy to be bothered with them. An assistant principal in the same school recalls ushering a set of parents into Mr. Jamison's office for a prearranged conference, and discovering him with his latest protégé, demonstrating some opening combinations.

Penny Alberto, an encrusted battle-ax with nearly forty years behind her in public education, guides and counsels in an intermediate school that is well integrated, both numerically and spiritually, but she refuses to speak to any but the white children. Her practice of pulling the entire white half of a class out of math and into her office to talk about "them" was eventually curtailed by her principal after several little Italian girls appeared at his office and complained that "Mrs. Alberto is gettin' to be a pain in the ass."

Mary Jackson enjoys a long-standing reputation as a counselor of great compassion and understanding, but her closest associates warn that she has yet to outgrow a ferocious and unpredictable temper. On one memorable occasion she was observed walking slowly down an empty corridor with her left arm draped over a distraught young man's shoulder, pouring soothing words into his unwilling ears. Well down the hallway and beyond earshot, she suddenly grabbed him by his left arm and flung him against the wall, slapping him about his face and his head. He reeled about in a state of shock at her unexpected outburst.

Lenny Easenberg, whose beat is an integrated middle school, spends the time the position provides in smoke-filled rooms with the superintendent and his deputies, where he stays on the inside track of the politicking that invariably goes on, always with an ear cocked for information that might better his lot. For a man on the move, counseling provides more than enough free time to touch all of the appropriate bases.

Lisa Deliterio, beleaguered by parents who insisted that their "gifted" children be given more homework more frequently, began telling each of them in the solemn, confidential manner she had cultivated over the years that it was a great mistake for them to insist that their children work so hard. She openly urged that the "gifted" slow down. Her unusual and audacious line of attack was reinforced by the husband of the president of the PTA, who slipped to her side while his wife was conducting a meeting and whispered, "I'm always encouraged coming to these meetings and hearing of the great number of gifted children in our school. I look forward to the day when the streets will be filled with gifted truck drivers."

One counselor assigned to do work-ups on a number of children with learning disabilities who were suspected of having brain damage sent a form letter home to the children's parents. It began:

Dear _____,
Over the past week I have been watching your son/daughter _____. He/she appears to have the following forms of Learning Disabilities:
— doesn't pay attention to his teacher
— talks too much
— fools around constantly with other children
— is disrespectful

Rarely does a principal quibble with the activities of his counselors — or rather, with their lack of activity — but once in a long while a hardy soul attempts a shake-up. One principal made a strong push with the local school board to have his counselors relocated in churches and in storefronts throughout the community with schedules that included at least two evening shifts a week and an ultimatum to "get off your buns and find out where the hell all these

kids who *aren't* coming to school *are* spending their time and why."
Furthermore, he wanted any counselors who bucked his reno-
vations shipped out on the morning train.

He dared the Contract. And lost.

Subbing

When we had a substitute teacher a boy named Bill (whose birthday is on the 27th) took a garbage can and put it over the teachers head.
— Jeanette, aged ten, from her autobiography

SUBSTITUTE TEACHING in the New York City schools is masochism in its purest form. A sane man would sooner tackle an aggravated Larry Csonka than a class of thirty-three thirteen-year-olds. Substitute teachers are whole-body transplants for other human beings; and just as a foreign heart is vigorously rejected by the host body, so is a substitute teacher rejected by the class.

Substitutes provide their students with an outlet, a Pavlovian release for a bountiful outpouring of frustration, kinetic energy, and all too often, bitterness. Children regard their substitutes as embodying all the most despicable characteristics of their regular teachers and feel a compulsion to exact fitting punishment. ("There's a substitute for Mr. Palmerston today, let's tear the motherfucker up" is the way I was greeted as a substitute one morning.) New York City spends better than $60 million on its substitutes each year.

Substitutes are hounded unmercifully by their classes, often pushed to the point of cracking and breaking (every period). But once the substitute has been eased to the brink and has hysterically called upon the administrator, the teacher across the hall, the custodian passing by — anybody — for assistance, the rudest shock of all awaits him. What he can expect is a shrug of the shoulders. Most schools regard substitutes as marginal people, not worth the slightest investment of time or compassion, totally expendable. There are some grounds for their collective coolness: few substitutes ever return to the same building twice, and since administrators have ample problems on their hands with the regular teachers, few can justify devoting precious time to the transients. One principal, however, demonstrated a novel attitude in his contention "My school is only as good as its worst substitute." He practiced that philosophy by creating a corps of ten regular substitutes who worked almost daily. He included them in the affairs of the school, provided them with mailboxes, and made certain that they were introduced to the faculty and made to feel part of the fold. (When word reached him that several of them were sleeping with several of his *regular teachers* he was delighted.) Few principals are so enlightened.

Although any licensed teacher may sub at any point in his career, substituting is often left to the lunatic fringe.* Wise men and women taste of the waters and realize, thankfully, that substituting is not for them. Those who remain appear to take an unhealthy pleasure in the scorn and abuse they suffer daily. Many adopt eccentric habits, practices, and modes of dress that suggest to the children that they are different. To take a closer look at a few of the most extreme of these characters:

One young man used to sit quietly on the top of the teacher's desk and stare serenely toward the back of the room while the cauldron bubbled around his feet. Bloodshed and anguished screaming failed to distract his trancelike gaze. Children were constantly turning around in their seats, suspecting that something was coming up

---

*This was particularly true in 1977, when the pay was a mere $40 a day. It had been reduced from $72 a day in 1976.

behind them. They used to poke at him and pull his coat in an effort to evoke a reaction, to find out, at the very least, what his name was and what his voice sounded like. This was the most unnerving aspect of the man — he seemed not to have a voice. Children who came into his classroom and found him seated on the desk, and who had had him before, feared him. One class, well versed in his widespread reputation, sat staring back at him for a full forty-five-minute period. The principal, passing by the classroom, poked his head in and commended him for doing a magnificent job.

The kids nicknamed him Speechless. One class entered a room, knowing that Speechless was in for their math teacher that day. The room was empty but they sat down and quietly awaited his arrival. They were intrigued by his absence, knowing that he was rarely anywhere but seated cross-legged on top of the desk like a hood ornament on an old Packard. Slowly the door to the teacher's coat closet opened and Speechless emerged. He drifted silently to his perch, expressionless, unconcerned by the shudder that went through the classroom. At the conclusion of the period he returned to the closet, closing the door slowly, and clicking it shut from the inside. He never went to lunch. When the principal arrived to investigate the matter, as dutifully reported by the entire fourth-grade class, the cupboard was bare. (That account is provided through the courtesy of one Larry Moses, aged nine, who with his classmates swears to its validity.) I was unable to track down the principal, who had since retired, but his secretary said she did remember "somethin' like that." One superstitious little girl, who broke her arm in the gymnasium when the wall separating the boys' half from the girls' closed on her arm, told her mother (who went and told the principal) that "Speechless had put a curse on her."

Kids rarely cut a substitute's class, much to the chagrin of the substitute. There is no reason to cut. Children cut, among other things, to avoid the anxiety that teachers instill in them; but the presence of a substitute inverts that situation. The anxiety flow reverses course. The games that are a great part of hanging in the hallways can easily be relocated to a substitute's classroom. In fact, the most lenient, laissez-faire substitutes often find themselves strapped with an additional fifteen to fifty kids who are seeking a haven from the purge of the third-floor halls. In one substitute's room the kids set a trash can on a desk at each end of the room, cleared the rest of the furniture to the sides, and played a full-court NBA game with a crumpled, mimeographed spelling quiz as the ball. Although the substitute did make a lame effort to call a halt to the game, he was conned into refereeing the contest and discovered that his popularity had soared. Throughout the building, "The Ref," as he quickly became known, was regarded by the students as the best possible replacement for an absent regular. Secretaries told of days when scores of students would check into the main office to determine where The Ref was working that day.

There is one widely known substitute in the borough of Manhattan whose reputation extends even into schools where she has never worked. Her trademark is that she wears no underpants and advertises the fact. The kids call her No Drawers. She walks inconspicuously into an eighth-grade junior high school class (she prefers older children), sits carefully on the front edge of the desk, props one foot up on the back of a chair, and begins reading aloud from the likes of *The Sensuous Woman*. She always wears relatively short skirts and in the position she characteristically assumes, she leaves little to the imagination. No Drawers wears no drawers!

Kids in her classes, although glued to their seats for fear of disrupting an outstanding performance, are beside themselves. They constantly drop pens, pencils, books, hats, watches, anything, on the floor to have an excuse to bend down and pick them up. She seems oblivious to the commotion she creates (obviously she is not oblivious), never deviating from her accustomed pattern, never showing any awareness of the intense pleasure she generates in overheating thousands of young men and women every year.

At least one principal closed his eyes to the audacity of No Drawers because, for once, the halls were clear and empty throughout the day. On one occasion a boy whom the kids called Superfly (not because he dressed "bad" and sold cocaine, he didn't; but because they thought he was gay) stood by the door selling two-bit homemade tickets to her classroom.

I did some research on No Drawers, tracing her career to the first school she ever substituted in, the first day she ever worked, and the first child who discovered her tantalizing demeanor. I think I found that child, a twelve-year-old (at the time of the discovery), redheaded little black boy from the Lower East Side whose name was Ivy Anderson. He told me what he remembered of his earth-shaking discovery in the fall of 1969:

"I went to math class during second period and found out that Mr. Baron was sick. A young white chick with long brown hair was sittin' on the edge of the desk like this. [He demonstrated.] She said, 'I'm going to read you something from this book and I'll bet you find it very exciting' — or somethin' like that. Anyway I didn't really feel like listenin' but I ain't had nothin' else to do so I sat down next to Dante Vásquez and started to listen. The book was nasty! Then I looked up for a minute and couldn't believe my eyes. The bitch ain't had on no drawers! I was lookin' right up into her pussy! I whispered to Dante and he checked it out and almost fell over backwards. Pretty soon the whole class was hip to it. By the end of the day she was like a Broadway star. Everybody was talkin' 'bout her and callin' her No Drawers."

To the best of my knowledge, No Drawers is still working her magic.

Another well-known substitute was a storyteller par excellence. He claimed to have been attacked and bitten by every frightening creature in the natural kingdom and lived to tell about it. He had had adventures in every corner of the globe; he had traveled all seven continents and been to the depths of the oceans; he had grappled with disciples of the Devil and agents of the Supernatural. Or so he told the children.

He would walk into a classroom with a plain white candle in his left hand and a book of matches in his right. He would quickly light the candle, turn off the lights, and announce to the startled class, "Now sit down, I'm going to tell you a true story that is going to scare the hell out of you." They were already scared to death. He would spin some extraordinary tale of intrigue and danger, and conclude with an account of how an Abominable Snowman (or whatever the aggressor might be that day) had assaulted him, slashing deep wounds in his chest. Then suddenly and unexpectedly he would tear open his shirt revealing a lengthy scar on his shoulder and chest (probably a shoulder separation from high school football) and substantiating the brutality of the struggle. Invariably the kids were dumbfounded, too shaken to challenge his account, praying that the bell would sound so that they could escape the raconteur's eerie clutches (and tell the world!).

One afternoon two fourteen-year-old girls came down to the principal's office and blurted out that they wished to report a substitute teacher who had "gotten fresh" with them. Asked to elaborate on what they meant by "getting fresh," one girl explained that she had asked the man if she could go to the study class next door to borrow a set of checkers. The substitute had responded, they alleged, "Certainly, if you'll lick my dick first." The principal and the assistant principal (who also happened to be there) stood stunned. Both girls had reputations of being rather promiscuous and of "getting fresh" once in a while themselves, and both seemed to regard the incident as more amusing than anything else, so there was justifiable skepticism on the administration's part.

The assistant principal went up to the substitute teacher's classroom, which was the boys' metal shop, beckoned him into the hallway, and recounted the girls' tale verbatim. The sub denied it in its entirety, saying he would never do a "sick thing like that." Just as the assistant principal was turning to go, the sub remembered where the girls might have gotten the impression that he had said such a thing. He apparently had told his student that his real name was "Mr. Richard Licker" (it was not) and had gone so far as to write it on the blackboard. The boys in the class had immediately seen through his play and began shouting, "Hey, Dick Licker!" "Mr. Licker" was informed by the assistant principal that this was a very foolish thing to have done around adolescents and that in the best interests of both himself and the school he could complete the day but his services would not be called upon in the future. "Mr. Licker," showing no signs of either remorse or anger, willingly agreed.

At about two o'clock that same afternoon the assistant principal found two girls crying in his office, upset that "that man" wouldn't let them get through the hallway to Spanish class. "Mr. Licker" had apparently been trying to grab their behinds. That did it. On the way back to the metal shop the assistant principal came upon a crowd of little girls, all crying and terribly upset, who had encountered the same obstruction. He entered "Mr. Licker's" classroom, told him to get his coat and hat, and get in the wind. Which he did. On the way downstairs the assistant principal bumped into the principal, who was on his way upstairs with a bawling little girl whom "Richard Licker" had instructed to remove her pants. A check on "Mr. Licker's" application and record revealed that this was not his only experience in "getting fresh."

The regular fifth-grade teacher was absent on Tuesday from a well-reputed Manhattan elementary school. He was replaced by a previously untried young woman who assured herself a place in the annals of history with the same suddenness as No Drawers. She allowed her open-classroom students to pursue their own interests and projects much as the regular teacher did on a normal day. But while they busied themselves about the room, she seated herself on a couch in the corner and read aloud from a collection of Hans Christian Andersen's fairy tales to those children who showed an interest. Quite by accident, a boy sitting behind her, in following the words and pictures over her shoulder, let his hand drop innocently to her right breast. She protested not. Another boy seeing the hand lingering on her nipple rested his hand on her knee and slowly worked it up the inside of her thigh, closely observing her eyes throughout. She kept on reading. A third child perched on her left shoulder allowed his hand to drop down to her left breast. She wriggled ever so slightly but read on. The first boy, no longer innocently, began gently massaging her nipple until he felt it stiffen in his hand, a phenomenon he had not anticipated but was delighted by. Gradually the rest of the class caught glimpses of the frivolity on the couch and joined in. The final pages of "The Ugly Duckling" were read in an excited, high-pitched, feverish voice as the young lady writhed under the numerous hands that caressed and massaged her from head to toe. She protested only when one big-eyed Puerto Rican boy began unbuttoning her blouse.

When the regular teacher returned the following morning, he was greeted by a chorus of boos. Inquiring into their meaning he was told that the class had had "a real nice lady" for a substitute and they wished he had stayed out for another day. He pressed further, asking a bold little Dominican named José (who incidentally all but lived in the principal's office) what it was about her that was so special. He was told, "I would have liked to, you know, fuck her."

One young woman who frequented the same school regularly, but who was despised by the children, sent the following three scrawled notes to Assistant Principal Kelsey in the course of one morning's work:

Mr. Chelsea,
There are some big boys by my door throwing grapes at me. Please come help.

Mr. Kelsey responded to the call, which came during first period, and chased the boys out of the hallway. During the third period he received the second note:

Mr. Chelsea,
Some more big boys are at my door and they are throwing donuts at me.

Mr. Kelsey responded again. The boys were gone but he was presented with a napkin full of crushed grapes and donuts as evidence. Less than an hour later he received the final note:

Mr. Chelsea,
The big boys are back and they are throwing dictionaries at me and one hit me on the upper left thigh.

The secretary's warning to the prospective substitute, "It's rough out there, isn't it," is in fact a gross understatement. One sub, who spent the day ducking flying furniture and books, sat recuperating in the main office at 3 P.M. His charcoal suit was covered with eraser marks and a droplet of blood hung from the corner of his mouth. His white shirt was buttonless and torn around the pocket. He managed a broad smile, waved goodby to the secretaries, and said, "See you tomorrow." The regular subs are a tough bunch, with or without their eccentricities.

Regular subs are understandably difficult to come by, and many schools, particularly junior high schools, are faced with a shortage every day of the year. In the most extreme cases it is not uncommon to hear over the public-address system at the outset of each period the following announcement: "Will classes 6-232, 6-207, 6-319, 7-210, 7-273, 7-240, 7-360, 7-362, 7-364, 8-372, 8-B12, 8-B17, and 8-375 please report to the auditorium instead of to their regularly scheduled, third-period class. I repeat . . . " The pandemonium that follows is inevitable. Half the children supposed to report to the auditorium never arrive (they either head for the streets or take sanctuary in the confusion in the halls) and hundreds whose teachers are present seize the opportunity to cut ("but I thought our class was called to the auditorium"). Inside the auditorium scores of children raise the rafters while four or five teachers, assigned the ignoble task of keeping order, rant and rave in the name of peace and quiet for five minutes before surrendering to chaos for the final forty. What in the world would they do if the children ever *did* sit still and quiet? The same scene is repeated eight times on such days.

Schools unable to attract and retain reliable subs have devised a marginal means of coping with the situation. Teachers are assigned class coverages for one forty-five-minute period a day in place of their regular preparation period. Nothing does more to damage staff morale than a plethora of classroom coverages. Notice of such assignments is usually delivered by one special child, the darling of the office staff, who seeks the teacher's signature (thus formally accepting the coverage) and leaves his heart-sickened victim with a copy of his warrant; worst of all the drop is usually made while the teacher is eating his lunch. A regular teacher, hardened by years of experience and pain, is about to endure the abuse and frustration of the green substitute.

The teachers call this messenger the Angel of Death. Some refuse his offering, instructing him to deliver a return message: "Tell her [the programmer in charge] to kiss my wrist!" Most, fearing reprisal, accept humbly and await the anticipated humiliation.

An assistant principal responsible for telephoning substitutes each morning between 7 and 8:30 A.M. in a difficult junior high school called me one morning. I told him that I was unavailable that day but that I would be willing to work the entire next week. There was a moment's silence, and then he said in a small voice, "You just stole my heart."

Parapros

THE CLOSEST APPROXIMATION to a human hybrid is to be found in
the public schools. She (most of them are women) is called a *paraprofessional*, a word not yet included in the dictionary, whose
prefix, *para*, means "alongside of" and whose root, *professional*,
presumably refers to the teacher. Paraprofessionals are most frequently found in elementary schools, one to a classroom when
financially feasible. They are usually mothers of school-age children.
Like Clark Kent they lead dual lives. Before and after school they
can be seen ducking into telephone booths to prepare to leave one
world and enter another. They are constantly on guard, aware that
they alone have right of access to the two hostile camps — school
and community — that are separated only by the thin skin of the
school's walls. They are a cross between school people and community people, science-fiction creatures born of the Elementary and
Secondary Education Act of 1965. From one side teachers cultivate

99

them and form alliances with them in order to learn something of the lives their students really lead. From the other side parents pump them for information about the teachers. Paraprofessionals walk a double agent's tightrope, which is as much a part of their job as the work they do with children.

The theory behind the addition of paraprofessionals, a relatively recent development, was to add someone who might be able to help neutralize the restlessness of the children, someone who lived among the children and their families and perhaps could help fashion a tighter bond between the two coexisting but noncooperating worlds. A paraprofessional, it was thought, would be apprenticed to an experienced teacher, much as a young boy was once apprenticed to a blacksmith, and she would learn the ins and outs of the trade through imprintation and osmosis. Parapros, as they have taken to calling themselves, were given no training either in pedagogical wizardry or in curriculum theory and design. Their fortunes were inextricably tied to the teacher with whom they were paired. The amount any parapro learned depended largely on the luck of the draw.

After the paraprofessionals were added to the school system and their work could be observed, educators began to realize how valuable they were. Whereas teachers brought with them scientific and intellectual know-how, they often did so at the expense of being warm and compassionate. They had become too afraid of the disorder that might ensue should they relax too fully and grow too close to the children. The Board of Education handbook for beginning teachers suggests that new teachers adopt a formal, impersonal manner in dealing with their students at the beginning of the year, advice designed to help the teacher save face at all times. The addition of paraprofessionals has in most cases neatly complemented the deficiencies of the teachers. Although unstudied in the hows and whys of learning theory and classroom management, most paraprofessionals provide a stabilizing influence on their classes.

At her very best, a parapro becomes a source of inspiration for her students and her teacher alike. She has rare natural gifts of insight and understanding, and can command attention and respect from even the most difficult students without screaming and threatening. Sasha Duval is a black woman in her late forties who in a matter of months in a large elementary school knew every child in the building by name. The children seemed to sense where she was and to be able to seek her out in moments of despair, to touch her skirt, and to hold her hand. She had a magical quality about her which other teachers and paraprofessionals tried vainly to imitate. Although no teachers were able to duplicate her special personal qualities, she was bright and sensitive enough to learn their trade quickly. By April of her first year she was, according to many teachers in the school, "the finest teacher in the school." When Sasha Duval was absent the class of third graders all but fell apart. Sasha assumed control in a quiet commanding way that made her students feel comfortable and at home. They were more productive and happier than on days when they shared their affections with another adult.

Because of the impact of paraprofessionals like Sasha Duval, a number of colleges, graduate schools, and foundations are busy creating Bachelor of Arts programs that will accredit some of the classroom experience these women have had. The programs will enable parapros to become teachers, with a corresponding increase in authority and salary (at present, parapros are compensated minimally for their work).

By no means are all paraprofessionals worthy of the accolades heaped upon them, or of college degree programs fashioned in their honor. When the parapro and her mentor are comparable in competence, friction can develop, which may disrupt the classroom for the better part of the year. At their worst parapros present teachers with disciplinary problems more severe than those attributable to the children. They create divisive little cliques within classes and incite individual children to long periods of acting out. They turn entire classes against the teacher and make real learning accidental. Like so many teachers in the trade they can be lazy to the point of negligence, arriving late and leaving early.

One paraprofessional strolled into the crowded main office at ten-thirty, nearly two hours late. The payroll secretary made the unfortunate mistake of asking her why she was late.

"You talkin' to me?" the parapro replied rhetorically, tossing her head back and glaring out of the bottom half of her eyes.

"Why, yes I am." The payroll secretary bristled as she answered, feeling the hair rising on the back of her own neck.

The defiant parapro was in no mood for pleasantries. "I was fuckin'!" she bellowed and strutted proudly from the office.

Another parapro had the habit of standing in the hallway outside her miserably chaotic classroom (the teacher inside was a floundering rookie who desperately needed her assistance), mopping her already-dry brow with a handkerchief and performing for any adult who might chance to be walking down the hall. She halted the principal on one occasion and, motioning over her shoulder with her thumb, asked, "Where'd you find that sweet young thing?" The principal was not amused by her comment and ordered her back inside.

The relationship between teacher and paraprofessional is critical. If it is a close one, based on mutual respect, they will have an enjoyable year. If each lacks confidence in the other's ability, both are consigned to failure before the year begins. And complaining of each other's inadequacies accomplishes nothing: principals are reluctant to make changes in teacher-parapro pairings for fear of a consequent snowball effect. The two are in for a long and unhappy year.

One young gentleman, on opening day of his first year of teaching, found that the parapro assigned to his class was endowed with a body like Gina Lollobrigida's. Furthermore, he soon discovered that her daily wardrobe was restricted to skin-tight jumpsuits (only the color varied) and that she was preoccupied with talking about her body and her lust for sexual fulfillment. He sat through long erotic tales of how her marriage had gone bad, of how her husband had gradually lost all interest in her body, of how she had taken to serving dinner in the nude to stimulate his ardor, of how she had littered the apartment with pornographic paperbacks, and of her eventual divorce. By November both teacher and paraprofessional were disappearing for lunch at her apartment every day. She was transferred to another school the following September.

The one change the paraprofessionals brought to the city, which few people anticipated, was their effect on the politics of education. Their strong link to the communities in which they lived and worked gave them a surprising amount of power after the advent of decentralization. They became, in fact if not in name, the anointed representatives of their respective communities. They freely dispensed information about the shortcomings of the schools, and when the shortcomings turned into grievances, they became advocates for their communities in filing complaints. Community control elevated them from being Santa's Helpers to positions of remarkable influence and leverage.

That Albert Shanker saw fit to woo the paraprofessionals was a reflection of their potency and a compliment to their remarkable achievement of respectability and power. After the Great Strike in 1968, he recognized that his union stood in a very bad light with the school community at large and that he, as its spokesman, had emerged as Public Enemy Number One. His tactic for offsetting this development was to champion the cause of the paraprofessionals. With one swing of the bat he began a vigorous campaign to bring the paraprofessionals under his security blanket as full members of the UFT. He was banking on the belief that if he delivered the financial goods, the parapros would let bygones be bygones. Shanker inundated soul radio, soul press, and soul television with soul brothers and soul sisters saying foxily, "Al Shanker is my main man!" By the time his teachers ratified the decision granting membership in the UFT to the paraprofessionals, Shanker was being hailed from Bedford–Stuyvesant to Morrisania as a "blue-eyed brother of soul." Overnight he had restored the luster to his tarnished image in poor communities throughout New York City.

In 1973, paraprofessionals and a machiavellian educational politician determined a superintendency in a well-integrated Bronx school district. The competition for the job eventually boiled down to a runoff between two men. One was the assistant superintendent, who was black and a longtime resident of the community. His opponent was the white head of all the federally funded programs in the same district, a man who was a longtime community wheeler-dealer. As the showdown loomed closer, the latter contender succeeded in securing a significant sum of federal money for the district. He quietly distributed the funds to the most vocal and uncompromising of his adversary's supporters in the form of paraprofessional jobs. By the night of the community school board meeting, in which public debate was to be entertained on the merits and demerits of the two contestants, numerous paraprofessional positions had been created and filled. Not one parent arose either to support the black candidate or oppose his white counterpart.

The longevity of the paraprofessional corps is perilous at best. There were 32,660 in 1975 and 26,752 in 1976. The parapros depend for their survival on federal funds, and it seems in 1978 unlikely that this tenuous funding will be maintained in the difficult economic years ahead. It seems equally unlikely that Albert Shanker will risk another strike in the paraprofessionals' behalf, should they be cut from the federal nipple and turn to the city for help.

Therefore the Clark Kent/Superwoman phenomenon that the paraprofessionals provide as they dart between two polar worlds might also go the way of Superman himself — off the air.

Decentralization

WHEN THE NEW YORK STATE legislature convened in late 1968 with an ear cocked toward the beat of the tomtoms coming out of New York City, and with a mind to revamp the governance of the city's schools, virtually anything was possible. The degree to which the schools had become institutions of failure had precipitated, first, the experiment in community control and now a legislative session dedicated to articulating Phase II. Community control, an experiment designed to reawaken traditional American values emanating from the New England experience — smallness amidst bigness, town meetings, and local control of local institutions — had opened a Pandora's Box of unfathomable proportions.

Out had popped fire-breathing Helen Teastamark, who would use her vault to national prominence in a series of organizing campaigns; David Spencer, hot on her heels in snatching up the pieces of the I.S. 201 Community Control District, terrorizing suburban America with his unusual looks and brash talk; Rhody McCoy, who looked like a Harvard professor in faraway Oceanhill-Brownsville and who, with his preacher friend Reverend C. Herbert Oliver, would precipitate the most devastating teacher strike in American history; Luis Fuentes, a relative child in the struggle, who raised his head first as an assistant principal in Oceanhill-Brownsville but gained notoriety in the third of the demonstration districts, Two Bridges on the Lower East Side, and has kept the fires burning almost single-handedly for the past six years; and, of course, Albert Shanker, who emerged in the capacity of president of the United Federation of Teachers as the counterpoint to the people's struggle for control of their schools and who was the architect of the Great Strike(s).

The result of the legislature's deliberations, which could have run the gamut from a wide variety of manifestations of decentralization of power, or delegation and subdelegation of functions, to a stronger, centralized, state-controlled construct, passed in heated debate the celebrated Decentralization Bill of 1970. The act, which took effect in July of that year, carved New York into thirty-three districts (roughly, 242,000 persons to a district), relatively equal in size, each equivalent in population to Syracuse. The bill included a mandate to each district to elect a community school board, which in turn would appoint a community superintendent. Between them they were to go about the business of running their districts, each one of which had some twenty-five thousand students and twenty-five schools. High schools were excluded from the transfer of power because they lacked the local feeding pattern characteristic of the elementary and secondary schools. The central Board of Education, the previous kingpin in the power structure, was anything but abolished and hung on in an ambiguous limbo, a condition that was bound to provoke future controversy as the spoils (and responsibilities) were gradually ironed out in the communities and in the courts.

Principal among the oversights of the decentralization legislation was the muddled demarcation of the powers to hire and fire administrators, teachers, and paraprofessionals. As one might expect, a series of battles and court cases ensued between localized and centralized forces in an effort to fill the many voids in the law with legal precedents. Furthermore, the distribution of federal monies earmarked for the city sparked numerous skirmishes, many of which also landed in the courts in a host of suits and countersuits. But the most provocative characteristic of the bill, in part related to its ambiguity, was the creation of the community school boards and the political plum they represented. As the courts handed down a series of role-clarifying decisions in favor of the community boards, it became increasingly clear to the likes of Albert Shanker and Rhody McCoy that the elections held at three-year intervals could become the real theater of the war. Nine seats are contested every three years on each of the thirty-three community school boards.

The collision between the UFT and community interests in District #1 on the Lower East Side of Manhattan stands as the epitome of a series of brawls that have erupted in other districts. There, Community Superintendent Luis Fuentes, appointed amidst a firestorm of controversy in 1970, incurred the wrath of every UFT chapter and all loyal rank-and-file UFTers during his initial term. Consequently, the union generated its own candidates for the community school board and ran its own slate in the 1973 elections, compaigning on the platform that, if elected, Fuentes would go. With voter turnout very low and extreme confusion as to who was to vote where, the UFT slate was elected (five of the nine votes) and Fuentes was given a boot in the pants. But charges of irregularities in the election process were upheld in court and a second election was held. Fuentes got his position back in the interim. The same scene was repeated. The UFT won the necessary five seats and Fuentes was given a second tail-kicking, made a little less painful by the fact that his $37,500 salary was intact for the final two years of his contract. But what the courts had failed to resolve through litigation, the community undertook to resolve with left hooks and roundhouse haymakers. In 1974 a District #1 board meeting was held behind closed doors but televised via closed circuit into an auditorium packed with angry pro-Fuentes people. It landed on the front pages of the New York dailies after the television cameras and screens were smashed and the sequestered meeting was stormed.

The community school board elections in all but a handful of the thirty-two districts have proved a great disappointment. Turnout has been embarrassingly light: in some districts in 1973 less than ten percent of the eligible voters voted. (Eligible voters include all registered voters and all parents of school-age children.) As a result, the selection process has placed some virtual unknowns in positions of considerable power, men and women whose two-line statements of educational philosophy in brief campaign blurbs have been adequate enough to garner them the necessary hundred or so votes to office. Each district has had to suffer through at least one totally inappropriate selection. In District #43, pony-tailed Paul Slater, who was studying English in graduate school by day, found himself sitting on the board in a highly volatile district and serving as its treasurer. For those of the community who attended the meetings, and for himself, the experience was a disaster. By the end of the first six months of his three-year term, it had become evident to the public at large that he knew little about either public education or New York City. He was heckled and mocked every time he reached for the microphone. "Don't let that punk speak!" buxom women were heard to yell from the rear of the hall. Yet he often was called upon to cast the deciding vote on a given issue. His most memorable public statement came when he was confronted by an angry parent who demanded to know if he had observed the program in the school about which he had just spoken so critically. He replied to her charges, "No. I have never gone into any of the schools in the district. I am afraid that if I did it would influence my decisions. That is my own personal policy."

The fury that the central Board of Education was subjected to during the late sixties was mild in comparison to the collective abuse that the community boards have suffered since the advent of decentralization.

The members of one of the Boards, surrounded by a mob of more than five hundred enraged citizens, were corralled into a closet by the mob and told that they would not be released until they agreed to vote on a certain issue. They were not set free until the wee hours of the morning.

Another Manhattan board contends that most administrative tenure votes taken over the past three years have been accompanied by a ritual overturning of the board's tables and the scattering of its papers.

In another district, in 1971, a black and a Puerto Rican were pitted against each other for appointment to the community superintendency, and at the meeting open to public debate, most of the local precinct had to be called in to stand guard as speaker after speaker shouted bitter racial invectives.

In still another district, three popular and well-respected board members announced their resignations from what they described as a "position of constant turmoil." A fourth, disliked and distrusted by the community he purported to serve, arose and said, "I know that what I am about to say will greatly disappoint most of you, but I must report that I have decided not to resign."

An assessment of the educational merits of decentralization is difficult in 1978, if only because of the intricate interplay of forces that are a part of anything as complex as learning. That decentralization has altered the political character of New York's public schools is undisputed. The shift to locally elected boards has served to localize the community's wrath, to raise ethnic consciousness, to create a new genre of administrators hired by new, more informal, parochial machinery, and drastically to change the nature of the superintendent's job and longevity in office. In a single post-decentralization year (1973) seventeen of the thirty-three community superintendents were fired. In one Manhattan district, the school year 1975–1976 saw five community superintendents come and go.

Whether all the bustle and activity that a new political plum has created will eventually improve the New York City schools is open to debate. The gulf between learning and the politics of education is sufficiently broad to trip up the most dynamic political scheme. The greatest threat to the decentralization experiment is decentralization itself: the abuse of the powers delegated. In 1974, the central Board of Education assumed financial control of three districts, charging them with financial mismanagement and the collective loss of millions of dollars. In 1976 the chancellor superseded the authorities in eleven districts, more than the total number of supersessions in the five previous years of decentralized operations. The trend forebodes at worst the demise of decentralization; at best, another wrenching political conflagration.

Writing (As Opposed to Acting) Out

IN AN ENVIRONMENT where each party is constantly acting out for the benefit of all the others, catching a glimpse of what lies beneath a carefully cultivated facade is refreshing. The following excerpts came from a class of Harlem ten- and eleven-year-olds, who were encouraged to write about themselves, their thoughts, fears and experiences, and to do so at home. There, because they felt no compulsion to put on a display of bigness and badness, they could write of their anxieties and perceptions in a way that would have been impossible for them to do in school.

I have made a diligent effort to avoid introductions and commentary, allowing the words to be read as they were written — for once without interruption.

Lois: That's how come I took my diary and locked myself in the tiolet bole and wrote my diary.

Dear Diary on Oct. 5 1975 my mother found out what I did on Oct. 4. 1975. Because I left my diary at home. And she was fixing up the house. And she found my diary. So she started read it and I got hit with the frying pan.

Dear Diary,
On October 23, 1975 My sister was fighting over an egg. She cried for two hours and a half. When my mother got sick and tire of hearing her crie she took a pan and took her clothes of and beat her ass.

Charlotte: At the party I met a boy named Jr. To tell you the truth I don't think he's very handsome, but he's charming. He asked to go with me, I said no, I am going to finish school before I think about boys. Any way, he don't even go to school.

We have something like a club on 124th st. If anyone from another block comes around 124th st. and starts trouble with one person the whole 124th st. is going to jump on that particular person. You see I should know because I live around 124th st.

When I grow up someday, and if I live to see this day come, I want to be a nurse. Deep down in my heart it says that I want to be a nurse. Since I was a little girl I wanted to be a nurse. I want to be a nurse so I can help sick people, old people. I want to help everyone that needs help. Of course I have to be smart and finish school before I can be a nurse.

The mid-term test was for us to be promoted at the end of the semester. By the way semester means the end of the *year*. It really means *year*.

Mr. Bell is a nice teacher. He said he won't cut his hair until I wear my afro to school. He really digs on my groovey afro.

Marie: I am playing hopskotch with my girl-friend and tage and other games. I am going to my cousin's house now to play with her. it is 8.00 soon I will be going home and in bed. Tomorrow is another day with the help of All mighty God.

I would like to hurry up and get through high school and all. I'm not in all that much of a hurry because if I was I wouldn't know what I am doing, I would be all mixed up and confused, Right Darling?

Gladys: We talk about Mr. Brooke breathe the first time he talked to me, I almost fainted. His breath will knock a mouse out.

On the 19, of September all of the 6th and 5th graders were in the auditorium. And we all heard fire bells ringing but no one really paid any attention to it. And I said I smell smok, then I said Mr. Davis its a fire. Then Mr. Wilbur [an assistant principal] said we are going to have a fire drill and I heard Mr. Epstein [the principal] said The fire is in room 211 on the second floor and the hallway was full of blak smok. And I said Mr. Davis I want my coat he said will you wait a minute. I was so mad because my coat got stuck up on the second floor. I was trying to get back in but no one will listen to me. Mister Epstein said everyone go home and we will see that everyone will have their coat put in the cleaners. The next day I asked for my coat and they said someone must have stolen it. I told my mother what they said and she said they better dig up $15.00 by the time I get there.

My third grade teacher was the best out of all of them. And she had a daughter. Her name was Shelly. She was big and FAT.

This story is about how i was in second grade. My teacher was Mrs. Karpool she was like the 50 foot women. She was mean. Everyone had hated her. And one day Mrs. Karpool came to school and beated all of us but not me I went and got my mother my teacher and her had a fight. And I was surprised to see my teacher make up with me and kissed me. And she never yelled at me or hited me with the ruler again. And she invited me over to her house.

And every since me and Sally keep on seeing him to much his face kept on getting ugly by the day. So now we call him frog face. And now he's so nasty every girl he sees he looks down at their legs and — well I'm not going to say the rest but you know how fresh boys get once in a while. And the one he really bothers is Debby. But you know how debby is nice, clean, normal city girl, oh boy when it comes to fighting that girl will LIGHT YOUR FIRE!

Lisa: One night I was peeling my toenail some of it came off and some din'nt, and it was hurting. One time me and Bertha was coming from school and I was going around trees, and she said that is bad luck. One day me and my friends were playing doubledutch and I couldn't jump in. One time we were playing straight rope and I jump in and slip in the mud. One day I kept feeling downstairs. When I got up in the morning I urinate and then get my clothes ready for school. It all apend when I had just woke up and my two little sisters and my baby brother and sister woke up. So my mother went downstairs to get some bananas from this man and I wanted to fix my baby brother and sister some baby food and then my gown had went in the fire and then it started to burn. So it came up so high, I ran to the sink and throw a glass of water on me, then I ran in our bedroom, and feel on the bed. I hurried up and got off, because I thought the bed was going to catch on fire. So I went in the front room and rolled over and over then I got up and ran down the stairs. I ran to the second floor and to men were there and they riped the burning clothes off me, but I still had my panties on. That's funny ain't it.

Priscilla: My name is Priscilla. I am 12 years old. I am in Mr. Richard's class. I like some of my friends in there but not to tuff.

But soon we're going to move and I'll be glad because this house I live in now is very small and I have so many close and no were to put them.

stop calling me Prissie. My name is Pricilla not Prissie and I hate the name Prissie.

Peter: In the fifth grade I graduated. I also had another certificate for the same thing. My father was there. He wore a blue suit and a white shirt with cuflins. My mother was out-of-sight. She wore a blue dress with earing, necklace and braclets. I wore a morowne colored suit with cuflins.

My mother is also an excellent house wife. She can sew, cook, clean up the house, straighten the house, dust the house, and wash the windows. My mother can sing and dance.

Margaret: Dear Diary,
   Today I went in the Aditorium and I saw a movie then later on in the movie they show apart that I was scared and I hid my face in my hands and when I look back I saw the fish back in the jar and it ended groovy.

Vincent: I am a boy. I like to play ball. I like to play 1st base. I sit next to a boy in school. I do not have any sister or brother or mother.

O.J. Simson got hit again and had that funny sepll again but practice was over. the Doc ass O.J. Simson was anything rough o.j. simson said no. And then the Doc. said for o.j. simson to stop by his office. So the Doc. said you will have to have a check up or you will not play in the game saturday. So o.j. simson said it is nothing rough with me. So the Doc. said will you want to have the check up now or later or tomorrow. And then o.j. simson wife came in and said less go honey. And so o.j. simson said one minutes baby. So they went home and came back tomorrow. o.j. simson wife went to work and o.j. simson went to the Doc. office to get his check up but the Doc. ass o.j. simson did he want the check up and o.j. simson said to the Doc. you is the Doc. I take what you give me not what I want.

Gail: I live on 125th st. To me I hate that block. Why. Because nothing happen around there. You can't play games or nothing without people running or telling you to move. You can't run

races without people getting in your way. You can't sit on your
stoop without people looking at you like you are crazy can't sing or
anything without people looking at you. If you play rope people
excuse me walking through the rope giving you a look when they
say excuse me. It's annoying if you know what I mean.

Today at school we went to Spanish the 8 period well we was
jumping and talking not working so Mrs. Perkins told us to sit
down but we didn't listen. Jessica was messing with Donald like
she was going to fight him. Mrs. Perkins said that's what you need
a big boy to kick your ass and we was laughing and asking her can
we get it. And she started laughing like she did something.

Me, Myself, and I

To me I'm smart enough to be where I am. I am fasted in math so
so in reading. I'm bad at times good at times but all ways talking.
I'm not too fly but dog if I'm ugly. tall and fat. Dress pretty nice.
hair comb. teeth brush. so if I must say I'm ALRIGHT

This lady name Eleanor is crazy. Everything happen she laugh
she had the nerve, the odesaty to say I'm dumb I say like wow she
had it backwards.

Robin: I saw Dorald and his friend went behind the car and spy on
me. So I made Dorald jealous and I put on a show for him and I
got closer and closer to Hugh and Dorald was just peeking. Then
when Jay and Hugh left, Share told me that Dorald said he didn't
go with me. I went up to Dorald face and say Dorald it's quicks.

I could spend the night with her and come home Monday cause
we don't have to come to school on Monday because we celadrge
Columbus Day. But Columbus Day is Sunday I don't understand
why we have a day off Monday?

When we went to lunch Mr. Brown ate lunch with us. I was scare
to eat lunch. So all I did was milk and ate my apple. We had frank,
milk, fried fry, bread, lima bean. I say Mr. Brown the lima bean
didn't tatse good. He say. Guess what he say. Mr. Brown say I

things the whole meal taste good. I say I think the whole meal
taste nasty.

David: Hello my name is David Franklin Jr. I live in Harlem on
128 street. I'm used to this neighborhood. This neighborhood is
fixed for some Black people like one: VIOLENCE! the dopeatics:
two: people who rap and kill 3: COPS!!!

My best sport is swimming. Swimming is a lot of fun but *always*
read the *safety rules* like I. drowning. Drowning is very searess
because many children lost the lives because of drowning. My
second best sport is basketball. Basketball is very searess to because when you jump up for rebounds the other guy jumping with
you have his legs under yours and you won't know but when you
hit the concrete you will know. Football is a DANGEROUS
game. you could get your wrist snap, arm broken, leg broken,
nose broken, black eye, back broken, crush toe, neck broke, and
lose your LIVES. now finist my sports let see about my hobbys.
No. one: reading Marvel comics and collecting them. No. two:
Down South choping wood. Choping wood is good.

Jeanette: I was born in Antigua West Indies on March 10, 1957 in
my mother house. I have five brother and 1 sister. I hate all my
brother except 2.

I had a bird before and it die and I bury it in our back yard and
every year I dide it up but this year I did not dide it up because
the skin went away and I did not want to take it up from the grave
again. I want it to had a nice quiet peace ful rest until everything
come back alive again.

Beatrice: Dear Diary. Some boys was bother me and Amy Friday.
We were talking about some other boys when a boy named Arnold came alone and now the other boy want to fight the other
boys so me and Amy call Arnold Mr. Newsreporter.

I said I go with Karl and he said you won't be around him all the time I said I see that boy every day like I see the fingers on my hand.

So I'm not sure when my first kiss will be with Karl but when it do I hope he kiss good.

Lorie: When I was 5 I was a tomboy because all I had to play with was boys I had no sisters it was a lot of fun playing with boys because they do a lot of good things they play baseball, football, shoot clips. I would have gave anything for a cowboy suit or a baseball or a football I hate dolls I called them ugly and everything. By the time I was 7 I like dress skirts dollars pocketbooks and all those things seven was a good age for me seven turned me into a real girl who liked all the girl things and all that jass. I learned how put my own clothes on by myself how to light a match all about what fire is and how it can kill you. When I was 8 I had a boyfriend in my class his name was Steven he use to tell me my work and I use to tell him his. I thought he was the best boy in the whole world then he movied away and he was the first boyfriend I ever had and from then to now there have been about fifty boys in my life and I know I am to young to say this but some boys when you get stuck on them you are really stuck because I was stuck before so take my word for it please try not to get stuck on any boys because they will break your heart.

On these pages I am going to write about how I think myself is I think I am good in my work sometime but sometime I ant I think my behavior is poor because I run in the hall and play with boys I still be bad in class when my teacher talk to me about what I do I don't listen I talk back and that is one of my main problems I have too much MOUTH!

Everything I wrote in my book about the way I would fix up my block is true. There would be no fights or nothing everybody would be friends with each other and they will laugh and dance and play not steal and kill and fight.

Freddie: When I was four I knew where I lived. I knew how to spell my name perfect and I knew how to fold my clothes perfect all of them. I was very small and skinny and bright and smart.

When I went to kindergarten I was a little artist. Oh boy I had a gay time in kindergarten.

Ruth: Dear Diary on Oct. 11, 1975 my cousin came over. I can't stand her. Her name is Sharon. She think she is cute. She act like a woman. She and my other stink sister were in the bathroom talking about some boy named Ralph. My cousin is only eleven years old and she got a mind like a teenager. I got a sister she is sixteen and she also think that she is cute. I hate all of them. She be smelling herself all the time.

Dear Diary,
    All I did today was play and fighting. That was no fun man. At first when I saw Mr. Drake I thought he was a squard man and Friday I found out that he was'nt. he is real nice to use and he can ice skate good. he could be on t.v. makeing better money and be a star.

Mr. Drake always wear bell bottoms. That's all he wears. he loves some Bell Bottoms. he wore a jacket today with his bells. he look kind of nice in them sometimes.

Sue is not my friend for real. I hate her real bad. I hate the table she sits at.

Patty: Dear Diary,
    One time I wanted a party. The girl downstairs. Her party was boss. we slow drag with the boys. and we had a contest. some kids played spin the bottle. I don't play spin the bottle because I don't like to Kiss Boys. we had pop cone, ice cream, potatos ships, prunch, and the worse pine apple ice cream cake. Therefor I throw all of the cake a way and every time that girls mother give me a piece of cake I throw it a way.

Lucille: When I was nine my behavior was very good. My teacher name was Mrs. Shepherd. She wuld take us on a lot of trips. My work and report card was good. One day a girl in my class set a desk on fire. That summer I went back to camp.

Margaret: My name is Margaret Iron. I was born to Mr. and Mrs. David Iron on June 16, 1959 at 7:45 a.m. At the age of one I was a very sweet little girl said my mother but I was the worst thing when I was outside said my father. When I was 2 I was a little devil.

And in the foruth grade I was in 4-1 and my teacher name was Mr. Walton. But he was working in the office and they gave us a nother man teacher and his name was Mr. Slones and he was a Dope and I mean a real Dope.

Barbara: I had a sister she will be seven years old in 1975 and she dies she was two years old She got hit by a truck. I was taking her to get some candy I stop to tie my shoes she knew that we was going to the Drug Store. So while I was tieing my shoes she ran across the street and before I could catch her she got hit. I ran in the house crying and got my mother and she started crying and so did a lot of other people. This was the sadest thing that ever happen to me in my life. I will never forget this as long as I live.

My mother has a friend name: Mrs. Winnie she's married to a man name Mr. Tommy they last name is Chappell. They had six children they all have African names. Mrs. was going to have seven but she had a misforget. I like them very much but it one thing I don't like about them they don't believe in God I ask them why and they said because there is no God. I said yes there is with out you are helpless. So I ask them who made the great, great, great, etc. they said first there was a fish and they came on land then they formed into a monkey, then they formed in a dinaur then to a ape then to a human bean.

Then I didn't say anything.

SCHOOL LIFE

Little Red Schoolhouses

POST–CIVIL WAR legislation made public education for all Americans compulsory. The states were compelled to provide the facilities, the materials, and the teachers; parents were compelled to send their children to the schools; and the children were compelled to go.

What the framers of the legislation may not have anticipated was that, ipso facto, they made not only attendance compulsory, but compulsory in a *particular building*. A school and all it connotes should be distinguished from the building in which it is housed. At present (the late 1970's) the kind of building in which a child will spend over fifteen thousand hours of his life coming of age, as opposed to the kind of school he attends, depends entirely upon where he happens to reside. Should forced busing ever enjoy widespread acceptance in the North, and the recent reception in Boston suggests that legislators and judges will not willingly risk their careers making such moves too often, the actuality of being compelled to patronize the particular school building nearest one's residence will undergo modification but not change. The modification will further specify the sentence: a child will not only be compelled to serve time in a particular building but also to ride a particular bus to get to that particular building.

Having to spend a considerable portion of one's childhood in a particular building (there are 1,205 such buildings in New York in 1978, including about fifty slated for shutdown), much as a convicted criminal is forced to spend a considerable portion of his life in a particular prison, makes the condition and appearance of that particular building all the more important. In New York, parents in search of a new and better school building are typically more willing to move across district lines than to lobby for additional construction monies. (Actually, the easiest and perhaps the most common tactic is falsification of address.)

The condition of the school building one is likely to inherit in a given neighborhood often fails to correlate with the condition of the neighborhood. P.S. 1212 in an affluent Manhattan neighborhood was forced to close its fifth floor on account of excessive leaks in the seventy-year-old roof. The leaks have yet to be repaired. The response of those in power (three successive community superintendents) has been to reduce the number of children in attendance rather than to "waste" money repairing the roof. When heavy spring rains fall, parents can expect their children home by noon. In the most dilapidated, crumbling sections of dilapidated, crumbling East Harlem, two magnificent multimillion-dollar intermediate schools have arisen, air-conditioned beacons to the poor yearning to breathe free. In P.S. 1000, a Chinatown structure fifty years older than its neighbors, the gymnasium is on the ground floor and has sixteen gargantuan pillars in bounds on its basketball court and a ceiling only eight feet high.

Drawing an attractive school is like drawing an attractive blind date. The chances are slim. Most schools have features equivalent to crossed eyes, buck teeth, and obesity. Although the Board of Education appears to have made and continues to make a diligent effort toward endowing its latest structures with novel and tasteful exteriors, little imagination has been devoted to rethinking the interior space, which is unfortunately where the law compels the children to spend all those hours. The practice suggests that the schools are built more for the passersby than for the passers-through.

The magnificent new intermediate school on Park Avenue and Ninety-fourth Street was built on the ruins of the renovated Squadron A Armory (for horses). Although its exterior is eye-catching, its interior is sterile and routine. The hundred-year-old concept of endless boxlike spaces called classrooms opening into long straight corridors prevails within this extravaganza as it does in its ninety-year-old neighbor five blocks away.

School interiors are further bowdlerized by a nauseating set of off-color colors that paint manufacturers seem to reserve exclusively for the Board of Education. A creamy pink à la farm pig, and a grayish yellow approximating the color of a dying tooth, are two of the favored hues. When confronted by them many teachers are overcome by nausea and opt to paint their own rooms, a practice many administrators quietly endorse. One young man, after painting his classroom in his first year of teaching, discovered that he had been switched to a new room in September of his second year. Undaunted, he painted this room as he had the first. The following September he was again transferred to a new classroom. Realizing at this point that the principal was surreptitiously and systematically having the building painted at no extra cost, the teacher negotiated a trade with the tenant in his original room, a maneuver that went unnoticed by the principal until late May.

A cagey junior high school principal, whose building desperately needed a fresh coat of paint but who lacked the funds to underwrite the job professionally, hired four high school students to do the job over the summer. On the fourth day of their sixty-day contract, a game of the Dozens broke out, resulting in a paint-throwing free-for-all that left one painter without two of his teeth and one classroom drowned in brilliant orange (a color that the principal later informed his staff was "Enlightenment Orange"). Enlightenment Orange covered the top half of every classroom; "Fingerprint Brown," which the children called "Dukey," covered the bottom half. Most principals are too busy waging war on graffiti and graffiti artists to be concerned about fresh coats of paint. Many pump into their custodians and matrons flowers, pies, cakes, and scotch to ensure that they remain loyal for as long as the graffiti wars endure.

Much of the workmanship in the construction of New York schools reflects gross corner-cutting. I once heard a principal describe the contractor whom the Board of Education had hired to do the building as "the kind of guy who would try to sell you an umbrella on the corner of Forty-second Street and Broadway on a sunny summer day."

One large intermediate school in neighboring suburban New Jersey, where most competitive estimates ran in the neighborhood of $5.3 million, was built for $3.4 million. The pipes carrying the hot water for the heating system were not properly wrapped before their burial in the ground around the building. Eight short years later, they began bursting. Mud volcanoes erupted and sapped all the heat from the building's interior. The repair job cost a half-million dollars and took an entire year to complete. Any approximation of education was disrupted because a new system of pipes had to be installed in the corridor ceilings. Workmen complained constantly of stolen tools. They often had to remove from their ladders children who had donned welders' masks and were busily scorching the exposed portions of the pipe with torches. A twenty-foot length of two-foot stone pipe disappeared into a pond behind the school. Similarly, a much-heralded New York intermediate school, some ten years in the hopper from drawing board to finished product, found that its air conditioning, a specialty unheard of in New York City schools, was inoperable from the day the school opened. The workmen had apparently sabotaged the project by stuffing debris into the network of air ducts that ran throughout the building. Eight years later the problem remains only partially corrected.

The blandness that typifies the New York public schools is reinforced by the system's nomenclature. Although each New York school building is assigned the name of a man or woman distinguished in the arts, letters, the sciences, or the humanities, and although each school stages an elaborate dedication ceremony to confer the name on the edifice formally and officially, the central administration's subconscious preoccupation with the impersonal is too formidable. Few if any of the buildings are able to shed the numerical "names" they were assigned in the planning and construction stages. The Emily Dickinson School remains P.S. 75, the Arthur A. Schomburg School remains I. S. 201, despite the best efforts of their respective principals.

Educators advocating radical changes in teaching methods are struck by the existence in New York of over one thousand individual buildings, many of which would have zero resale value on the open real estate market should the current system of education ever be scrapped. The buildings created by one philosophy of education now frustrate all others. The amount and arrangement of interior space dictates the size of schools, the number of children they can house, the internal classroom structure, and the number of children each classroom will contain. Desirable innovations calling for large open spaces or small private niches must necessarily be bypassed by a system of schools wedded to the configuration of its buildings.

Buildings known as schools exercise in and of themselves great control over the character of life in New York City. In addition to enjoying a cause-and-effect relationship with educational philosophy, they create and destroy neighborhoods. Neighborhood children are faced with the unfortunate proposition of either accepting them the way they are or of moving away. In too many instances throughout the city, children are sentenced to aging fortresses, the unlikely progeny of Little Red Schoolhouses, whose best days are well behind them, and whose spaces engender little more creativity than Riker's Island.

"O-O-O-O Sit!"

I stole some of your property Tony. What are you going to do about it?
Peasant!

— Graffito on a desk in I.S. 44

NEW YORK CITY has always boasted its own characteristic twist of the
English tongue. "Brooklynese" dominated the first half of the twentieth century. Gas station managers told their attendants named
Earl, "Give the Buick a quart of earl, Oil." At Ebbets Field one
afternoon an outfielder by the name of Hoyt attempted a catch in
deep center field and injured himself diving into the wall. A fan
leaned forward and uttered with grave concern, "Hurt's hoyt." This
was an era when "goils had poisonality" and cops chased "poipe-
trators." But the dialect that once surrounded the Dodgers headed
for the suburbs at about the same time that the Dodgers beat it for
the West Coast.

Language in New York has remained anything but a static commodity since the decline of the Brooklyn dialect. The proliferation of
new and large minorities in the city, particularly southern blacks,
has contributed unique and rich variants of the English language.
The argot has spread through the public schools in all directions

128

from the South Bronx, Harlem, and Bedford–Stuyvesant, and has assumed its position as The Language of the public schools, spoken as freely by the sons and grandsons of European immigrants as by its authors.

As the school and the community have evolved into two separate camps, so too has the language representative of each furthered the gulf between them. Most teachers are confounded by individual words, phrases, and accents that they encounter in their first few weeks in the New York schools. Parents also are shocked by the violations of standard English their children bring home from school; they had expected improvement, not the opposite. As with clothing, the question arises as to which "side" will exert the greater influence on the other. Will tomorrow's street corners be crowded with loiterers talking the King's English, or will the elite of New York carry on in their drawing rooms conversations punctuated by outbursts of "O-O-O-O-O sit!"

Creative additions to their own argot is a crucial activity for New York children. They feel that it is *their* language and that it must remain so, must not be superseded. Although they attend classes in formal English and make a genuine effort to learn to manipulate what is for them a second tongue, aware that mastery is somehow related to higher education and employment, the children make no effort to speak it. It is not their own.

While the argot includes new vocabulary and new expressions, much of it is simply a rearrangement of traditional grammatical patterns into what amounts to virtually unrecognizable configurations. No amount of space could do justice to the scope of these new usages. (Several books have already been published on black English and English as a second language.) What I will offer here to the uninitiated are a few of the more common expressions and aberrations: a tiny lexicon of guideposts to assist the curious in their meanderings through public schools.

Probably the most common expletive (besides "motherfucker," which is used as noun, adjective, and verb with boring frequency), is "O-O-O-O-O *sit!*" *Sit* was once a purely derogatory term, literally defined as "human feces," and was used in describing distasteful people, places, and things. In those days *sit* was pronounced "shit." *Sit* is generally preceded by the attention-getting utterance "O-O-O-O-O." The expression enjoys an unlimited number of applications, but is usually used to express wonder and admiration for accomplishment, either major or minor. A few examples:

The Monday following Easter, Esther arrives in school dressed totally in lavender: lavender pantsuit, lavender hat, lavender high-heeled shoes, lavender lipstick, lavender bracelets, lavender earrings, and lavender nail polish. Brian, the boy who happens to be seated nearest to the door when Esther enters the classroom, turns to his mates and exclaims, "O-O-O-O-O *sit!* Check out motherfuckin' Esther!"

During gym class, Ernie cradles a basketball elusively behind his back and begins his takeoff for a breathtakingly graceful lay-up. "O-O-O-O-O *sit!*"

Francine raises her hand to answer the teacher's question, "What is the capital of Vermont?" By the time her hand is recognized six of her peers have entered guesses ranging from Los Angeles to Montana. Francine says, "Montpelier." The class: "O-O-O-O-O *sit!*"

In an effort to defuse a potential in-class war, Mrs. Gifford urges Randolph to cooperate by sitting in his assigned seat. The usually reserved Randolph spins on his teacher and screams, "I'll sit where I wanna sit!" The class responds in chorus, "O-O-O-O-O *sit!*"

Carl listens intently to a tale told by his friend John, a tale he knows to be a preposterous exaggeration. He finally loses his patience and interjects, "Aw, come off it, man. You talkin' boosit!"

Mr. Douglas, a white Anglo-Saxon Protestant sixth-grade science teacher in his sixties, checks into the main office to collect his regular paycheck. He is informed that the checks have yet to arrive. As he turns and retreats from the office he is heard to mumble under his breath, "O-O-O-O-O *sit!*"

Charlene and Darlene are separated after a battle royal in the privacy of the girls' room. Darlene commits the final affront by tossing a clump of hair into the air and gloating as the hair floats lazily to the floor. Her seconds respond softly, "O-O-O-O-O *sit*. Darlene *bad!*"

Bad assumes the meaning of *good*. Actions are judged to be so good, so outstanding, that they are bad. *Bad* connotes both accomplishment and daring.

James Pearson is overheard discussing the talents of the 1973 New York Knicks: "Bill Bradley? Yeah, he runs a lot and he gets open a lot and he can hit the 'j' [jumpshot], yeh, he's bad. So is DeBusschere, he's a stronger rebounder and he sets bad picks for the rest of the Knicks, and he's got a bad outside shot too, although you don't hear so much about it. Willis Reed is real bad when he's around but his knees are so bad [bad!] that it's hard to say if he'll ever be his old bad self again. Monroe can be one of the baddest dudes on the court when he gets fired up and feels like shakin' an' bakin'. But Walt Frazier is my main man. There ain't nothin' that Walt Frazier can't do on a basketball court. He is truly *terrible!*"

A new teacher, who was walking into his school building for the first time, recalls being struck by a scribbled message on a barren hallway bulletin board: "Miss Weisser is a hoe." A hoe? A garden hoe? An explanation was not long in coming. He overheard two eighth-grade boys discussing the whys and wherefores of a girl named LaChelle. "You got down with LaChelle. That don't mean nothin'. Now you're just the same as everybody else. LaChelle ain't nothin' but an old hoe anyway."

Another of the most common classics is *ax*. *Ax* no longer refers to a woodsman's mainstay; after all, what would children who grow up among concrete, bricks, and mortar know or care of axes. Now, *ax* is used exclusively as a verb. A child presented by his teacher with a question he is unable to answer responds, "Why you axin' me? Don't be axin' me. I ain't raise my hand! Ax Audrey."

The most severe violations in construction are found in the usages of verbs and in possessives. The language the children have created juxtaposes combinations of helping verbs and main verbs that confound the unaccustomed ear. Says a class in unison to a rookie math teacher who announces that they will begin the year with long division: "We been done had that." Says a young boy in response to the question of whether a character in a mystery acted wisely: "He shoulda hadda oughtta but he di'n't." Says a young girl to her substitute teacher when confronted with the fact that someone is sitting in her assigned seat: "Teacher, ax him to move, he be's sittin' in my seat."

Consider a brief sampling of some of the more common new forms of the possessive. A class president explains to her homeroom teacher what sparked an argument between two children in the class and their French teacher: "They ain't want to take off they coats, but she be's yellin' at 'em to take they coats off in her class." She also reports that another argument cropped up in a later class, when Richard snatched a math book from José, screaming, "This book be's mine's! This be's mine's book! Teacher make him give me mine's book, sit!"

New York children have institutionalized a word game (previously mentioned) that requires of its participants great quickness, imagination, and verbal dexterity. The game is called the Dozens. Despite the unfortunate drawback that a game of the Dozens often evolves into a fistfight, it serves as an entertaining form of impromptu theater for teachers and students alike, a critical element of the acting-out syndrome. The game pits one child against another in an exchange of insults usually about each other's mothers (not surprisingly, fathers are rarely mentioned in the Dozens). The insults are designed to sting one's opponent but must be cut with enough humor to keep him from irretrievable anger. The Dozens is designed to be appreciated by the multitudes, and is therefore rarely played within the privacy of such places as the bathrooms. Rather, it is designed for the classroom, as a diversion for all those present, and improves with a raucous, appreciative audience, one that punctuates each barb with outbursts of "O-O-O-O-O sit!" Segments of a typical game of the Dozens may include a few of the following:

"I saw your mother on a Hunnert an' Twenty-fif' Street yestiddy, she ugly!"

"Oh well, if we're gonna be talkin' 'bout people's mothers I'll give you a few minutes to go out and dig yours up!"

"Your mother rides shotgun on my local sanitation truck!"

"Yeah, at least she don't wear no combat boots!"

"I saw your mother 'round my block the other day. She was beatin' the dogs to the garbage cans."

"Yeah, well at least my mother ain't a man!"

"They tell me your mother knows all the roaches in your apartment by name!"

"Maybe. At least that way they don't carry the TV out the house like I seen over at your building."

"Your mother makes Pig Pen look cleaner than the Board of Health!"

"Yeah, well at least she don't chew tobacco."

"Your mother attract flies."

The exchange can go indefinitely, but all too often, as each participant exhausts his repertoire, the game is reduced to the basic

"Your mother!"

"Your mother!"

"Your mother!"

and what began as an exchange of words deteriorates into an exchange of fists.

"O-O-O-O-O-O-O *sit!*"

"Please Excuse This Interruption ..."

GOOD TEACHING IS LIKE good music. Both gather momentum, rise to great heights, ease back to earth momentarily, then rise again. Both involve the human soul and are largely emotional expressions.

> *Teachers, please excuse this interruption. Will the owner of a white Buick, license plate number YVL–621, please move your car. The sanitation truck can't get by.*

Both are beautiful at their very best. They are acts of perfect timing and grace. They lighten the mind and inspire each man to the limits of his individual capacity. Both reach startling and unspeakably beautiful climaxes, acts so close to love as to be love.

> *Mrs. Jones, Mrs. Jones, please report to the main office, there is a long distance call for you, Mrs. Jones, Mrs. Jones to the main office, please.*

But as a loudly crying baby can unnerve a symphony orchestra, so too can an overused, abrasive public-address system disrupt the

> *Will the following students please report to the music*

room at the end of period six: Dawn Davidson, Juan Rivera, James Jennings, Susan Schachter, and Kim King.

most rhythmic and poetic of lessons. Public-address systems are the playthings of administrators. The very best administrators rarely employ them. They understand leadership to be made of sterner stuff. Their influence is exercised as they move

There will be a cake sale in the main lobby at three o'clock today. All students are welcome. Proceeds will go toward the Christmas Dance.

about their buildings, truly inspiring and leading those who work directly with the children. The most capable and enlightened administrators understand the incredible annoyance that abuse

James Buckley, Hector Diaz, Juan Acevedo, Rachel Allentelli, Angela Seabrook, and Danny Harley, please report to Mrs. Calabrese's office immediately. I repeat . . .

of the public-address system creates. They turn to it only in the direst of emergencies, and when their voices come booming out its speakers through the building, people listen.

The periods for tomorrow's professional half-day will be as follows: 1, 3, 7, 4a, 4b, 5a, 2, 8, 4. I repeat, 1, 3, 7, 4a, 4b, 5a, 2, 8, 4.

These are men who understand the fable of the boy who cried "Wolf!" They make their presence felt in more human, vital ways.

Teachers please be reminded that your pink IBM attendance cards are due in the main office no later than three o'clock today. I repeat . . .

But New York is not gifted with many of their kind. In most schools the public-address system becomes the lazy man's shortcut. Children are paged to the main office because administrators are too self-indulgent to walk to the classrooms

I pledge allegiance to the flag of the United States of America and to the Republic for which it stands . . .

and pick them up in person. Children are paged to guidance counselors, to nurses, to speech therapists, to enter the building, to leave the building, to breakfast, lunch, and dinner. Teachers

There will be a joint rehearsal of the morning and after-

noon choruses today during period four. Teachers please
do not mark chorus members cutting.

are urged to answer telephone calls and to correct roll books. On
occasion the public-address system becomes the vehicle for lengthy
extemporaneous political harangues. One principal spoke

Will all teachers please step into the hallway, there is an
intruder in the building, and to the intruder I say I am
coming upstairs and you will not get away with this.

at vehement length about the Senate's failure to confirm Judge
Carswell's appointment to the Supreme Court. Calling it the most
significant day in the lives of all those listening, he wound

Please disregard the fire alarms, I repeat, please disre-
gard the fire alarms. Teachers please keep your classes in
their rooms.

himself to a fever pitch in a spiel that lasted upwards of an hour. A
weak administrator uses the loudspeaker as a means of inflating his
ego, of creating the illusion of omnipotence

Keith Erickson, please report to the main office, your dog
has followed you to school and is in the building. Keith
Erickson to the main office immediately.

and omnipresence by bellowing into the farthest reaches of the
building, privately aware, however, that few are really paying attention and that his ability to lead is negligible.

Administrators are not the sole heirs to the rights of the

Tickets for the Easter Dance are on sale in Mrs.
Washington's office, Room 421. All tickets cost seventy-
five cents. Refreshments will be served and cost extra.

public-address system. Teachers are allowed their day, calling students to meet at unscheduled times and places, assembling unscheduled choral rehearsals, gathering casts of one-act plays,

Will the following students please report to Mr. Brad-
sky's office with their high school preference sheets at
once . . .

and participants in assembly programs. In the most exaggerated
cases the public-address system serves as the medium for an entire
program, hastily constructed, honoring Martin

> *Ellen Kramer please report to the main office to pick up*
> *your lunch money. Your mother brought it in since you*
> *left it home. Ellen Kramer to the office.*

Luther King's Birthday, Rosh Hashanah, or Black Solidarity Day.
The public-address system represents education's effort to board the
technological bandwagon, to utilize some of the media that Marshall
McLuhan has talked about understanding.

> *Will one of the custodians please come to the main office*
> *at once. One of the custodians to the office please, this is*
> *an emergency!*

Children are also allowed their inning before the microphone,
reading endless lists of before-and-after-school events,

> *May I remind you that this is the last day that the blue*
> *lunch tickets beginning with the number 227 will be hon-*
> *ored in the cafeteria. Please turn in all extras today.*

calling wrongdoers to the principal's office, postponing meetings of
the Rocket Club, canceling meetings of yearbook committees, ad-
vertising cake sales, promoting ticket sales to the sixth-grade
faculty-student

> *Yearbooks will go on sale this Friday night after school in*
> *Mr. Metzger's room. Yearbooks for eighth graders who*
> *did not sell boosters will cost three dollars.*

basketball games, calling their friends to the office (for no other
reason than to enjoy the walk home with them), announcing sales of
bus tickets, reading eight-digit numbers of stolen (and therefore
void) lunch tickets, sharing

> *Because of the weather, today's track meet with Wagner*
> *has been canceled. Correction: because of today's*
> *weather, today's track meet with Wagner has been post-*
> *poned. I repeat . . .*

results of close elections, declaring winners of talent shows, mumbling the names of forty children who do *not* have to go to the Red
Cross on Tuesday, pinpointing locations of yearbook sales,

> *Whoever just pulled that fire alarm, I personally am com-*
> *ing to get you! All teachers please step into the halls! I am*
> *on my way upstairs now!*

begging colleagues to try out for cheerleading, urging participation in co-ed touch football, campaigning for office, praising God, and reminding their peers to tell their parents not to

> *The following classes should move quickly and quietly to the auditorium now: 6-319, 6-262, 7-219, and 7-314. Please see that your doors are locked and your windows are closed.*

forget to bring their cars to the car wash this Saturday. Secretaries, too, are granted their say, although most do so meekly and unwillingly, fearing that the impact of their message is trivial next to that of their many competitors.

> *Will Angela Kransky please report to the main office. Angela Kransky to the main office immediately.*

Few persons ever pay the slightest attention to these constant interruptions and many people, teachers and students,

> *May I remind all students to please listen to WINS radio tomorrow for any announcement of school closing. If the snow is light we will be open.*

talk back vehemently to the infernal machines. One young teacher who in frustration had actually torn the speaker from the wall of his classroom was sent an official reprimand by the principal. Talking back to the "box" when the

> *Will the owner of a green Dodge Dart parked on the downtown side of West Seventy-seventh Street please go to your car. You left your lights on.*

principal makes a series of unnecessary announcements becomes for teachers and students a form of therapy. They regard it as an opportunity to come together briefly and vent their emotions and frustrations, which have been mounting between themselves,

> *This is Mr. Edison speaking. I will wait a minute. It is only fair to tell you that each fire alarm has been sprinkled with a special powder that will show up under a special light. Any person ringing . . .*

at the defenseless, inanimate object. It presents an ideal form of release, an opportunity to let the principal know what they really think of him, to tell him off "good," to cuss him out without fear of reprisal. Thus, using the public address system

> *I would like to remind all teachers that Mr. Schneider from the 110 Livingston Street Office will be visiting our school this afternoon. I don't have to tell you how important . . .*

affords the principal an illusion of power, and at the same time ironically provides his underlings with a similarly grandiose illusion, not of power but of revolt. Attacking the nagging loudspeaker is the underdog's supreme moment of ventilation. The weakest teacher appears potent before a class of thirty, abruptly snapping his head in the direction of the speaker and barking at the

> *Please excuse this interruption, all students are encouraged to watch a special program on Channel 13 on Saturday at 8 p.m. entitled "The Louisiana Purchase: A New Look."*

principal to shut his "damn mouth."

Voices are not the only forms of interruption in our increasingly technological era that grate on the patience of those confined to the classroom, a captive audience if there ever was one. Certain loud, clanging bells ring periodically, a signal to the custodian that he is to report to the main office, pronto, to cope with some unforeseen emergency. Tones sound at the conclusion of each teaching period: the first denotes the end of class, the second is the warning bell for tardiness to the next period, the third ends the three-

> *Any seventh-grade girls interested in trying out for* West Side Story *should report to the auditorium right after school today. I repeat . . .*

minute interlude of passage from one class to the next, and the fourth and final tone tells a student that he is late and reminds teachers that students should not be accepted beyond

> *All students who were given the green and white polio inoculation slips and have had them signed by their parents should report to the left side of the cafeteria at this time.*

that point without a pass. Fire alarms sound constantly in most junior high schools, bringing secretaries and administrators to the microphone to confirm or deny their authenticity. Clearly some children take great pleasure in hearing the alarms sound four or five times every hour.

Public-address systems are constantly breaking down, but

> *Hi! You all know me. I'm Lisa and I'm running for president of the school. Vote for me, and remember, "We're red, black, and green and we say what we mean!"*

rarely die a silent death. Some let out moaning hums that remain unchecked until help finally arrives. Others utter brief but brutally piercing shrieks that send droves of children to the nurse's office, convinced that their eardrums have been shattered, complaining of throbbing headaches. Secretaries are forever leaving the amplifier in the "on" position, permitting

> *Teachers please excuse all boys coming late from gym. Please accept all late students into your classes. I repeat . . .*

typing and idle gossip to filter through the building until some frustrated teacher elects to leave her classroom unattended (a cardinal sin) and storms into the office telling them to turn the "damn thing off!" On other occasions the public-address

> *Will Anibel Terry please report to the main office with your books and coat. Anibel Terry to the office at once. You are going home.*

system will begin its own involuntary hums and buzzes as if offering loving courtship to a similar system in a neighboring school. Just as mysteriously as these noises crop up, they fade and die. They seem to endure just long enough for a service man to receive the desperate cry for help and get out on the road. Once he arrives, the sounds are history and none of the secretaries are quite able to reproduce the proper pitch and volume.

> *Bus and subway passes for the month of March will go on sale this Wednesday right after school in the guidance counselor's office. I repeat . . .*

The medic performs a cursory check and returns to headquarters before the machine acts up once again.

Music can be transmitted over most systems but is a rarity.

> *At two-thirty today, in the middle of the eighth period, all students and teachers should report to their homerooms to pick up report cards. I repeat . . .*

Principals seem to feel that music has no place in school, that technology's partnership was designed not to soothe and relax but to command, startle, and coerce.

> *All students interested in signing up for an after-school karate class should give their names to Mr. Antelli in Room 417 before three o'clock. I repeat . . .*

Teachers can speak of public-address systems only through clenched teeth. The more accomplished they are in their particular art, the more poignantly they resent the brutality of interruption. Constant interruption violates nature.

> *Mrs. Hartack, please report to Room 362 immediately. You class is waiting for you. Mrs. Hartack to Room 362 now!*

Interruption encourages discord and disrespect. Interruption mocks the quiet beauty of harmony and process, momentum and magnitude. Interruption segments life, forcing artists to

> *Mrs. Lamendola's African Dance Troop dress rehearsal scheduled for seven o'clock tonight has been canceled. African Dance is canceled for tonight.*

endure the distortion or ruin of the orderly presentation of ideas.

Interruption is as brutal to the artist as it is to his work. He grows disappointed and discouraged; he is forced into compromises he would not otherwise accept; his talents are dissipated.

> *May I have your attention for the afternoon announcements. Alphonso Green has been elected president of the school for the second year in a row. Today is Mr. Waldenberg's birthday, so be sure . . .*

In extreme cases his spirit is broken and he finds himself forced, if he is to survive, to abandon teaching for another career.

This is Mr. Hansen, your principal. I would like to say once again how much I have enjoyed working with all of you this year and wish you all a wonderful summer. When the bells sound, the 1974–75 school year is officially over.

The Bathrooms

THE GREATEST DEPRIVATION any New York City child suffers is the absolute unavailability of private space. Offshoots of this condition are the pent-up anger, hostility, and frustration that force children to seek affection and understanding through channels that seem aberrant and deviant to the rest of us, but that make perfect sense to the children themselves. Similarly, the difficulty a child encounters in correcting this imbalance is a reflection of the freedom he does not have.

Consider the day-to-day existence of so many New York children: They walk crowded streets in the morning and board crowded subways and buses to get to school. They sit in overcrowded classrooms in overcrowded schools. There may be as many as forty children in a room designed comfortably for twenty. Gym periods in junior high schools typically include ninety girls on one side of a dividing wall and ninety boys on the other. The children eat lunch in noisy, crowded cafeterias and have recess on unbelievably crowded play-

143

grounds. One junior high school of more than one thousand students sends its children after lunch to a single playground not eighty yards long. The children return home on the same crowded subways and buses, climb stairs in crowded buildings, and enter their own crowded apartments. Few enjoy the privacy of their own bedrooms; most share the space with three or four siblings. Small rooms further crowd large families and shrink space. Children find themselves least comfortable in the confines of home, a place too small and too packed with humanity to allow either for letting off steam or for relaxation. They return to the crowded streets for a few hours of play, or to a park, also crowded, where they have a chance to get into a crowded basketball game. If a child is lucky he will be given a chance to go to camp in the summer for two weeks, but there he will find the same congestion that so dominates his life in the city. Summer camps typically operate at two to three times their capacity because the need of city children for fresh air and green hills is so great.

A new breed of humanity is quietly evolving within the great cities of the world: people, in the millions, who never experience solitude. Access to private space implies control over one's life; a lack of it generates patterns of behavior and types of personality with which the rest of us may as yet be unfamiliar.

Another important phenomenon, in evidence throughout the New York City public schools, is the establishment of an order of dominance. A study on the behavior, growth and habitat of the wild baboons of Africa had broad implications for anthropologists and sociologists alike. The study explored the phenomenon of dominance within a single baboon troop and charted the various phases through which individual baboons, male and female, moved as they ascended or descended the dominance ladder. The "pecking order" was perfectly established. The laws that prevailed were as clear to the baboons as if they had been typed and tacked to a tree. Maturing males had to demonstrate physical dominance over mature females before they could make a move toward the top spot in the troop. At the top there was only room for the three stoutest males, and their stay in that position was always subject to challenge. The symbolic gesture that signaled a challenge and the rules governing the challenge itself were neither arbitrary nor malleable. The entire troop observed each potential adjustment in the dominance order with keen interest and anticipation. They studied young rising baboons with the enthusiasm of baseball scouts in search of promising talent. All of the baboons were in agreement about the precise order at any given point in time.

So it is also in the public schools. Each class gradually creates its own order of dominance, by playing the Dozens and by fist fights. The greatest number of fights occur in junior high school classes composed of sixth or seventh graders, all from different elementary schools, and therefore new to each other. The dominance order must be established from scratch and teachers discover that violent fights and arguments mark the months of September and October. Needless to say, if a child transfers from one school to another, he feels considerable anxiety until the first blows have been struck and his position has been established.

A child's position in the order of dominance determines the extent of his freedom of speech within his classroom. He can give directions and orders to all those below him without fear of reprisal or refusal while at the same time recognizing that placing demands upon those above him will lead to trouble. Conversely, he is prepared to live by the wills and whims of his superiors, but never to let a challenge from below go unanswered. Always it is understood that dominance is in no way related to academic achievement.

The search for private space in schools and the compulsion to establish dominance are realized in the same location: the boys' and the girls' bathrooms. In several respects, the bathrooms are the most important places in the school, particularly in junior high schools. There, certain phases of school life go on unnoticed by most educators. The children can rest assured that no teacher will ever violate that space. The most intrusive interruption the children can expect is a knock at the door or a messenger sent to urge them to hurry back to class. But the bathroom is the only space in the school that "belongs" exclusively to the children. The bathrooms reflect their codes of behavior and fair play regardless of what the school may preach.

For many children, the bathroom becomes their clubhouse, their base camp, their toehold in the institution. Accordingly, the real fights in schools, the fights which determine true superiority, must, by their very nature, take place in the bathrooms. All children are aware that fights in the classroom, despite their apparent ferocity, will ultimately be broken up by the teacher. Conversely, they realize that fights in the bathrooms never end with even a whisper of ambiguity; there must be a clear winner and a clear loser; no fighter will compromise his wrath until he and the many onlookers have exacted a clear surrender.

Gregory and Carlton met in the bathroom during the third period, accompanied by a host of "reporters." Gregory was new in the school, a quiet, shy boy from the Deep South. He had indicated that he had swallowed all Carlton's goading that he could stomach and that he was ready to go to war. Although only twelve years of age, Carlton was tall and lithe, with quick hands and fast feet. He was a boxer and had earned bragging rights as a boxer. Gregory was shorter and thicker but lacked the grace and fluidity that Carlton demonstrated in all sports. Gregory had refused to fight for so long that the heckling and name-calling had become an all-day, everyday occurrence. He was unaccustomed to violence in any form and felt uncomfortable entering the bathroom. He had seen many others risk their titles in the very same arena over similar issues, but had always assumed that he would be spared such attention and anxiety. Gregory was nervous and Carlton sensed that and continued to ridicule him as they walked down the halls together to the appointed forum.

As the battle began, Gregory balled up his fists and raised them in front of his face in imitation of others he had observed in similar fights. Sensing Gregory's unfamiliarity with the art of boxing, Carlton probed his inadequate defenses with lightning jabs and combinations to the body and face. He stung Gregory hard on his cheeks and around his ears with crisp, accurate thrusts. In the process Gregory's dander rose. He discarded his stylistic affectations. He unclenched his fists and dropped his hands from in front of his face. Then he charged his aggressor. His approach seemed to take hours, and Carlton landed several clean blows on Gregory's chin and around his eyes. But once in close, Gregory was a different fighter. He locked Carlton's neck in a vicious vise and squeezed it in boa-constrictor fashion, while Carlton swung his hands in vain. Gregory then whirled him around and banged his captured face first into the walls, then onto the floor, and finally against the toilet. When Carlton appeared close to drawing his last breath he signaled defeat and Gregory relaxed his grip. Carlton fell limp to the floor, gasping for breath, his left eye already closed. Gregory seemed more embarrassed by his victory than proud. He had presented a convincing demonstration to his classmates and to himself that the shy little boy from down South could hold his own. It would be a long time before he would be called upon to answer another challenge. The witnesses spread the word of his achievement quickly through the building. His position in the order of dominance was at last established.

Just as the students are banned from entering the special retreat of the teachers, the Teachers' Room, so too are the teachers excluded from the private world of the bathrooms. Each army in the daily wars that characterize public education in many schools is afforded a place in which to fall back and stop acting out. Much of the activity in each domain is similar in nature and degree. As teachers retire to their sanctum to smoke, drink coffee, gossip about the romancing taking place among the teaching staff, and to criticize parents, principals, and pupils, so do the children retire to their bathrooms: to smoke, drink soda (and occasionally wine), gossip about romances among the students, and criticize the principal, their teachers, and the school. It is unfortunate that no way has yet been discovered to merge the two, often-adjacent environments or erect two-way mirrors in the walls. Each group would be fascinated by a glimpse of the other. Teachers would discover restless, inattentive little boys sitting and listening to their peers or copying telephone numbers from the walls. Students would find men and women whom they assumed to be universally evil, laughing and joking with their friends.

The gossiping that takes place in the boys' and girls' bathrooms is facilitated by bountiful graffiti, which are more up-to-date and better read than the school newspaper. Old romances are crossed out entirely. Names of different partners are added above erasures. One principal checked the graffiti in every bathroom in his school each afternoon before he left at five P.M. He was looking for new additions. He claimed that he could anticipate and prevent fights by spotting a fresh challenge ("Joey T. is a punk faget"), and he insists that he sidetracked potential pregnancies by keeping his most trusted guidance counselor informed of the latest pairings. On occasion he even corrected spelling, once adding a *t* to *buch* in "Sharon Graves is a buch." Students characterized as nonreaders peruse the bathroom walls daily and diligently for any happenings they might have missed. The walls become the vehicle for communicating new nicknames as well:

> *Calvin as Sweet-Movin*
> *Charlene as Peanut*
> *Anthony as the King of Bad*

The graffiti-covered walls become the grapevine that no student active in the goings-on-about-school can afford to ignore.

Bathroom apparatus provides a rare fascination for school-age children. Microscopes, although intrinsically capable of far greater fascination than toilets, lose some of their clout because teachers constantly harp on their proper usage and manipulation. Toilets usually float a wide assortment of unlikely articles and artifacts that curious children have attempted to choke down the pipes. Many schools have switched from rolls of toilet paper to single sheets after discovering that the children were placing the end of the roll in the toilet, oiling the rolling fixture, and testing which toilets could imbibe the most paper in a single flush.

Kotex dispensers in girls' bathrooms excite similar passions. One school installed such devices after months of pressure from parents, only to find sanitary napkins all over the school by 3 P.M.; some were set on fire in classrooms, some were crammed down overflowing toilets in the girls' room, others matted the bottom of the urinals in the boys' room. At their venomous worst, children use toilets as means of corporal punishment for their "friends" and enemies alike. In one instance, Mr. Dayton devoted a period of his seventh-grade social studies class to a discussion of the purges in the Soviet Union under Beria and to an analysis of some of the more unseemly tactics used in extracting information. Included on his list was the practice of placing a man's head in a toilet and flushing it repeatedly until he drowned or talked. Not ten minutes after the class had ended, Michael Green was recuperating in the nurse's office after being rescued from repeated flushings in the second-floor boys' room.

In the more difficult schools in the city, particularly in the junior high schools, children attempt to gain the same uncontested control of the hallways that they have of the bathrooms. If successful, they expand their private space and virtually take over the school. The affectations of the bathrooms, graffiti and the like, spread unchecked into the hallways, often with increased vigor and vitality since boys and girls are no longer separated. Once the children take over the halls, usually consuming the principal in the process, they grow accustomed to manifestations of freedom they have never enjoyed before. They then provide remarkable guerrilla resistance to any effort to retake the corridors.

The bathroom-hallway phenomenon that afflicts almost all secondary schools deserves as much of the educator's attention as new textbooks and new systems of teaching addition. The lack of private space that many children growing up in New York and other cities experience, and the effect it has upon their lives and their attempts to redefine and re-create that space in the confines of the bathrooms, profoundly alters the best-laid plans of the best-intentioned educators.

The Trenches

ARCHITECTS OF SCHOOL BUILDINGS have little understanding of the relative importance of the space they set aside for hallways. They envision that space being used exclusively for the smooth efficient transit of double lines of children as they go back and forth, like so many walk-in-line Madelines, between the classroom and the gymnasium, the cafeteria, the auditorium, and the great outdoors. Architects are concerned that hallways be wide enough to accommodate classes passing in opposite directions, and that they be well lit and decorated in bright colors. Architects base their concepts of school corridors on memories of their own schooldays. How shocked they would be today!

The hallways have become the most controversial pieces of real estate in the New York schools. In many junior high schools the administrators all know that regardless of his educational philosophy, professional schooling and experience, and ability to train and lead teachers, his tenure will turn almost exclusively on his ability to take and hold the halls.

Administrators of elementary schools generally do not share the problem of the hallways with their intermediate and junior high school colleagues, although the first symptoms of the affliction are to be found in corridors devoted exclusively to fifth- and sixth-grade classes. They avoid the problem (or are avoided by the problem) for three reasons: first, the children in question are younger, smaller, weaker, more easily intimidated ("If you go out there, you'll probably get beaten up by the bigger children" — or eaten or whatever) and therefore much easier to control; second, elementary schools are organized in contained classes, which give the children little occasion to be in the halls in the first place; and finally, the rise of Open Corridor programs converted many hallways into extra classrooms with regularly appointed teachers assigned to use them as laboratories. (Although by 1978 Open Corridor was slipping quietly out of vogue and out of sight.)

But a plan so ingenious and subtle as Open Corridor, which subversively places the control of the hallways in the hands of the school authorities while creating in the minds of the children the illusion that they have gained access to a place once feared and forbidden, has failed to gain widespread acceptance in the secondary schools. There control and dominance of the hallways is a never-ending struggle that taxes the wits and patience of the most gifted administrators and the most ornery, acting-out children. The number of students roaming the hallways at any given point in time, and the activities they become engaged in while in the halls, represent the barometer by which the host community evaluates the school. The only other indicator that parents and the general public will place an iota of stock in is the standardized reading test, but the exposures of recent research have so damaged the test's reliability that the matter of the hallways has taken on even graver concern. For most taxpayers, the importance of maintaining order and control in the hallways, of communicating a *sense* of security, safety, and stability, outweighs any measure of cognitive success or failure. A school characterized by raucous, bawdy play in the hallways between and during classes may boast reading scores in the highest percentiles in the city, but when the time comes for the community school board to deliberate on tenure for the principal, it is a virtual certainty that the man in question will find himself out on the street. On the other hand principals who control and patrol their hallways with Prussian military precision and authority soon find themselves seated in the community superintendent's comfortable chair, despite the fact that most of their former students can't spell *cat*.

Many junior high school students regard a school corridor as a prize worth working for, as a Bastille worth storming, as a Hill 481 worth taking. They are willing to pay the price it may cost in parent conferences, suspensions, and in extreme cases expulsion, for the privilege of roaming the halls in groups of up to fifty, kicking classroom doors, and singing "Doctor's Orders." They see themselves as engaging in trench warfare with their teachers and administrators (who are paid to fight), as being locked in hand-to-hand combat and needing a prize to show for their efforts. Their goal is to extend the privacy and absolute control of the bathrooms to all the corridors and stairwells in the building. Their numbers, once small, seem to increase yearly. In some junior high schools it is difficult to find any children who *never* "walk the halls."

In such schools new teachers refuse to walk the halls alone. They are too often encountered by hordes of marauding children; they are verbally harassed, occasionally poked, and in at least one instance "goosed." Non-hall-walking children (still the majority in the majority of schools) live in abject fear of their hall-walking peers and avoid having to use the bathrooms until they arrive home, shortly after three, on the verge of exploding. In such schools, parents and visitors, strangers to the immediate school community, are considered fair game by the masses of children who "hang out" in the corridors for six consecutive hours, five days a week. Administrators, ashamed to show their faces, barricade themselves in their offices to update their résumés, informing their crack secretaries to buffer any assault on their self-imposed exile. Such schools are characterized by confusion, bitterness, chaos, and, in the extreme cases, terror.

A new administrator, inheriting a disheveled junior high school, as many do each year in New York, finds that he has to wage a well-planned, well-manned campaign to regain control of his building. He has to take individual corridors one at a time; drive invaders (alumni and alumnae) to the streets and the bathrooms, areas he knows he will never control; hold those corridors and begin his assault on others. No wonder one New York principal adorns his office walls with portraits of military heroes of foreign campaigns. He has continually to rally and bolster the troops at his disposal (doorguards, male aides, gym teachers on their free periods, and volunteers), knowing that the slightest indication of retreat or regression could so discourage morale that they will break ranks and hide behind contractual grievances, excessive sick days, and locked doors. He has seen the process in other schools and must be an accomplished psychologist to make certain that it is not repeated during his reign. He is fully aware that the struggle will be long and costly, that it may consume the bulk of his time for as much as a year, aware also that his job and career depend on it. He must prevail. When he senses that the corridors are secure, he will isolate and cleanse individual stairwells and hiding places throughout the building. His taking control of the hallways automatically rejuvenates teachers and staff. Right away they feel again the power that consorts with ownership and control. The lurking, slinking gait that had characterized their passage during the years of student occupation is metamorphosed into a tall, bold strut. The principal is revered for his accomplishment. Socrates assumes Caesar's robes.

The hallways have become a demilitarized zone. To many parents and educators, schools plagued by mob student rule of the corridors are deemed "bad" schools; those whose halls are empty and quiet are considered "good." A single classic struggle has reduced the evaluation of men and their worth to a momentary gander down a lengthy corridor — a test so simple and yet so revealing.

Strategies that administrators draft to retake their buildings reflect their imagination and approach to a relatively simple, clear-cut problem. In general they have but three alternatives at their disposal: to bull the kids out of the corridors; to con them out; or to lure them into the classrooms with either the most noble of intentions or blatant chicanery.

The first alternative, simple coercion, the choice of most principals, is the messiest and probably the least effective. The principal augments his forces with relentless use of the public-address system and several mass-arrest tactics, smacking of Stalin's purges. In one school he suddenly bursts out over the public-address system: "There will be a roundup on the second floor in one minute. All students on the second floor not in their classes will be caught and severely dealt with. I repeat . . ." Panic follows as student hall-walkers barge into the nearest classrooms and gesture the intimidated rookie teachers to silence. Sixty seconds later, deans, gym teachers, guards, counselors, and assistant principals seal off bathrooms and stairwells and systematically sweep the halls. The unfortunates trapped in their net are herded into the auditorium like so many cattle, and detained until a family member (or next of kin) comes to claim them, sometimes as late as nine or ten at night. But this tactic rarely has lasting effectiveness. The children sense that it is more of a drain on the staff than on themselves and after two or three days of self-imposed curfew, they are out on their familiar beats again. In another school, one in which the staff sensed the principal's impotence in dealing with the hallway theater, the teachers assembled to form vigilante committees to improve the climate and to elect a field marshal. A tough, battle-hardened veteran of twenty years in the girls' gymnasium was nominated, but she declined, asking, "Do you want me to head this committee in this school or the one I'm transferring to?"

Principals who recognize the futility of reclaiming space through coercion will attempt a sleight of hand to get the job done. Morality has no bearing on a struggle so intensified as that for control of the halls. One wily junior high school principal rounded up the biggest, meanest, most feared ninth-grade boys and girls in his building, acknowledged to them that they were getting absolutely no education in school, and that they might as well join the staff in its effort to make the hallways livable once again. They were understandably flabbergasted, but flattered by the offer and willing to extend their services. The principal publicly played his hand to the hilt, supplying each child with a desk at the end of his appointed corridor, decorating each with a tinny little badge that read "Sheriff," and giving each a formal man-by-man introduction (à la Super Bowl) at the faculty meeting. The faculty, too, seemed delighted to find themselves suddenly teamed with those who had brought fear into their lives for the past five months. (It was like having Dick Butkus traded unexpectedly to your Pop Warner football team.) After the meeting one young female teacher was embraced by a girl nicknamed Porkchop, who had once trapped and terrorized her in the girls' bathroom for over an hour. Privately, the principal encouraged ruthlessness in his green troops and implied that they would be evaluated by their ability to keep the halls empty.

They understood him perfectly. Transgressors were often kicked and beaten before being returned to class. One boy was warned that if he appeared in the halls again, he would be shot. He believed it. An adorable, four-foot-tall, sixth-grade girl stepped into the halls with a pass to the bathroom. Not more than ten feet down the corridor she was charged by a "Sheriff" screaming, "Get out the mutherfuckin' halls, bitch, before I break your ass!" She fled back to her classroom before wetting her pants. Other problems soon surfaced. The halls became ominously quiet and the "Sheriffs" ran out of things to do. They couldn't prop their feet up on their desks and read the sports section of the New York *Times* because they couldn't read. They couldn't wrestle with homework because they had been excused from all classes. (This is probably the last way they would have chosen to while away the hours anyway.) They couldn't play chess or checkers because they were alone.* They had been perfectly conned. They were so effective that they bored even themselves. Some started popping in and out of classrooms, telling kids to "sit down and shut up and do they work," realizing that the teachers were too afraid to object to their rude entries. One sat quietly behind his desk and rolled, sold, and smoked cigarettes.

The principal suddenly transferred the whole lot, replacing them with guards he had hired off the streets for the same purpose. The

---

*Thanks to a new era of outdoor park furniture, including poured concrete tables with inlaid checkerboards, many New York children are masters of these parlor games.

coup was magnificent. Unethical and devious but perfectly executed. The building had been returned to his control. Possession in the eyes of a public-school faculty is nine tenths of the law.

The only long-term alternative includes a massive, costly, time-consuming retraining program for the staff (with no guarantee of success) in an effort to make what goes on in the classrooms interesting to the students. Most schools make at least a few token efforts at teacher training, either during daily "workshops" or in after-school centers. Because these programs are expensive and usually draw on outside sources, they have become an early target of budget cuts.

The intention behind retraining is to make the lure of the classroom more magnetic than that of the street life of the halls. For several obvious reasons, retraining is rarely the course an administrator follows. His own job and personal well-being are too insecure for a protracted entanglement; he opts for a slugfest in the trenches.

Schools that are able to control the flow of traffic in their hallways institutionalize that control with a complex system of passes and permits. Some schools insist on identification cards with full-face photographs, which must be shown at the entrance door (they are mandatory in the New York high schools), and issue wooden or written passes for travel in the halls during class periods. Wooden passes usually have the teacher's name carved into one face and the room number on the reverse side. They are easily duplicated at home, and an accomplished seventh-grade whittler can make a hearty moonlight income if he is careful not to become too prolific. Written passes come in all colors of the rainbow and are color-coded to destinations: pink for the nurse's office, green for the counselors, blue for the main office, yellow for the library, and so on. They are essentially one-way tickets, while wooden passes are reserved for round-trip sorties to lockers, bathrooms, and drinking fountains. Teachers are constantly out of whatever color of pass the moment ordains and must substitute the backs of worksheets, scraps of notebook paper, and trash off the floor. They are out of their allotted stacks of paper passes because the craftier kids, set on walking the halls, steal them. Written passes are chock full of information: time, destination, ETA, date, room number, mission, height, weight, and the appropriate teacher's signature or initials. Forgery of the latter separates the mediocre artists from the greats — another in-school hobby that nets certain children pocket money. One, Sarah Zarkin, claims that she was able to sell enough forged passes to pay for lunch every day of the year. Pride usually consumes the forgers, however, as they carelessly wager with their teachers that they can duplicate their hands.

Passes are only significant if there are adults in the halls to read the passes. Some schools use teachers on duty periods, some use volunteer parents, others use guards and paraprofessionals. Almost all are easily buffaloed by counterfeit passes. A school rampant with successful forgers may sometimes end up with as many students in the halls as a school that has lost the war.

Ingenuity can still beat the system. One young man used to have a cigarette or two in the boys' bathroom between classes, stroll to his classroom door, knock, and as it opened, look back down the hall and say, "Thanks for the escort, Mr. Sims" (the principal, of course). The teacher, realizing that the principal's power transcended the insistence upon passes, would stick his head out into the hallway to thank Mr. Sims for safely delivering his prodigal charge, and find the hallway empty. By that time the boy was seated and at least feigning work and his teacher usually elected to avoid a confrontation.

Regardless of who wins the war, the corridors are the stage set for some of the liveliest events of the school year. Fights in the corridors are usually memorable, if only because of the huge crowds they are able to attract. A brief verbal exchange in a deserted corridor can suddenly be transformed into a title bout when classroom doors are flung open and students quickly take ringside seats. Female teachers are advised to avoid a hallway fracas — it can get out of hand; male teachers are encouraged to be rough and tumble to discourage the combatants from a return challenge.

In one school, while Ethel Kennedy was being given a red-carpet tour by the administration, daring Hank Hawkins, an established second-floor roadrunner, rounded the corner hotly pursued by his homeroom teacher, Mr. Fox. Almost at the visitor's feet Mr. Fox went airborne for a breathtaking open-field tackle on young Hawkins. His arms pinned behind him, Hank apologized to Mrs. Kennedy (who had her back to the momentary drama and may have missed it entirely), "Sorry lady," and was dragged, struggling and protesting ("Get your motherfuckin' hands off me, mister!") back to class.

Ten students from a suburban New Jersey school visited a New York intermediate school to put on a public-speaking performance. After the program had ended, each child was assigned a guide from the host school and was on his own until after lunch. By noon, most of the visitors, all but one of whom were black, were pleading to go home. One little girl named Theresa had had her hat snatched by a boy she claimed looked "awful." He promised to return it if she gave him a big kiss. She let him keep the hat. Another girl was approached by a group of girls who had apparently seen her perform.

"Is you one of the girls from New Jersey that was on the stage?" one of the locals asked.

"Yes I was," Delta said proudly. "I hope you liked the performance."

"Well, let me tell you somethin'," the bigger girl continued. "I don't think I like the idea of a bunch of niggers from New Jersey comin' over here to steal our men. You think you're so damn cute, bitch, but I'm warnin' you, you even look funny at one of these boys, and that's your behind!"

The one white boy among the visitors was such an oddity that he was accorded special treatment and was the only one who wanted to stay longer. At one point he joined a line of about twenty students waiting for a drink of water. His guide snatched him from the rear of the line, yanked the lead drinker away from the water, and deposited his guest at the fountain head, warning those in line not to "mess with this dude." "This dude" was red-haired, freckle-faced, and chubby.

An account of life in the hallways would not be complete without paying some attention to two unique phenomena: bulletin boards and intruders. Teachers are assigned bulletin boards in corridors outside their classrooms and instructed to keep lively displays up throughout the year. All teachers put up one bulletin board during their careers but few decorate a second. A freshly frilled bulletin board seems to excite the worst in the hall-walkers. The board is either shredded or set on fire shortly after the unsuspecting teacher turns his back. In one case a teacher kept a watchful eye on the bulletin board from her classroom door while trying to control her classes; even the slightest tear was stapled, repeatedly, back into place. Her obsession with the maintenance of the board seemed to consume her. By Christmas she no longer had much rapport with her classes, but the board had become a mass of staples, a huge reflecting rectangle whose original design had long been obscured by the sutures.

"Good" schools have no traffic in the hallways. "Great" schools have bulletin-board displays whose colors are permitted to fade and grow yellow with age.

"May I have your attention, please. This is your principal speaking. There are three intruders in the building. Will all teachers please step into the hallways and detain these young men. I am on my way upstairs. I repeat, I am coming upstairs." No teacher in his right mind answers that kind of plea over the public-address system. He realizes that there are big guards at every entrance to the building, and the incursion of an intruder means that he is (or they are) even bigger. Some teachers believe that intruders exist only in the mind of the principal, who periodically makes such announcements in order to plead helplessness to those higher up in rationalizing the deplorable state of his building or some act of violence that has recently occurred.

In 1974 the West Side was terrorized by a man whose police sketch appeared in virtually every store window. He had dismembered several small boys. The children called him Charlie Chopoff and the most perverse teachers and principals used the fear of his presence to help keep their halls empty. One principal announced calmly over the public-address system, "Teachers please count your students. There is a possibility that Charley Chopoff is in the general area."

The Teachers' Room

THE TEACHERS' ROOM is like a backstage room used for rehearsals. Many teachers feel that good teaching is like good drama, that good teachers are good actors. Their classrooms become their stages; their pupils are their audiences; the forty-five-minute class period determines the length of the performance. And perform they do. Such teachers plan their wardrobes well in advance. They review their daily scripts time and time again before the bell sounds and the classroom becomes the theater. They anticipate the reactions of their audiences; they weave in laughter, tragedy, and pathos. They learn to utilize every second allotted to their forty-five-minute spectacle. They let the sound of the bell replace the falling curtain at the close of each performance.

Teachers who act work themselves into a state of concentration and intensity before they "go on." They are momentarily unrecognizable to their colleagues. Their faces reflect the anguish that even the most confident Broadway performers feel before they face each

160

new audience. They fantasize interruptions of every sort: from loudspeakers, from untimely knocks on the door, and from children within the classroom. They dread such violations of their art, knowing that a supreme moment may be forever lost.

They are truly not themselves. They exaggerate their motions and the modulations of their voices. They rant like Laurence Olivier in *Othello*; they punctuate long silences with melodrama that Gregory Peck might envy. Though they have no style of their own, they create original collages of the many performances they have seen. Their material is often dreary: proper nouns, dangling modifiers, and fractions with unlike denominators. They defy a seasoned professional to do better with an equivalent script.

Teachers as actors personify eccentricity. One, Mr. Hart, wore outlandish, out-of-date clothing that riveted the attention of his young audience to his person and allowed him to begin a performance without a moment's hesitation. On one occasion he wore a way-too-snug jumpsuit that hugged his every contour with unbridled truth. Mr. Hart carried a long, silver, collapsible pointer, which he continuously extended and contracted to underscore thoughts and to emphasize his thoughts. His audience lived in fear of his domineering, unpredictable behavior, yet revered his ability to capture and hold their interest. He made the forty-five minutes fly by.

Peter Tracy would leap unexpectedly to the top of his desk and deliver near-hysterical, rambling soliloquies to his stunned pupils. Once he felt that they had grown accustomed to such antics, he would just as suddenly dart underneath a table or desk and continue his ravings from there. (On a trip in Central Park one afternoon he caught two of his boys throwing rocks at a squirrel high up in a tree. He made both climb the tree and spent ten minutes throwing rocks at them.)

Teachers as actors involve their audiences in the play, reaching out to them with probing, unexpected questions, catching them slightly off guard. These teachers charge the atmosphere in the room for forty-four and a half minutes. They achieve startling crescendos and reach incomparable climaxes just a fraction before the bell sounds and the theater empties. The room quickly fills again and the performance is repeated. Applause can be thunderous and spontaneous. The children are aware that they have been treated to a show that others would have to pay to see.

Teachers who act, as enlightening and entertaining as they can be at their best, are exploitive and dull at their worst. They are granted their audiences by law not from love of the theater. Their students have no other choice. And what is more unbearable than squirming through a performance by actors who can't act? For every virtuoso on the classroom stage, there are probably a hundred impostors. They too perform before packed houses, particularly as schools have become so overcrowded of late. Furthermore, the audience is never free to raise criticisms for fear of having parents called or being sent to the office. Imagine Clive Barnes's mother receiving an irate telephone call to the effect that because of some candid criticism he made he will not be permitted to attend another performance, at least until the offended party and Mrs. Barnes have had an opportunity to sit down and talk the matter through. What is at stake, of course, is the teacher's ego, and in such matters the right to free and honest criticism is understood to have been surrendered.

As resolutely as the dramatists believe that pedagogy and theater are inseparable, so do other of their colleagues believe that the school's primary function is to teach discipline, order, and an appreciation for the American way of life. They believe in tough, militaristic tactics within the classroom. Bob Rucker periodically orders his eighth graders to forty-five minutes of silence "because it's good for them." During the curfew, Mr. Rucker will stand squarely in front of the classroom, arms folded, and glare from one student to the next, saying little or nothing himself.

These teachers believe in corporal punishment and regard its illegality as a tragedy in the annals of educational philosophy. "Every kid," says Mr. Walker, "could do with a good kick in the ass or a belt in the mouth once in a while." Like "closet queens," the advocates of corporal punishment are becoming increasingly daring and outspoken in their defense of force. They join corporal-punishment lobbies, affix bumper stickers advocating all forms of legitimized violence, and maintain a constant buzz in the school to keep the issue of "belt-in-the-mouth teaching" alive. They come in both sexes and in all colors and rise mightily when one of their own has been singled out and chastised for what they regard as justifiable behavior. They find allies on the U.S. Supreme Court. In 1974 the New York *Times* carried an exposé of two deans in the South Bronx who were paddling behinds to get their messages across.* The students were so familiar with this practice that they had named the paddle "The Smoker." Most schools conduct similar practices, although in the majority of instances individual teachers do so without the knowledge or tacit consent of the administration. It is not uncommon for students to give nicknames to these practices and instruments; in one intermediate school a paddle was known as the "Board of Education." What neither the New York *Times* in its exposé nor the central Board of Education in its quick removal of the accused deans had anticipated was a flood of letters and protests from teachers and parents (particularly the parents whose children had been victimized) urging the chancellor not only to reinstate the guilty parties but to allow them to continue their practices.

Such teachers will not tolerate a moment's disorder. Their classes form double lines before entering the classroom, with the shorter students up front and sequentially taller ones in the rear. They march in and stand behind their designated desks. Mr. Davidson gives the signal with his right hand and each child passes his coat up his row to the front child. The children in the front row then hang all coats in the closet. Mr. Davidson begins his regular morning spiel: "Sit down!" "Pick up that paper!" "Take out your homework!" "Spit out that gum!" "Get in your correct seats!" "Shut up!" The routine rarely varies; nor do the clothes Mr. Davidson wears to school; nor do the predictable wisecracks that emanate from the unbroken colts in each of his classes.

Like the actors in the teaching profession, the generals, too, work themselves into a special state of mind before the day begins, and maintain that state in "pupil-contact" periods for the duration of the

*Deans in the junior high schools are supplemental disciplinarians.

day. They have developed a reputation for toughness that they themselves realize was neither natural nor easy to cultivate. Their lives have become completely absorbed by the effort to maintain that reputation, to save face at any cost, to cast a long, broad shadow before those of their colleagues whom they regard as "limp-wristed fairies and silly old ladies." Whatever their internal chemistry may be, they understand that their egos are at stake whenever they confront their classes. They live in fear of provoking reactions in their students that could lead to massive uprisings. They are uniquely paranoid, knowing so little about the children they "teach" that they sense unrest and conspiracy when there are none. The feverish, defensive posture they assume in the classroom is as contrived and artificial as the demeanor of their theatrical counterparts. They are no more warriors than their colleagues are performers.

Another in this constellation is the moralist, who feels that it is his inherited duty to preach the gospel of goodness and truth to his students. His efforts are no less exploitive than those of his theatrical and militaristic colleagues. He, too, goes through a daily ritualistic warmup to prepare for meeting and inspiring his students. They attend his church not because they have been touched by the word or seek repentance but because their mothers and their principals have conspired to decree it. The moralist speaks in a soft even voice, drawing lessons and meaning from every minor incident that takes place in the classroom. Although classes will grant such would-be pulpiteers an occasional sympathetic and curious ear, for the most part they will rampage through the room for the duration of the period like so many uncircumcised heathens. Said Charlotte of Mr. Bell, "He's my favorite teacher because we can play around in his class every day and he never gets mad. He's nice."

There is only one location within each New York City school building where all the teachers are drawn together for brief but illuminating moments during the day. That haven is known as the Teachers' Room.

The Teachers' Room is off limits by edict to all students and off limits de facto to all administrators. It is, in the fullest sense of the term, the Teachers' Room. Hair comes down within the sanctity of its walls. All the various actors toss their costumes into the corner and become themselves for a brief intermission without fear of retribution or confrontation.

The physical manner of the teachers changes. The straight backs assume the contours of the old but comfortable second- and third-hand Salvation Army couches and easy chairs. Each teacher plugs a nickel or a dime into the coffee or soda machine, and slumps down into a chair with his feet up on a coffee table, cup in one hand, cigarette in the other.

By eleven o'clock the Teachers' Room is filled with cigar and cigarette smoke; chewing gum wrappers and used paper cups are scattered about the floor; ashtrays overflow onto coffee tables and the arms of easy chairs; and cigarette butts are everywhere. No teacher would tolerate his own classroom in such a state. But because the Teachers' Room belongs to everyone and no one, membership carries no responsibility for cleanliness.

On only one occasion have I seen teachers upset at the condition of their retreat. In this particular junior high school the day before the Easter Recess was designated Student Takeover Day and students were encouraged to exchange roles with the adults in the building. They became teachers, paraprofessionals, guidance counselors, deans, and custodians, and their near-perfect mimicry of the adults whose parts they played embarrassed and angered the teachers. (It is only fair to note that several of the teachers did not lose the opportunity for good sport: they turned into students and were discovered hiding behind stairwells, smoking cigars, and shooting craps. Others sat in classrooms provoking confrontations with their replacements.) The Teachers' Room on Student Takeover Day was overrun with small children, who sat with their feet propped up on the coffee tables and read newspapers, smoked cigarettes, drank coffee, and littered the floor with their refuse. The teachers cornered the principal and demanded that the activities of the day be suspended and the perpetrators made to clean and scrub their quarters. The principal, as the only other person besides the students excluded from the teachers' sanctuary, laughed openly at their hypocrisy and ordered the band to play on.

The Teachers' Room is a forum for truth.

There is a bar on the West Side of Manhattan that looks to all appearances as if it were managed by the ghosts of Bobby Kennedy and Martin Luther King. The bar is so perfectly integrated that it appears that quota systems must secretly be enforced. Blacks and whites come in together laughing, talking, and carrying on. The more intimate two-seater tables are crowded with mixed couples, representing all mathematically possible combinations of blacks, whites, Latins, and Orientals.

But a trip to the men's room in this same bar throws the theory of the paragon of melting pots into disarray. The walls are plastered with bitter racial obscenities. "The only good nigger's a dead nigger." Below that is printed in bold capital letters: "I guess that's why all the white bitches in this place have turned to niggers for good lovin' — faggot!" Et cetera, et cetera. So lengthy is the exchange of challenges that the walls read like a page from *Dutchman* by LeRoi Jones (Imamu Baraka). High at the top of the same bathroom wall, breathes Robert Frost's rural sanity: "Something there is that doesn't love a wall."

A friend of mine, Roy Blount, who fancies himself a country song writer, contributed the following lyric appropriate to the discussion in the Teachers' Room.

> *When you said you were on my side*
> *You lied.*
> *When you said I'd be satisfied,*
> *You lied.*
> *When you said your love would abide,*
> *You lied.*
> *But when you said you'd hit me and knock out my tooth*
> *You told the truth.*

The Teachers' Room becomes the place where all true feelings, thoughts, and words are expressed. Conversation naturally revolves around those who are excluded. Little children, who are called "youngsters" and "students" in the hallways, become "niggers," "wops," "spics," "schmucks," and "wasps," in the Teachers' Room. There are no holds barred when teachers begin to talk about what they care to talk about where they feel free to talk. The most benign confess the urge they normally suppress to "kick the living shit out of Samson Sorruellas." One elderly woman who emanated love and kindness in the common grounds of the hallways, offices, and classrooms, once announced to her startled colleagues that she would like "to tear off Porkchop's arm and hit her with the wet end."

The favored topic of conversation is, not surprisingly, the principal. It is inconceivable to envision a smoke-filled room full of teachers sitting amidst their cluttered droppings, heaping accolade upon accolade upon him. Each of the teachers has some ax to grind, be it a personal memo in her mailbox or an interruption over the public-address system. Each teacher knows that she will find a sympathetic ear in the Teachers' Room. There she can describe vividly how she intends to confront or humiliate the principal. Everyone present is aware that such braggadocio has evolved into an institutionalized charade and that when the actual confrontation takes place the teacher will be fawning, obsequious, and apologetic. But no matter. The love of such sport transcends the prospective reality. The realization of the threat matters not.

Once the teachers have finished professionally lambasting the principal, usually during the first half of a given period, the talk will turn to his private life and matters of sex and intrigue (any teachers who are not present are similarly discussed). One Manhattan principal provided his staff with an endless string of affairs (at least one of which resulted in childbirth) with teachers, parents, and paraprofessionals. The teachers assigned lookouts each morning to determine the direction from which the principal approached the school. They spent the remainder of the day hypothesizing about whom he might have spent the night with. Although he was married and the father of two, it was well known that he had not spent an evening at home in the past three years. One teacher, noted for her venomous attacks on the principal in the comfort of the Teachers' Room — she went so far as to criticize his breath and his underarms — lost all credibility that same year when several teachers noted the principal leaving her apartment building in the morning, altogether too frequently for coincidence.

Regular visitors to the Teachers' Room go through observable cyclical changes within each period spent there. They fall into a state of complete and quiet relaxation within the first few minutes of their allotted forty-five-minute respite, then engage in loud and lively conversation for the bulk of the period, and finally trail off into a few minutes of nervous preemergence as the clock ticks closer to the final bell. The time for truth has ended. They don their various masks once again and return rejuvenated to the fray.

Puberty

"I ain't no fuckin' virgin!"
     — Paulette D., twelve years old, in a state of anger and puberty

NEW YORK SCHOOLS have been type-cast as such utter failures that they are full of both suspicion and guilt. Teachers are skeptical of parents, students, administrators, and fellow teachers. Parents distrust anyone connected with the schools. Paraprofessionals, as teacher-parents caught in a squeeze between two different worlds, view even themselves with suspicion. Reactions like these are characteristic of any failing institution.

Elementary schools suffer less because their failings are, not surprisingly, less exaggerated. The yardstick for evaluating performance in schools has become, for better or for worse, the grade equivalent scores on the standardized reading test. School-by-school results are now published each spring (like traffic deaths over Labor Day used to be) by the New York *Times*, and individual parents have the right of access to their children's scores without obstruction and obfuscation by the principal's office. That measure of candor in itself represents a significant change in the New York schools. While stories abound of junior high schools in which the school population as a whole averages three or four years below grade level in reading performance, elementary schools rarely have to suffer such ignominy. Which is entirely logical when it is realized that a child can't possibly fall three or four years below grade level until he's been in school for three or four years. But this apparently basic piece of logic escapes most New Yorkers, to the great relief of the elementary school administrators, but to the chagrin of their colleagues in the secondary schools. In the words of one frustrated intermediate school principal, "Where the hell does the public think all these ignorant kids come from in the first place?"

Suspicion, anxiety, and frustration run highest in the secondary schools, which bear the brunt of the most taxing pressures in the system. The hell-raisers who slipped unnoticed through elementary school and who in all likelihood will drop out of high school are in secondary school every day — raising hell. The teachers incessantly blame each other for their own lack of success. Administrators absorb mountains of abuse from the public, the parents, and the press. Parents are roundly criticized for the clothes and attitudes their children bring to school, the homes they provide, their morality or lack of it, and the lives they lead. Publicly each entwined party blames the others, while privately each blames itself.

The one villain that usually escapes unnoticed is Puberty. Almost every child enters the intermediate school in a prepubic state and leaves, at least physically, as a young man or woman. Although schools cannot reasonably take much credit for the bodily changes their children manifest while passing through, they can certainly blame the children's shortcomings on the stresses that Puberty brings to bear. Puberty to twelve-year-olds is synonymous with sex and sexual awareness, and begins with the discovery of what one little girl described as "my first public hairs."

Puberty unnerves junior high school students. It excites passions in them that they never anticipated and have no conception of how to deal with. Momentarily it jumbles the pecking order. Girls mature earlier than boys and settle briefly at the top of the dominance ladder, necessitating their physical displacement as the boys gradually catch up. Puberty quadruples the number of fights young boys and young girls find themselves embroiled in. There is always one young girl in every sixth-grade class (you remember the one in *your* class) whose glands have worked their magic earlier than those of the rest, and who sits unnaturally among a class of small children with a chest fantastic enough to stop traffic on Fifth Avenue. Some such well-endowed twelve-year-olds struggle vainly to hide their natural gifts, wearing bulky wool sweaters throughout the summer and refusing to remove their overcoats in winter. Others flaunt their bounties before their teachers and peers: "How come you ain't got none if you're supposed to be so bad?" In either case they are a constant source of distraction to every child in the class. Little girls hide their jealousy behind a pretense of disinterest, although they are often caught staring wide-eyed across the room while unconsciously rubbing themselves where theirs belong. Little boys become completely distracted; nature urges them to tweak, poke, grab, and fondle the "wondrous curiosities" (which many of them do) but also warns them that such tampering can be dangerous. One little boy who sat open-mouthed, drooling on his homework for the better part of a year, murmured, "I still can't believe *she* is supposed to be in my class."

Wearing a bra to school is a mark of considerable status for every secondary school girl. Most sport a bra well before they begin to blossom, caught in the mounting pressure from the girl across the room, who established the bra standard at the end of fourth grade. Boys notice bras and are embarrassed to "go with" a girl who doesn't wear one. Girls destined to avoid Puberty's clutches until their late teens wear shirts sheer enough to see through so that their young admirers will note that at least a bra is being worn. The most desperate sixth graders will experiment with multiple forms of falsification: from crumpled-up sections of the *Daily News* to athletic socks. In one such case a girl removed the socks from her bra and wore them for volleyball and Snatch-the-Bacon, then returned them to her chest all wet and funky from the ninety minutes of play.

Boys are generally confronted with an evaluation of their sexuality in only two locations in the secondary school: the locker room and the boys' bathroom. Many of the more immature twelve- and thirteen-year-olds cut gym class weekly to avoid the embarrassment of the inevitable "short-arm" inspection and the banter that goes on in the showers ("Hey, Willie *still* ain't got no dick!"). Mothers come to school and complain hysterically to the gym teachers that they have bought their sons four sets of gym clothes during the year and on each occasion their child has reported them stolen. Little does the mother understand that her son probably placed his uniforms in the Lost and Found himself.

In the other private haven for little boys, the bathroom, the play turns more serious. The bathroom becomes the arena for those fortunate enough to mature at a young age. In such cases masturbation is the order of the day, often spiced with competition among as many as ten energetic contestants and with as many spectators as can possibly squeeze into the available space. Time is of the essence as passage between classes is brief. Most of these events are scheduled hours, sometimes days, in advance and begin promptly at the end of period six or seven. (I talked to a winner one time who claimed it was easier to "jerk off" on a full stomach.) As many as fifty boys will inconspicuously race to the second-floor bathroom opposite Room 270 and scramble for ringside seats. Most teachers only pretend they don't know what's going on. The winners of such competitions are quickly circulated about the school on the grapevine as the masses pour out of the bathroom and scurry to their next class. The winner's identity is anything but a secret to the girls, who adoringly congratulate the newly crowned king.

"Did you hear that Ernie beat everybody this afternoon. Again!"

"O-O-O-O-O *sit!*"

Puberty creates considerable problems in classroom management. The pairings of who is "going with" whom are constantly being shuffled and reshuffled even within the space of a single class period. A little girl who said on a Tuesday, "I can't stand that ugly little toad — he makes me sick," found herself "going with him" on Thursday. Honor and its defense become critical issues in every seventh-grade class. Arguments that erupt into full-scale battles are sparked by ardent lovers' quarrels. In the custody of the assistant

principal, who adjudicates these conflicts, combatant Melvin Craw-
ley pleads his own case:

"See, here's how it all started. I go with this girl named Natalie,
you know her. [Who could help but know her. She was the one
whom Puberty had struck first.] Anyway, everybody says she's too
big for me. But I like 'em big. Anyway, Jeffrey [the other pugilist]
started talkin' some mess about how I would suffocate if I was slow-
draggin' with Natalie and I got my head stuck between her titties
[Natalie is at least a foot taller than Melvin and probably fifty pounds
heavier] so I told him to take it back. He didn't say nothin' so we
went to war."

Most assistant principals in the intermediate schools have to listen
to variations on the same theme several times a day.

Teachers frustrated with the failure of their students ever to do
homework and rarely to take a word of notes on whatever is being
discussed in class, usually pick up dozens of love notes from the floor
in the course of a week's work. Although the spelling usually reflects
the inadequacy of the job the school has performed, the messages
convey deep affection and the confusion of Puberty. One archetypal
example skimmed from the floor of a sixth-grade class serves as
representative:

> Dear Cheryl,
>   I love yo. I really love yo. I want to go with yo. I
> love yo very much. Will yo go with me. I love yo all
> the time. I love yo. I love yo.
>   Give me some pussy after class.
>
>   Love,
>   Robert

One student in particular comes to mind. Her name was Karen.
By the sixth grade she was a marvelously proportioned *woman*, five
feet four inches tall. She radiated sensuality, less to her classmates
than to her teachers and the larger, "badder," boys in the eighth
grade. Her mind never wandered from devising ways of pleasing
her body. When she talked to her teachers she made a point of

trying to run her breasts affectionately against their arms, chests, or backs. She made the most stoic and old-fashioned of her teachers take notice. When she stood talking to her teachers in the classroom she almost always stepped on their feet and touched them lightly with her hands. The principal was afraid to go near her. Afraid less of her than of himself. Karen Minor inflamed passions in all who crosssed her path.

Her teachers held a perfectly solemn meeting one afternoon during which they explored possible means of incorporating her lust into the teaching of mathematics. Karen never let learning interfere with her pursuit of pleasure. Her mother claimed that she had to shoo the street urchins away from her door like stray dogs overcome by the scent of a bitch in heat. And Karen Minor lived in heat.

One eighth-grade hall-walker named Red, who periodically terrified teachers and administrators alike with his longshoreman's mouth and his violent, unpredictable temperament, caught Karen's scent and was driven blind by its magnetism. He once sent a messenger to the door of her classroom. The teacher protested that the class was busy and that he would have to wait until the bell rang twenty minutes later. The messenger pleaded innocently that it was an emergency (it was of sorts, knowing full well that if he failed in his mission Red would "whip his bunky"). Karen squirmed in anticipation and began pleading with her teacher to let the young man speak. The rest of the class, which took great vicarious pleasure in the exploits of Karen Minor, joined in the chorus of pleas to the teacher. The teacher, too, had undoubtedly grown more curious by then and he finally consented. The emissary stepped not more than one foot into the classroom and called in Karen's direction, "Red says he wants to meet you on the roof of his building right after school. He says he wants to get down with you." The teacher all but fainted. Karen hid her blushing (but smiling) face in her hands, then slowly raised her head, nodded in agreement, and beamed shyly at her peers. Her concentration was lost for the remainder of the day.

Virginity becomes a highly controversial topic during the junior high school years and the occasion of more than a handful of girl-versus-girl fisticuffs. What is at stake is a young lady's honor, although the connotations of that honor vary from school to school. In the quieter, more traditional, "better" schools in the city, a fourteen-year-old girl is ostracized if she loses her virginity ("She ain't nothin' but an old hoe"); whereas in schools at the opposite end of the moral spectrum ostracism is reserved for those who still cling to their virginity. One confused young lady, caught in a semantic trap, cursed at her adversary in the midst of a knock-down, drag-out, hair-pulling, clothes-tearing, shin-kicking fight, "I ain't no fuckin' virgin!"

Pregnancy becomes a matter of concern for intermediate school girls. Again the connotation the condition carries differs from school to school and from neighborhood to neighborhood. A bulging belly can mean anything from sheer disgrace to immense pride depending upon what street corner you happen to find yourself on. (No wonder New York children don't understand *The Scarlet Letter* anymore.) One eighth-grade girl, newly elected to the presidency of her school, proclaimed during her inaugural address that she was already formulating plans for a second election to be held in January, as she would be leaving at that time to have her "first child."

Another pregnant girl, who spent the first seven years of her life in school instigating fights, began instigating pregnancies. Using her two older brothers as studs she threatened "friends" with bodily harm if they, too, didn't become pregnant. The threat was unnecessary, however, as most of the girls regarded a baby as a symbol of womanhood and were more than willing to listen to her encouragement. Before the guidance counselors grew wise to this young lady's ploy and removed her from the school, four girls were on their way to becoming young mothers.

In junior high schools the most difficult aspect of sex for the uninitiated to become accustomed to is the openness with which most supposedly private phenomena are approached. The set of values that prevailed twenty years ago and presumably still prevails in large stretches of the country is inverted in the New York public schools. Acts of affection usually reserved for the privacy of a living-room couch, a bedroom, or at least the back seat of a Rambler are now performed routinely in crowded school corridors. It is not at all uncommon to stumble on young couples passionately kissing and petting in stairwells crowded with children moving from one floor to the next between classes.

An assistant principal of one New York junior high school came upon a huge third-floor crowd he assumed to be viewing a fight. He plunged headlong into its midst, hurling protesting bodies left and right, to reach its epicenter, raising cries of foul as he went, never generating even the slightest sympathy or cooperation from the onlookers. Once in the eye of the storm he found no fight at all, but instead two fully clothed couples feverishly "dry-humping" on the hallway floor. (Perhaps competing or racing?) He tapped each, opening their eyes locked shut in passion, and indicated that the party was over. All four participants arose sweating and disheveled, mumbling "Aw, come on, man" and "You ain't right" to the assistant principal, and acknowledging the raucous approval of the crowd.

Humping, bumping, grinding, and slow-dragging are the fare at junior high school dances. Administrators dread these occasions and use every imaginable excuse to avoid harboring them, knowing full well that they will be forced to concede at least one dance to salvage some peace and tranquillity in the building. Once it is established that a Christmas dance is to be held, every teacher and administrator utilizes the threat of cancellation or individual exclusion to maintain order. A lively dance is an occasion replete with all the pomp and excitement of a Broadway opening or the seventh game of the World Series. The anticipation that builds as the weeks count down to days and the days to hours ultimately destroys the loftier purposes of the loftier of the city's schools. Good dances become good theater. The school momentarily legitimizes sex. This is to be Puberty's finest hour.

Principals beg teachers, parents, any adults, to attend. They assemble forces of volunteer police to man the exits in an effort to keep strangers, usually older boys, from infiltrating. Dances are never without firecrackers, wine bottles bootlegged into the boys' and girls' bathrooms, and a slight scent of marijuana, whose origin can never seem to be located (probably just breath). Teachers on assignment as chaperones, often compensated for their generosity, arrive straight-faced, ready to wage war. Other teachers, the younger, first-year cotillion, arrive sky-high and come to dance and carry on, to "Party!," with the sixth and seventh graders they teach. Shy unassuming little girls paired with equally shy unassuming little boys appear to be trying to move their bodies *through* each other. The flamboyancy of the Bump, the Loose Booty, the Robot and the Hustle gives way to a euphoric pulsation that exhausts twelve-year-olds of both sexes. It is no longer the overly promiscuous who engage in it, but all children. They clench their teeth in ecstasy/agony, bear-hugging their partners with veins raised on the backs of their hands, arching their backs grotesquely, and grinding their hips with every ounce of energy they can generate. The whole gymnasium bumps and grinds mercilessly until the record ends or the entwined collapse. On one occasion a mother and her new boyfriend, both of whom had come to the dance to chaperone her young daughter, had to be forcibly separated in the dark corner of the gym ("Throw cold water on them," suggested the principal) by two strong teachers who reminded them that the dance was given for the students. Principals stand by the record player or band (depending upon the budget) throughout the evening, pleading their case for fast records because they know that their telephones will be jumping off the hooks in the morning if the music slows.

Well-rounded behinds and full-sculpted chests do not go unnoticed by male teachers. Public opinion to the contrary, female teachers are also keenly aware of the assets of some of the young men in their classes. Many prospective teachers avoid high schools as an endangering temptation; others select high schools for the same reasons. Although physical characteristics have undergone few, if any, significant alterations in the past several years, morality and the degree of allowable promiscuity exercised on both sides of the fence have undergone drastic transformation in the current laws of "what goes" in public schools. In 1974, an article in a suburban New Jersey newspaper alleged that there were twenty student-teacher couples in one high school and that the practice of dating one's teacher was widespread. (The reaction of a secretary in that school to the article was "Oh yeah? I can only think of eighteen.") The practice is by no means unique to New Jersey.

Two teachers, haggling over who was the best-looking girl in a school, reached an impasse because only one of them was familiar with Samantha Dawson. To settle the argument Samantha's teacher sent her with a sealed note to the other teacher's classroom. The latter noticed the strikingly beautiful young messenger as he opened the note, which was written in a familiar hand. It read simply, "*This is Samantha Dawson.*"

A teacher who had taught for fourteen years on the Lower East Side, and later became a teacher trainer, warned his protégés of the temptations that would entice them as teachers of ninth-grade students. He offered a lengthy personal saga of a sixteen-year-old Chinese girl who had tantalized him for the better part of a year, writing him suggestive notes, mailing him declarative letters, even calling at his apartment late in the evening. He told of the many defenses he had employed in warding her off and suggested several that his tutees might follow in the event they were plagued by a similar situation.

He paused reflectively as he completed his tale and launched into a different area of discussion. One inquisitive trainee interrupted him and asked if there had been a denouement to his titillation by the girl; had he eventually stopped speaking to her or informed her parents of her fixation? "Yes," he slowly confessed, "there was a denouement. In June when I thought I could stand it no more, I took her back to my apartment one afternoon right after school and gave in."

Lust and licentiousness don't end in the administrative circles; there they reach their greatest heights. In one junior high school, a newly crowned assistant principal was warned by his teaching colleagues to be careful "down there," a reference to the administrative team of guidance counselors, assistant principals, and the principal himself, who held the collective responsibility for running the school. He assumed that his confidants' warning referred to cut-throat political maneuverings in the inner circle that were best avoided. How wrong his speculation proved to be! There were cut-throat maneuverings all right, but they were hardly political. In a system where there is little loose money up for grabs, the spoils proved to be more pleasurable. Although most of the fifteen "educators" were then married (and all had been married at one time or another), the number of sexual unions that were created and liquidated was mind-boggling. Every morning the participants seemed to enter the building in new and different pairings, arriving from different directions. Telephone numbers changed weekly. As the principal told his young accomplice, "You'll get more pussy in this job than you can shake a stick at."

He was no idle jester. He had slept with virtually every eligible female on his staff and made no secret of that fact to anyone but his wife and kids. His favorite ploy was to appoint the best-looking rookie to be in charge of the Book Room each September. This meant that only he and she had the keys to this windowless but spacious nook that was graced by a well-worn couch. He would then offer a series of playful amorous advances before cornering his prey in the confines of the Book Room regardless of the time of day. A curious paraprofessional, wise to his capers, nonchalantly borrowed the Book Room key from one such designee one year and had duplicates made, which she distributed to her gossip-hungry friends. Noting that the principal was disappearing into the Book Room one morning during third period, she marked off ten minutes by the clock and then followed him in. Both he and petite Pam Steed were stripped to the waist on the couch, lights on, breathing asthmatically, and glistening with sweat. "Oh my! Excuse me!" the parapro interrupted, feigning great embarrassment. "I was looking for the Bank Street Readers." She make her exit as abruptly as she had entered and rounded up her colleagues, who waited casually for their leader's disheveled departure.

One custodian who claims he has a gift for catching teachers in the act says, "Hell, when you really come down to it, there's more fuckin' in this here school than learnin'. Why, just last Thursday, I come on Mrs. Green and that new fella from the boys' gym down in the back of the Library, and everybody knows Mrs. Green's gotten it from someone in every department in the school."

PTA parents who have the time and the willingness to be in school often find themselves caught up in the Peyton Place web that prevails in many city schools. One outstanding teacher, exploited by her principal for her accomplishments with difficult children, found herself unceremoniously transferred to another school after a protracted in-school affair with the president of the PTA.

The most outlandishly bizarre episode that I have been able to unearth involved a gentleman whose rise and fall proved to be as meteoric as that of Spiro Agnew. In 1973 he was a substitute teacher who worked in a single Brooklyn elementary school, where he soon found himself sleeping with the PTA president. In early 1974 she was elected to the community school board. Three months later he became the interim superintendent of the district at an annual salary of $37,500. Within the next four months, he made amorous overtures to his deputy superintendent, which she willingly went along with. When his double-dealing was discovered by his first lover she called an emergency meeting of the board and had his contract terminated overnight. The New York *Post* ran a brief account of the transfer of power the following afternoon, citing his insubordination in refusing to fire his deputy superintendent as the board's reason for his sudden dismissal.

Plumage

Evahbody dressed deir fines' — Heish yo' mouf an' git away,
Ain't seen no sich fancy dressin' sence las' quah'tly meetin' day;
Gals all dressed in silks an' satins, not a wrinkle ner a crease,
Eyes a-battin', teeth a-shinin' haih breshed back ez slick ez grease;
Sku'ts all tucked an' puffed an' ruffled, evah blessed seam an' stitch;
Ef you'd seen 'em wif der misters, couldn't swahed to which was
    which.
Men all dressed up in Prince Alberts, swaller tails 'u'd tek yo' bref!
I can't tell you nothin' 'bout it, y' ought to see it fu' yo' se'f.

— Paul Lawrence Dunbar, "The Party"

IT IS THEORIZED that as a result of spending thirteen years in school the children of New York City will have assumed the middle-class values of their middle-class teachers. So much for theory. More often than not it is the teachers who gradually discard "isn't" and "ask" for "ain't" and "ax" and develop a taste for double and triple negatives, and unprintable combinations of unprintable words.

One critical indicator of this process is the clothes that teachers and students choose to wear. Nothing excites more controversy and interest in middle-school-age children, knee-deep in puberty, than creating and wearing loud, outlandish outfits to school. Matching colors is of marginal concern to a thirteen-year-old coquette who sports bold orange slacks, a tight turquoise top, and six-inch yellow, red and chartreuse platforms; her eyelids are plastered with glittery eye shadow and lengthy lashes, her lips smeared with blood-red lipstick, her cheeks rouged miles beyond the limits of good taste,

181

her nails a kaleidoscope of color, her wrists burdened with several pounds of loud jingly bracelets (most of which were once table settings), her hair teased à la Pointer Sisters, spot-dyed gruesome colors, and brushed back to expose reflecting plastic earrings the size of small shoetrees, hung through ears that were pierced when she was three months old. The little boys, for whom the outfits are undoubtedly contrived, double-take at such spectacles, exclaiming, "Bad!" "Outta sight," and "O-O-O-O-O *sit!* Have you checked out Yolanda today!"

The first day of each school year, the day after Christmas vacation, the day after Easter, Graduation Day, and the evenings of all school dances become the occasions that no dedicated fashion critic can afford to miss. The style shows of new items and bizarre combinations, particularly displayed by the girls, but also by the boys, are altogether breathtaking. These are the only days in the course of the entire year when an administrator can be reasonably sure that no fights will occur.

Children are as fascinated by the bland, conservative clothing worn by rookie teachers as the teachers are by their students' regalia. New teachers are constantly berated for their "mismatch" shirts and ties and their "high-water" pants. (New teachers are stumped by the origin of the latter term, which refers to slacks and trousers with legs ending an inch or so above the shoe. The unabridged edition is "You can put away your high-water pants now, the flood is over.") But years in the profession tend to relax the tastes of even the most staid. Low-heeled shoes yield closet space to their platformed brethren. Wool jackets and coats are discarded at the expense of their equivalents in leather. In short order students discover that it is the teachers who are outpacing them in the quest for the bizarre.

Mr. Young goes jumpsuit mad (tight-jumpsuit mad at that), including one overly snug number in shocking pink that leaves little to the imagination. Mrs. Terry discards all of her expensive Bloomingdale woolens for faded blue jeans, blue-denim jackets, and homemade blue-denim skirts all adorned with Op Art patches. Mrs. Zabido adds a new piece of jewelry with each new day on the job:

sporting as many as a dozen turquoise rings, an armload of bracelets (make that two armloads), gaudy concentric-circle earrings, a loose silver chain draped around her left ankle (which looks as if it might have been a necklace that has somehow slipped down; but that just can't be), and a tiny pearl pinned to the exterior of her right nostril. She presents compelling evidence, perhaps even the "smoking gun," that it is the children who have supplanted the teachers in dictating taste and in all likelihood a good deal more.

Outfits serve several practical purposes for youngsters in public schools, from classifying social status to screen-testing adventures in creative costuming. No function is more weighty, however, than attracting the attention of members of the opposite sex. Just as nature endows her creatures of the fields and of the air with bold adornments of color, young children dress in wild, eye-catching hues to attract their mates. The phenomenon is unisexual. Little boys are as conscious of the little girls' embellishments as the little girls are of the little boys'. Although autumn is generally characterized by a mixed bag of fashion lures, the winter and spring terms have all but institutionalized "must outfits" for enticing young counterparts. Both boys and girls absolutely refuse to remove their overcoats in winter, verbalizing the fear that they will be lost or stolen. What teachers who often engage in hand to-hand combat with children over coat-removal policies fail to comprehend is that it is the coat that *is* the plumage for a period of several dark, dreary, winter months. A child, or more accurately, his mother, will invest exorbitant sums in "hip" coats for the winter, aware that none of the underclothing will ever be seen and will in no way influence the child's ability to attract and hold a mate. It is no wonder that leather coats — maxis, minis, midis and wetlooks — enjoyed such prosperous sales among school-age children. No overcoat, worn twelve to fifteen hours a day, survives to a second season, even as a hand-me-down, so the market for new and alluring models at the advent of the annual fall frost is limitless. Manufacturers who consulted either the children or their savvy teachers would come to the realization that by giving up a hair in warmth and durability and by weaving in a taste of the outlandish. they would be offering a virtually irresistible item to New York's style-conscious, conspicuously consumptive schoolchildren.

Springtime brings with it recklessly daring cuts of cloth that young girls are anxious to model. It comes as no surprise to school people that miniskirts, hot pants, and bra-less halter tops enjoyed such widespread acceptance among adolescent girls. Crowds of boys gathering at stairwell landings to gain advantageous views of young ladies as they strut up the stairs in their miniskirts and hot pants have to be dispersed and reprimanded. Spring fashions throw entire buildings into disarray (heat) and make it largely impossible for business to be conducted as usual.

School fashions enjoy an inverse relationship with familial wealth. Sons and daughters of successful doctors and lawyers wear the same T-shirt and the same pair of patched, ragged blue jeans and the same pair of ratty sneakers day after day after day while the offspring of the indigent welfare-receiving, single women stroll through school in togs labeled Bloomingdale's and Saks Fifth Avenue.

In the purest tradition of acting-out (or out-acting in this case) each stratum imitates what it presumes to be the tastes of the other.

Theotis Davis (and Others)

NEW YORK CITY offers her children few opportunities to take part in organized athletics. One double period of gym (ninety minutes) one day a week is typical of an intermediate school student's fare. Classroom teachers consequently have to absorb the residue of excess energy. Whereas suburban kids channel their libidos into hitting baseballs and kicking footballs, city kids end up hitting and kicking each other.

One April, when I was a math teacher in an uptown intermediate school, I hung a notice on a bulletin board in the hallway outside my classroom, inviting any interested sixth-grade boys to try out for an "All-Star Baseball Team." The designated day was drizzly and dreary all afternoon. Eighty-seven twelve-year-olds showed up. Among them was Theotis Davis.

Theotis Davis was no stranger to me. He was a student of mine but I had hardly expected him to show up to play baseball. Earlier in the winter I had been trying to teach my classes how to multiply (or "times" as they insisted on calling it; that is, "times" as a transitive verb) by means of an ingenious method using fingers and thumbs. A teacher with whom I shared a room had shown it to me and claimed the patent for himself. (I later found it in a book that attributed its origins to the early Chinese.) He usually left my classroom in a complete shambles after using it for only one period each day, but on the day he taught his students how to "times" with their fingers the room was immaculate. I was persuaded. His nomadic plight is typical of public-school scheduling. He taught fourteen different groups of children in eleven different rooms on three different floors. His schedule varied daily; he was always late or lost; his pushcart laden with books and materials was periodically hijacked or looted; and when he did arrive for his appointed rounds he spent most of the period arresting the mayhem that had begun in his absence.

The math gimmick was designed for multiplying numbers between six and ten by numbers also between six and ten. The language of the game was simple. One finger held up on either hand was read as 6. Two fingers up as 7; three up as 8, and so on. Hence two fingers up on one hand and three fingers up on the other is read as 7 times 8. To arrive at an answer the "up" fingers are counted by ten (in this case 50) and the "down" fingers on the left hand (3) are multiplied by the "down" fingers on the right hand (2), in this case 2 times 3 = 6. These two partial sums are then added (50 + 6), giving the correct product: $7 \times 8 = 56$. It sounds far more complicated on paper than it actually is.

I had taught this method to several of my classes with great success. Parents had written me notes telling me that their children had in turn taught it to them. One alleged in writing that "timesing with the fingers is a mericle." Cheryl Wellington brought in a picture of then President Nixon flashing peace "V's" with both hands. She had written "49" on the bottom. I tried it in Theotis's class. I instructed each child to hold up two fingers on his right hand (that is, 7) and to tell me how many remained pointing down. The class answered in unison, "Three." Theotis Davis said, "One." Which was correct because Theotis Davis had only three fingers on each hand.

School life isn't exactly a "day at the beach" for a kid with three appendages on each limb. In addition to getting wrong answers to "timesing" with his fingers, Theotis was always having to kick other children away from his sneakers, which they were trying to remove. From the outside the toes of Theotis's sneakers looked empty.

His hands were actually claws. Each digit had three joints. One opposed the other two. Theotis could type, play the piano, and play third base. He made a baseball squirm on the throw over to first so I put him on the mound. He tried pitching several times but was wild and had a ferocious temper. I moved him behind the plate. In 1968 he was probably the best twelve-year-old catcher in New York City.

Our diamond was horrendous. It was littered with ground glass and pop tops and was bounded on three sides by highways and by a cement factory on the fourth. There was so much noise that when I stood behind the catcher and coached the batter, he was unable to hear me. One of my pitchers once hit me in the Adam's apple with a wild pitch from the bullpen (Theotis wasn't my only errant chucker). Although he and two other kids screamed at me while the pitch was on the way, I never heard a thing. I didn't regain my voice for what seemed like a lifetime. In addition to being unable to hear, I could now no longer talk. Practice was called off.

New York City schools provide no money for equipment, so that anything we had we cherished. The team made uniforms out of T-shirts decorated with felt markers (at least each kid had his name across the back) but they were stolen out of my Volkswagen when it was parked in front of the school one afternoon. Not long thereafter an aging drunk was spotted wearing one that read "Samson Sorruellas" across the back, and he was stripped and beaten to within an inch of his life.

A ball hit into the highway usually meant that the whole right side of my infield and my bench were over the fence and into traffic. No one was ever hit and we never lost a ball. Playing out on Long Island one afternoon against a well-to-do private school, one of the hometown boys hit a foul pop that lodged on top of the batting cage. My entire team started in toward the batter, who broke for his bench and the security of his coach, who stood open-mouthed and terrified. The umpire stood upright in disbelief, too stunned to realize exactly what was happening. My team went up the inside of the backstop, but only Theotis could travel upside down over home plate and recover the ball. Most catchers throw off their masks for high pop flies. Three-fingered Theo kicked off his cleats.

My All-Stars had never been razzed playing baseball. I guess city kids aren't accustomed to yelling things without having to back them up. During another game against another suburban school, this time in New Jersey, my team had the bases loaded with a chance to tie up a close game. Samson Sorruellas took a short lead off third base toward home plate. Their third baseman started riding our batter: "No batter! Batter can't hit! Pitch it in! No stick! Batter can't see!" Samson suddenly lost his cool and went nose to nose with the third baseman screaming, "How the fuck do you know? You ain't never seen the motherfucker before in your life! You wanna go with the hands?"

City kids catch on pretty quickly. By the end of our season I had a boy named Michael Wing who specialized in heckling. He sat up on the back of the bench with his hat on backwards and yelled at the pitchers:

"Your mother's a dog!"
"Your mother's ugly!"
"Your mother runs numbers!"
"Your mother snorts coke!"
"Your mother takes needles!"
"Your mother shoots crap!"
"Your mother's a hoe!"
"Your mother's a man!"
"Your mother! Your mother! Your mother!"

Michael Wing never missed practice and was never late to a game and never got in. He confessed to me that he preferred yelling at pitchers.

If you organize athletics in New York City you have to seek out competition on Long Island and in New Jersey. Our home field was so lousy that all our games were played away. Another convention about away games that the All-Stars never fully adjusted to was the refreshments that were served following the game. Dobson Bradley used to break from second base to the host team's school, sometimes even before the game was over, and steal all of the cookies. He had a sixth sense that told him where they were going to be, and with a good head start, it was a foregone conclusion that no one else would even realize that cookies had been served. He filled his baggy pants with Oreos and waited for the rest of his teammates in the decrepit, multicolored van that served as the team bus.

Coming out of Art and Design High School one evening I was met by my former ace pitcher, Emilio Vargas. He used to drive me insane on away games (and they were all away) because he preferred to swing on the swings and slide on the slides rather than to pitch. His mother once hit him across the back with a Willie McCovey bat which he claimed explains why he never fared too well in school but was a good baseball player. His temper was so unpredictable that the other kids on the team were afraid of him. He used to walk on the bridge railings above speeding downtown traffic en route to our field. The night I met him in front of Art and Design he was setting garbage cans on fire. The minute he saw me he ran up to me and asked if I would get a team together again. He promised to stay off the swings and the slides.

Transportation always presented great problems in managing a baseball team. Most of the city games required that we take at least two subways and walk several blocks. The equipment bag weighed well over forty pounds, too heavy for anyone but myself to carry. (Most of my players didn't weigh much over forty pounds themselves.) It contained for the most part extra gloves, extra hats, extra face masks, and extra chest protectors because several of my All-Stars invariably forgot their own. The sight of fifteen uniformed twelve-year-olds incited gang-war sentiments in many of the local kids sitting on stoops in the neighborhoods we traversed. It was not uncommon to have to break up fights stemming from violations of "turf rights" going to and coming from a game. On one occasion we ran into a team we had just beaten waiting on the same platform for the subway. A donnybrook ensued in which both managers ended up battered and bruised and both teams missed their trains.

Contact with parents of players increased as the season dragged on. Mothers, realizing that their children were talking favorably about the coach, began calling me up at all hours of the day and night to confide their problems to me. Mrs. Choate, mother of Bobby, who played a near-perfect third base and could get the meat of the bat on a low inside curve ball (whenever I was absent from school he would telephone me from a bar across the street and tell me he was going home), called me and arranged a rendezvous at the White Horse Tavern one afternoon after practice. I arrived on time, searching for a woman whom I had never laid eyes on, and found her at a dimly lit table in the rear of the seedy pub, outfitted in a short, clinging, leopard-skin dress and an enormous, ill-fitting wig. She was drunk.

The gist of her story, which apparently had little to do with her arranging the rendezvous, was that she was embroiled in an extended dispute with the "lady" across the hall (I never did get the origins of the matter clear) and that she was afraid to go anywhere without protection. When I pushed her into telling me what exactly she meant by protection she fumbled with the zipper on her handbag and eventually revealed a butcher's cleaver of regulation size, weight, and sharpness. I told her that I thought it best that I stay at arm's length from this situation but made many suggestions of whom she might ask for help. Not long after brandishing the cleaver, she fell asleep and I made my exit.

The All-Stars' first season lasted until late August and ended with a satisfying 18-6 won-lost record (against community centers, Boys Clubs, and the like — we were the only school team) and a fourth-place finish in our league: good enough for me to convince the

Vanderbilt Foundation to grant us uniforms for the following year. The new crop of All-Stars looked prettier than the originals but without the likes of Theotis Davis played less impressively. It is unfortunate that so few New York children have a similar opportunity.

Jym

My best subject *by far* is jym.
— Robert, aged ten, from his autobiography

THE PROLIFERATION of American professional athletics is having a profound impact on our nation's folklore. The epitome of the American Dream used to be that a poor backwoods rail-splitter from Illinois could work his way into the White House through diligence and industry. Today's equivalent is that a ghetto-born street hustler from Funky Philly can grow up to be the starting middle linebacker for the Cincinnati Bengals.

This shift represents something far deeper than a simple substitution of idioms. Values and value systems must also have undergone considerable change for such a rewrite to be widely accepted, as it certainly appears to have been. Honesty, hard work, pursuit of knowledge, and self-education have been brushed aside, giving way to ferocity, aggressiveness, recklessness, speed, quickness, good lateral movement, and mental toughness. It is difficult to say conclusively whether professional football created a market for such virtues or tapped resources with which urban America was well endowed.

192

In either case the athletes themselves have assumed the mantles of remarkable folk heroes, capable in the eyes of their followers of excellence in virtually all fields. They are rewarded for their ability to attract crowds and motivate entire cities and by six- and seven-figure contracts, particularly if they adopt a "bad boy" image in the press (another clear inversion of the old "always be polite" school). Unlike their predecessors of an earlier era, they do not spend it all on clothes, cars, and women, although most budget a chunk on such image-building, but instead hire fancy agents and lawyers to manage their investment portfolios. Many have already put their incomes to great advantage and have become genuinely wealthy. The sharper members of this new caste will in all likelihood never be called upon for a day's labor beyond their retirement in their early thirties. Compare this to the plight of the bumper crop of Brooklyn Dodgers, updated in Roger Kahn's *The Boys of Summer*, men who commanded an extraordinary following but who without the big salaries are now resigned to lives of selling used cars and mixing drinks. An athlete's money is now pumped into real estate, construction, municipal bonds, and blue-chip stocks. Much as the early show-biz world created a class of nouveaux riches, the new entertainment vehicle of Astro-Turf show biz is creating a similar stock of parvenus.

The deification of the individual athlete has not been lost on the children of New York City. In fact the new mythology has demonstrated a magnetism which has all but obscured an American past whose heroes were warriors, abolitionists, and statesmen. Earl Monroe and Walt Frazier exert a far more powerful pull than George Washington (or Mayor Koch or Crispus Attucks). The vehicle is identification. New York is a basketball town. This is not surprising when one realizes that there are few places in the city that can accommodate a crippled eighty-four-year-old woman throwing a Frisbee, much less a full-fledged eleven-on-a-side football game. But basketball is as ideal for New York as New York is for basketball. It can be, and is, played anywhere by anybody and everybody. Every alleyway, play street, and vest-pocket park is easily converted into an NBA court.

The growth of professional athletics and the consequent mutation of the values America once espoused for her children has had a considerable impact on the public schools. Success in professional athletics has had very little to do with success in school, and more and more New York children have come to understand this fact. The street set of values, as opposed to the school set of values, embraces professional athletes and their life-styles. Few children, if any, are able to manipulate both worlds. Success in the hustle of New York's street life, which includes the ability to maneuver a basketball behind the back and through the legs with flawless execution while racing down a crowded block, presupposes failure in school. Success in school — manipulating columns of mixed fractions and recalling the names of Middle Eastern sheikdoms — similarly forecasts failure in the streets. Most New York children are well aware of their personal strengths and shortcomings, and choose one of the two milieus with care and at a tender age.

Schools do provide an opportunity for children infused with the message of the streets to display their talents and demonstrate their worth on a scale they are able to cope with. That opportunity for showmanship comes but once a week in the secondary schools and is known as *gym*. Gym's infrequent appearance on a child's program card is as unfortunate for his teachers as it is for himself. Gym is the one chance a child has in a long five-day week to burn off steam, and the one time that teachers are able to correlate with less in-class acting-out. Just as the scheduling of a trip lures children off the streets and into school, so does the occasion of gym attract the truants. Children rarely seen inside the school, all but unknown to their homeroom teachers, arrive faithfully on the designated day, towel and gym suit neatly rolled and tucked into one armpit, and assume an unaccustomed seat while attendance is taken. As one teacher puts it, "If Champ is here, it must be Thursday."

Outside the gym bad little boys, schooled in the streets, line up patiently and cooperatively, disciplining their classmates (that is, threatening the hell out of them) so that they can get inside without wasting a minute of time. Once they are dressed and on the floor prepared to play basketball (few gym classes beyond the fifth grade do anything else), it becomes immediately apparent that the gym is no place for the earnest classroom student. The play is fast and rough, and those who are able to dominate put in scores of hours each week on the city playgrounds, sharpening their skill, while the students are confined to the classrooms. The era of the scholar-athlete has passed in the New York public schools. Serious basketball aficionados put away the books and turn pro at age eleven. The best of them are readmitted to high school several years later to compete in the Public School Athletic League (PSAL) and bargain for the many college scholarships tendered on the city playgrounds each spring.

School children, as opposed to street children, are often absent on the day the class is scheduled for gym, or they worm a pass to the library or the audio-visual center, or predictably forget their gym clothes and are forced to sit in the stands for an hour and a half. Although gym teachers and classroom teachers punch the same time clock and arrive at and depart from the same building, they often work with mutually exclusive clienteles. Outstanding classroom performers become armchair guards in gym class, while accomplished one-on-one artists assume profiles of truants, hall-walkers, and disrupters in class. Just as life in America has assumed an increasing specialization consistent with the dictates of industry and technology, children in urban public schools become specialists at tender, improbable ages. The era of the Renaissance man has died a quiet but decisive death.

An occasional school administration has seen fit to utilize the mystique of the gym to lure some of the school's errant flock back into the fold. In 1975, one West Side junior high school presented its thirty-eight most dissident thirteen-year-old boys with a schedule it called Major Gym. The schedule created for this unique homeroom one ninety-minute gym period each day (yes, *each day!*) and two such offerings on Friday — mouth-watering to say the least. The selected few agreed to sign what amounted to a contract to attend all regular classes in order to maintain good standing in such an ideal program. Uncharacteristically, the boys were delighted with the school for reaching out to them in their idiom and the school was happy with the boys for their willingness to agree to some form of rehabilitation. The math, English, science, and social studies teachers of the Thirty-Eight were less than enthusiastic about their assignment and the obvious challenge that the task presented, reason enough that few administrators have dared experiment with such a program.

From observing the extraordinary effort that street-schooled young boys invest in improving their skills on a basketball court in gym, and the level of achievement that is a product of that effort, I have become more keenly aware of the tragedy of modern public schools: their failure to generate similar enthusiasm for and commitment to the pursuit of knowledge. Too many people continue to come to school for too many different reasons. In the event that the needs of schools and the needs of students ever mesh, there is no gauging the long-term effects on the city of New York.

But schools and students are light years away from that today.

"Teacher, Man,
Change My Seat!"

NEW YORK CHILDREN are fascinated by smells. They seem to feel that they have an inherent responsibility to publicize the presence of smells to their friends and classmates. Taboos forbidding open discussion of bad breath, body odor, and farting have slipped clean out of sight in the New York public schools. Each school has its own characteristic smell, usually stronger than the normal funk created by gathering more than one thousand individuals in a single place. The two most pervasive and common odors are pickles and cheap perfume. So many pickles end up in already-cluttered desks — the pickle is the principal breakfast treat in New York — that the teacher, overcome by the smell, orders her class to empty their desks on the floor, root out the pickles, and either eat them on the spot or throw them out. As for perfume, young girls seem to feel an inexplicable compulsion to douse themselves with sprays, creams, rubs, and "69-cent showers" (as one teacher categorized deodorants), boldly mixing scents in defiance of the laws of nature and

197

creating widespread nausea. It is not uncommon to hear tiny José shouting out to his teacher, "Yo! Teacher, man, change my seat. I can't sit next to no Gwendolyn. She's makin' me sick with all that mess." Only the "coldest" of teachers would not sympathize with José's plea. Ruth, you may recall, wrote in her autobiography that she disliked her teenage sister because "she be smelling herself all the time."

Children differentiate teachers according to breath odor. Most science teachers wish they could generate half as much enthusiasm for the process of respiration as for the product. Nothing seems to excite commentary like bad breath. Just as New York schools are filled to the gills with teachers given to eccentricity of dress, so too are they endowed with teachers who have unusual culinary predilections. To name just one: garlic and limburger cheese sandwiches, a favorite of math teacher Bert Teser. Discussion of bad breath is not reserved for the solitude of the bathroom or the hustle of the halls, but occurs almost instantaneously following a malodorous exhale. Most teachers have suffered the embarrassment of leaning down to help a child and having him yank his head back in anguish and cry out in a voice loud enough for the entire class to take notice: "Mr. Betts' breath stink! You better do something about that mess today, man!"

Eleven-year-old Mary included the following entry in her diary: "One day when we were doing math in our book, I went to ask Mr. Rush about this problem and he start to get angry and open his mouth and let the bad breath out and I said I know the answer."

David Taylor, an art teacher whose breath was widely regarded by students, teachers and community alike as the worst they had ever encountered (one fellow teacher contended that it was "suicidal" to keep breathing that "stuff"), was assigned to my classroom on one occasion to help me proctor an exam. Throughout the test every child who needed help would raise his hand and await either me or Mr. Taylor. If Mr. Taylor spotted the hand and took a step in its direction first, the child, with a look of sudden insight, would immediately lower his hand until Mr. Taylor had turned his back. Then the hand would pop up again. Once, however, Mr. Taylor got close enough to bend down to Pamela and ask her which problem she was having difficulty with. She pushed his bearded face away with both hands screaming, "Not you, man, I don't want you! Your breath *stink!*"

Body odor, or that which extends beyond the acceptable limits of good clean funk, is as much a matter of concern to teachers as stale breath is to students. Teachers unfortunate enough to have classes scheduled to them immediately after gym bear the brunt of this unenviable condition: showers seem to have gone out of vogue.

Spanish teacher Tim Chapin recalls lecturing his sixth-grade homeroom class one afternoon about a condition he described as "unacceptable." Being careful not to name names, he devoted twenty minutes to the rudiments of personal hygiene, laying special emphasis on the bath and the bar of soap. One young man in the class, correctly assessing that much of the monologue was pointed in his direction, burst out in interruption of Mr. Chapin: "I know you ain't talkin' about me, mister, 'cause my mother makes me take a bath every Saturday night!"

In a similar situation, Mrs. Prentice sat down with her special-education students, numbering not more than a half dozen, and reviewed a host of basic essentials to cleanliness and good health. She warned that if there were no signs of improvement in the atmosphere of the classroom (it was the dead of winter and therefore too raw to open the windows) she was going to have to speak to each child individually. Nothing changed. She took each child aside and reviewed the particulars, devoting an extra few minutes to Christine Alston, whom most of the class recognized as the archvillain and chided as a "garbage picker." Christine had more than a sneaking suspicion that she was pivotal in this matter. She therefore relayed the classroom developments to her mother, who was insulted and incensed and escorted Christine to school the following morning to air the issue personally with Mrs. Prentice. The ensuing conference proved a heated waste of time. After it had ended and Mrs. Alston had disappeared downstairs and was well out of earshot, Mrs. Prentice told her assistant principal, who had refereed the bout, that "next to her mother Christine smelled pretty good."

Nothing serves to distract a class as effectively as a fart. Whereas rules of etiquette mandate that such should be greeted with little or no fanfare, a single fart evokes a reaction that will sidetrack a class for a full period.

Kenneth Sellers, struggling through his math work at a two-man desk with Willie Thompson, eases out a silent fart. Willie begins an outburst that ignites the whole class:

"Oh man, this motherfucker farted!"

"Oh *stink!* Teacher, man, change my seat!"

"I can't breathe here."

"Let's get outta here!"

"This dude shit his drawers!"

Before the teacher has a moment to gather her thoughts and decide what to do, the entire class is screaming, fanning the air with notebooks and paper, and rushing to the exits. Their faces are wrinkled in an apparent effort to seal off their noses without the use of hands and fingers, which are tied up in the fanning. It is not uncommon to find a rookie teacher out in the hallway trying to coax her class back into the room ten or fifteen minutes later.

The drama is predictable with a zero margin of error. Each fart sets off the identical chain reaction, and children who develop reputations as "farters" often end up being transferred from class to class and labeled by their guidance counselors as "disruptive" — certainly a unique manifestation of acting-out behavior.

It goes without saying that a teacher who farts in front of his class is a goner for however long he decides to remain in that school. Details of such a mishap are dutifully recorded on the school grapevine, just as an entry is made into a computerized data bank, and the teacher's reputation bears an indelible mark. This is not to say that teachers don't fart (although many students I have discussed this matter with steadfastly contend that teachers don't fart, period). They merely learn very quickly to develop strategies that will make detection a virtual impossibility.

Probably the most common strategic cover-up, confessed to by most teachers who are willing to drop their facade of "Farting? Who me? I've never had that problem" involves what one teacher described as a "quick, silent, deposit-and-run strategy." She confided that when she sensed a fart coming on she tried to hurry through the portion of the math lesson that involved explanation at the blackboard and to direct her students to their texts or folders. On the verge of bursting, she would then wander about the room helping certain students to get started on their work, and presently she would ease the deadly, colorless gas silently into space and then scurry to the far side of the room to feign assistance to another child and to wait. The reaction usually had a delayed impact of three seconds. One one-thousand, two one-thousand, three one-thousand . . .

"Oh man, this motherfucker farted!"

"Oh *stink!* Teacher, man, change my seat!"

"I can't breathe here."

"Let's get outta here!"

"This dude shit his drawers!"

And they're off, breaking for the exits, fanning the air with their notebooks and papers, wrinkling their noses, and pinning the blame on each other in a mad, disorganized, chaotic uprising, which the teacher innocently tries to suppress.

Another tactic was employed by a Manhattan elementary school teacher, Mrs. X, during the early months of her pregnancy, a time when she had difficulty silencing her emissions. She would dart into the hallway for a quick outburst, under the pretense of checking the time, and would then step back into the classroom. On one such occasion, with her class busily at work, she exclaimed, "Let me just see how much time there is before lunch," and stepped into the hallway, where she released a thunderous explosion. She fell to her knees in embarrassment when she realized that she was not five feet from a workman who was painting the walls.

Administrators, particularly the heavy coffee drinkers, confess to being caught in situations where there is no comfortable means of maneuvering out from under the pressures of gas that quietly wells up through hour after hour of conferences and meetings. One assistant principal recounted the following incident. He was in the midst of a conference with a guidance counselor, a teacher, a mother, and her son, during which the boy was under attack from all sides for his general demeanor and attitude in school. Although his mother had agreed to accompany him with a promise of support, the charges against him were too compelling even for her. She jumped the tracks, and began ripping into him with a venom that delighted his teacher, long a victim of the child's abuse. In the middle of the tirade, the assistant principal silently emitted some gas among the assembled. Although the boy restrained his urge to make the usual comments on such outbursts, his mother demonstrated less patience. The moment she had gathered a noseful, she exclaimed, "Oh Jesus!," grabbed her son up out of his chair, slapped him sharply across the mouth, and dragged him into the hallway and out onto the street, ignoring his denials throughout. Both teacher and guidance counselor were taken in by the performance and proceeded to put the incident on the day's agenda in the Teachers' Room, as the assistant principal breathed an astonished sigh of relief.

"O-O-O-O-O *sit!*"

Distractions

You were a very good boy today Darin, thank God
— Teacher's comment in seven-year-old Darin Still's notebook

NEW YORK CITY public school children have raised the knack of creating distraction in the classroom to the heights of true art.

Teachers start the day equipped with an agenda they call a lesson plan. Principals insist that lesson plans be written, and in many schools they inspect and initial them with awesome regularity. Teachers gradually come to understand that it is the drafting of the lesson plans, rather than the implementation of same, that influences an administrator. The supervisor who makes daily inspections of a teacher's planbook may never check to see if the lesson plans are actually followed. Since the appearance of order and purpose on paper is what counts, teachers gifted in writing convincing lesson plans receive endless commendation from those in high places, regardless of the chaos in their classrooms. (By writing extra plans for their colleagues, these teachers also have a second source of income.)

Other teachers, confident of their proficiency in the classroom,

203

refuse to write lesson plans. They depend for their longevity on strong parent support, daring the administration to proceed against them. They move naturally and spontaneously from topic to topic, certain that the rhythm that is so much a part of learning and understanding will carry them through the day. As long as a teacher demonstrates excellence in either the pretense of teaching (lesson plans) or the reality of teaching (classroom performance) his job remains secure.

Just as it is the objective of most teachers to get through a predetermined agenda in the course of a day or a period, it has become the objective of many children to see to it that the agenda is never completed. Teachers identify with the logo carved over the colonnade on the face of the Thirty-third Street Post Office: "Neither snow, nor rain, nor heat, nor gloom of night stays these couriers from the swift completion of their appointed rounds." Samson Sorruellases are easily substituted for the natural obstructions.

Schools have developed innumerable names for children whose efforts in the classroom run counter to those of the teacher. In seminars and conferences they are labeled "emotionally disturbed," "socially disadvantaged," and "disruptive," but in the Teachers' Room these same children are irreverently referred to as "pains in the ass" and "shitheads." The teacher who described Samson Sorruellas in an educational forum as "a socially disadvantaged youngster who desperately needs a good home abounding in love and compassion" confides to his wife that "the little fuck needs a good kick in the teeth!"

Distracting a teacher or disrupting a classroom varies in difficulty with the experience, stamina, and proficiency of the teacher. Raw rookies and day-to-day substitutes offer little or no challenge to the children. The subtleties and intricacies of their art go untested. With the uninitiated, the basic forms of disruption work more than adequately: loud talking, fighting, and throwing anything that isn't nailed down. Since novices expect resistance from their students but resistance manifested in more subtle and duplicitous forms, the unexpectedness of a frontal assault disarms them. Most substitutes find that they are unable to command the attention of their classes until they have worked for several days in the same school and have developed a reputation for resiliency. A substitute's only weapon against such an attack is uninterrupted wailing for each forty-five-minute period, a pastime that leaves the wailer unable to swallow. After school, substitutes queue up at the Italian Ices wagon outside the school to combat the rawness of their throats.

Unsuspecting rookies have few other weapons at their disposal, and they have little notion of the physical abuse they will suffer in the first month of teaching. The ones who grow frustrated and discouraged and lack the patience to win the screaming war run the risk of committing one of two unpardonable sins: they either break down crying or come out swinging. Either course of action, although effective for established veterans, proves disastrous for the tyro.

Prolonged weeping may capture the hearts of many sympathetic children, awakening in them guilt because they have pushed the teacher up to and beyond her breaking point, but in the long run a healthy crying spell establishes a vulnerability in the minds of the children that they will never forget. For the rest of the year their eyes will periodically warn the bawler, "You had better not push me, lady, or I'll make you cry again." Trying to complete a daily agenda under such pressure is an impossibility.

Green teachers frequently spot their experienced mentors smacking children who threaten disruption. The new teachers make the mistake of assuming that the strategy will work for them also. Once the first face is slapped or the first chest pushed, the rookie realizes that the preceding chaos was only a form of foreplay. He suddenly finds himself plunged into the "real thing." Slapping a child brings meaning to the word "class." Thirty-one children who seemed to be in cacophonous discord become united in an all-out assault on the aggressor. The children's logic is, and it is usually supported by the administration, that if the teacher throws the first blow, anything goes; no holds are barred. They will hurl all the furniture in the room in his direction. They will hit him with books, erasers, spit balls, bottles, chairs, and garbage. They will punch him with their fists and scratch him with their fingernails. They will create the most unholy disturbance imaginable to ensure that the principal will hear the ruckus and charge in to investigate it. When the door bursts open and the doorway is filled by the Boss, the children immediately halt their missile assault and huddle fearfully around him, describing in detail the provocation of the hostilities. In most instances a substitute will lose his welcome at that instant (not that he is dying to make a career there) and a new teacher will have one indelible strike against him.

On any given day in any given school the percentage of teachers who fall into the novice category is relatively small, and it decreases as the year advances and as the new teachers thicken their hides and grow out of their novice ways. To children with a proclivity toward disruption this means that more sophisticated forms of their art are called for.

Over the past six or seven years, distractions have taken on an institutionalized character. This phenomenon has induced even the shyer children to become involved and has consequently reduced the workload of the kingpins of the trade. Some past standards included one-legged jump ropes, portable radios, single-play record players, click-clacks, revivals of jacks and the yo-yo, and skate boards.

But most of the city's teachers are more than capable of maintaining order when subjected to pressures derived from such institutionalized mayhem. The wiser students realize that their ploys will have to be far more sophisticated to distract the wizened veterans. They will have to go to greater lengths to drive a wedge between a teacher and her lesson plan.

One bilingual teacher instructed her Spanish charges to repeat English sentences after her. She placed a textbook on a desk and said, "The book is on the desk." They said, "The book is on the desk." She placed the book on the floor below the desk and said, "The book is under the desk." They said, "The book is on the floor." She said," The book is under the desk." They said "The book is on the floor." She bellowed, "THE BOOK IS UNDER THE DESK!" They bellowed, "THE BOOK IS ON THE FLOOR!" And so on until she was so livid that she was on the verge of tears.

Snow is one of the favored forms of diversion. When hearing a class react each winter to the first snowflakes, one would suspect that New York was located in the tropics. Every productive classroom activity grinds to a halt. Children fall all over each other racing to the windows. The smattering of conversation that a teacher is able to pick up rarely varies.

"O-O-O-O-O *sit!* It's snowing."

"Hey man, look outside! Snow!"

"Ain't that snow out there?"

"Mrs. Collins, look at that stuff come down!"

"Look at that beautiful motherfuckin' snow!"

Teachers soon discover that the same scene is repeated with every snowfall throughout the winter.

A similar reaction is evoked when a dog appears in school. The streets of the city are cluttered with dogs. Strays lurk warily around garbage cans, bolting for cover at the slightest unexpected motion. And yet the presence of a dog in the hallway serves as a stimulant for unmitigated distraction. Again the snatches of comment capture the tone of feigned anxiety that characterizes a dog's intrusion.

"Hey man, what's that?"

"Ain't that a goddamn dog?"

"That's a dog, man! That *is* a goddamn dog!"

"Jesus Christ, there's a dog in school! Look, there's a goddamn German shepherd right here in school!"

"Let's get the fuck out of here!"

"No goddamn dog is gonna bite my behind!"

David Peason had a rather unique means of disrupting Mr. Champion's math class. He would work feverishly for the first half-hour of the period, finishing the work sheets Mr. Champion had prepared, then turn his eyelids inside out, roll his eyes back into his head, and run recklessly around the room, yelling for Mr. Champion's help.

One stocky veteran, a short black woman by the name of Mrs. Turner, whose classroom was an oasis of structure and order in a Harlem school rampant with lawlessness and chaos, did not let herself fall prey to any of the common modes of distraction. (When her students misbehaved she marched to the precinct during lunch hour and swore out a complaint.) She was far too seasoned to allow fights and loud talking to overcome her classroom, far too intimidating for children to dare bring in their institutionalized forms of distraction. Her doors were always shut and locked so the "dog-in-school" gag had no impact, and her classroom was located in the windowless basement so that the "snow" nonsense was meaningless. (Critics of the school's construction said that there were no windows "so the kids couldn't look out and be reminded of how crummy the neighborhood was and parents couldn't look in and see how crummy the school was.")

In short, it took a wily student equipped with a sophisticated but delicate touch to distract a woman of Mrs. Turner's caliber. K. B. Wilson was such a student. After lengthy study, K. B. discovered that she was endowed with a grandiose ego: she adored talking about herself, her childhood, her family, her interests, her hobbies, her religion, her beliefs, her life. K. B. said that the task then became a matter of delicately posing a question in such a way that it would appear he was asking a question related to her lesson, but actually he would be awakening the nostalgic egotistical impulses within her and encouraging her to go into a long extemporaneous reflection on some aspect of her life. In a sense K. B. encouraged Mrs. Turner to con herself off the mark. The class was left with no notes taken, no homework assigned, and an earful of Mrs. Turner's personal history.

A single example suffices. Mrs. Turner had an elaborate drawing of the innards of a frog on the blackboard. She was two or three minutes into an explanation of her artwork when she noticed K. B.'s hand held high in the back of the room. He asked, "That certainly is a beautiful drawing of a frog, Mrs. Turner. Educational, too. The kidneys look so big from even back here. Tell me. Were there frogs that big where you grew up, Mrs. Turner?"

"Were there frogs that big where I grew up, son? You can bet your bottom dollar on that! Why, down South where I grew up there were frogs so big . . ."

Lunch

We had wheat bread white ez cotton an' a egg pone jes' like gol',
Hog jole, bilin' hot an' steamin' roasted shoat an' ham sliced cold —
Look out! What's de mattah wif you? Don't be fallin' on de flo';
Ef it's go'n to 'fect you dat way, I won't tell you nothin' mo.
Dah now — well, we had hot chittlins — S'pose you'd been an' seed it
   all;
Seed dem gread big sweet pertaters, layin' by de possum's side,
Seed dat coon in all his gravy, reckon den you'd up and died!
Mandy 'lowed "you all mus' 'scuse me, d' wa'nt much upon my she'ves,
But I's done my bes' to suit you, so set down an' he'p you' se'ves."
              — Paul Lawrence Dunbar, "The Party"

THE PUBLIC SCHOOLS have begun to assume the job of feeding children as well as educating them. In fact, the schools seem to have cut back a bit of their concern with providing a good education and are devoting more time and attention to providing good meals. Recent exposés about inner-city malnutrition (and paint-chip diets) prompted the federal government to begin pumping funds into school breakfast programs in every poor neighborhood in America in order to put Frosted Flakes, milk, and hot chocolate on tables that up to then had been used solely for lunch. A third of the children in New York come from families on welfare. Fifty-nine percent of the children now qualify for hot lunch. Unfortunately, the success rate in this latest endeavor has been no more praiseworthy than that in the more traditional one.

The food served at lunchtime in the city cafeterias is often unrecognizable both in appearance and in taste. In 1973 Congress even came close to passing a bill that would have permitted the serving of

209

cancerous chicken to the children. Just as the delicate relationship that develops between a mother and her child is founded upon the mother's providing the child with food, so too the first impressions of government young New Yorkers experience are based upon the food they are offered. It is not inconceivable that the gradual disaffection of the American citizenry from active participation in the American experience (that is, from voting) is as much related to the quality of those first meals in kindergarten as it is to Watergate.

Faced with the food they know awaits them each noontime, New York children recognize three separate and distinct options.

A small number, usually the most docile, will capitulate to the whim of the school and submit to eating the lunches as served. These children recognize the bland, tasteless character of the food ("some brown meat") but prefer its convenience to the hassle of leaving the building for lunch and having to rush back to school for sixth-period class.

Another small number, either not particularly hungry or "brown-bagging it" for the day, queue up in the cafeteria for the sole purpose of amassing ammunition in the event that hostilities break out. Unchecked food fights leave a cafeteria in a state of total disarray: tables and chairs overturned, food blanketing most of the floor, and vegetables clinging to the walls in silent testimony to the dimensions of the rhubarb and the potency but inaccuracy of some of the throwing arms.

As a prelude to one pitched battle, George Peters hurled a canned peach directly across the table at Al Hills, who managed to duck. The peach went over his head and settled in Angelina Alexander's Afro. Without speaking a word, she did a quick about-face and deposited her entire chicken dinner, gravy and all, upside down in Al Hill's lap. A battle eventually involving over one hundred combatants was under way.

Nelson Tatum and Lisa LaFlore were ushered into Assistant Principal Sheila Jacobson's office after a similar fracas. Nelson was draped from head to toe in spaghetti and tomato sauce while Lisa was similarly "spinached."

A more difficult matter for administrators to resolve arises when a well-meaning teacher steps into the debacle and is buried in garbage for her efforts. Mrs. Lenore Peterson, a substitute teacher who made such an error at the outset of a donnybrook, appeared in Principal Hope's office in hysterics, her hair littered with green beans and turnips, and her blouse bathed in chocolate milk. Set-to's at breakfast are no less frequent but pale by comparison because the throwables are fewer and the attendance is poor. Most food fighters contend that the hairs and the debris they have uncovered in their meals in the past have contributed to their refusal to eat what is offered.

The third group, usually larger than the first two combined, storms the exits every lunch hour in an effort to go home or to the pizzeria or to the fast food joint. Although most intermediate schools now permit their children to leave during the lunch hour, the decision to change school policy was brought about by the behavior of the students themselves, rather than by a change in priorities. The expense of hiring a battalion of door guards, big enough and durable enough to withstand the relentless daily pushing and shoving, became too great. Part of the rationale behind sealing the exits in the first place was that children freed to the streets would irritate local merchants with their rowdiness and shoplifting, thus discouraging as much business as they created, and that they would return to school late or not at all. The change in the door policy, which the children wrought, has realized the schools' worst fears.

Life in the teachers' cafeteria is hardly less interesting than that in the students' quarters. Most teachers' cafeterias find that their business varies less with the quality and variety of their offerings than with the weather. Cold days and rainy days do more to perk up business than pheasant under glass. The food in the teachers' cafeteria is usually a little more appetizing than that offered to the children and considering its poor quality, it is very expensive. Says Mr. Detwiller, a veteran of cafeteria cooking (he admits he is too lazy to go out to lunch), "Stray dogs eat better."

There are noteworthy exceptions to the stereotype. Several enlightened schools, ones in which one or more distinct ethnic groups are represented on the teaching staff, have hired fancy chefs and earned well-deserved reputations as bastions of either Jewish or Italian or soul cooking. In these schools teachers flock to the cafeteria in unholy numbers. Good offerings in the cafeteria do much to strengthen a school's morale by pulling all its people together for a few minutes every day. One uptown Manhattan school with a soul cuisine that rivals Jack's Nest, regularly attracts ninety percent of the school's faculty.

Although teachers generally exercise more self-restraint than to throw their lunches as the children do, their better manners are probably caused less by the food's virtues than by the fact that they pay for it. Still, some unusual practices have been observed in teachers' cafeterias. Jim Cleveland, who had sat down at a table with a half-dozen close friends and his chicken dinner, was handed a message by a hall-walker-turned-errand-boy that he was wanted in the office for a long-distance telephone call. He rose quickly from the table, pushed in his chair, hesitated for a moment by the door as he cast a glance over his shoulder at his comrades and his steaming chicken, then returned hurriedly to the table, picked up each chicken piece and licked it with a vengeance, then bolted for the office, confident that he had dispelled any notions of petty larceny in the minds of his friends.

Teachers have a tendency to linger in the cafeteria beyond the allotted lunch hour, particularly if the food or the conversation or both are to their liking. This practice prompts a most embarrassing series of announcements: "Mrs. Brown, Mr. Gottlieb, Mr. Rush, please report to your classrooms immediately. Your classes are waiting for you. I repeat . . ."

The men and women responsible for preparing the food still manifest a great deal of pride in their work, a particularly strange phenomenon when one considers that the raw materials they are given to cook are so inferior in quality that failure is almost guaranteed. It is indeed ironic to observe the venom with which women trapped behind the steam tables assault anyone whose remarks are not complimentary. This pride in the all-but-inedible food can probably be understood as an effort to save face in the presence of wisecracking children, but it suggests the degree to which their egos are wrapped up in the meals they serve.

In addition, the lunchroom personnel are an anomaly among school people in that they are accountable not to the principal but to an outside agency. Their services are usually contracted for from outside companies, which bid for the job with the Board of Education. Consequently, they maintain a unique autonomy. They are free to confront teachers as well as students because they are representatives of the world outside the school. They may be the only persons trapped in the public schools who are not caught up in the pressures to "act out." They call children "little honkies," "little niggers," and "little spics" without overwhelming provocation, and turn on teachers without the pretense of respect that the milieu dictates.

Mrs. Forsano, a stocky veteran of several campaigns in the school kitchens, vividly recalls two encounters with teachers. In one the insults flying between her and a science teacher, Mr. Baker, became so heated that she shoved him out of the cafeteria and into the lunchroom, slamming and locking the door in his face. He then put his fist through the glass in the door in a fit of unchecked anger, an error which netted him six stitches, a tongue-lashing from the principal, and untold ridicule from the students, who had sided with Mrs. Forsano.

On another occasion, while dishing out hot ravioli, Mrs. Forsano was interrupted by a home economics teacher, Mrs. Klein, who raced into the kitchen screaming that Mrs. Forsano's son Pico had made an obscene gesture at her during study period. (He had apparently raised his middle finger in her direction.) Mrs. Forsano was incensed at her child, afraid that his behavior was showing signs that he had been corrupted by the other children, whom she fed but whom she also despised. Without so much as a word, she strolled into the classroom, gathered her stunned son up by his throat with her left hand and slapped him loudly across the face with her right. The class immediately rose in unanimous protest, claiming that the blame for the crime had been pawned off on Pico but that he was innocent. Mrs. Forsano recalls spinning toward Mrs. Klein to give her a similar "rap across her chops," but settled for making a series of vulgar threats that left Mrs. Klein in tears.

The lunchroom workers are the cutting edge of the world outside, proud of the hash they sling, unabashedly overt in their hostility toward disrespectful children and teachers. And yet, like the custodians and the secretaries, they develop some of the warmest and closest friendships in the building.

They are a refreshing group of people, whose independence sets them apart from a world of "acting-out" and "out-acting" that they neither pretend, nor care, to understand.

Trips

And when the first day of school came and I went to school and I met a lot of children. My teacher name was Mrs. Burnett. Mrs. Burnett was a very nice teacher, she took us on trips every to weeks. Then on March 18, I'll never forget this day, she had to leave the school, and the class started to cry. We got this new teacher named Mrs. Duncan Mrs. Duncan was very mean. She only took us on five trips throughout the year.

— Ellen, aged eleven, from her autobiography

MEASURING TEACHING PERFORMANCE (that is, "productivity") has gradually become the paramount concern of the New York public-education system. Several foundations have earmarked millions of dollars for research into that particular question. What is sought is a tool, a yardstick with new quantum markings, that will reliably tell a teacher how he is doing, that will assist a principal in making tenure recommendations, and that will generally improve the school system. Currently, teachers are evaluated by their supervisory administrators, former teachers themselves, and are graded according to classroom management, dress, neatness, the decor of their classrooms, the modulations of their voices, the aesthetic quality of their lesson plans, their motivation, lateness to school, attendance, and sometimes, most importantly, their cooperation with the principal. Had the quality of the schools not markedly deteriorated, this system of evaluation might have continued unnoticed and unchallenged ad infinitum.

Many parents would like to see teachers retained or transferred strictly on the basis of their ability to improve reading scores. Although there is certainly something to be said for their insistence upon making reading the prime concern of the system, several problems have arisen with the evaluative tests that limit their reliability as a means of assessing the performance of students as well as teachers. These problems vary from falsification of scores to volumes of data that substantiate different learning patterns in different children. The ultimate tool, if one is ever found, will inevitably be a complex one, incorporating a wide variety of educational variables. The tool will also be in need of annual evaluation and alteration.

Children in New York have a much simpler answer to this complex question. They see no difficulty in differentiating the "good" teachers from the "bad." "Good" teachers take their classes on many trips; "bad" teachers take them on none. The purpose and destination of the trips have little to do with the teacher's rating; the number of trips taken is the only variable worth tabulating. The children of New York would tell the foundations to save their money and "just count the trips." In the words of one fifth grader about her 1975 teacher, "She ain't no teacher! She don't take us nowhere!"

Trips are important to New York City schoolchildren, not because of where the children go and how they spend their time, but because of where they don't go and how they don't spend their time. As long as the trip takes them out of the school building, which all trips do by definition, the children are satisfied. Children act differently on trips than they do in school. They show a more tolerant, responsible, pleasant side than the one they manifest in the classroom. Trips bring teachers and classes together in purpose and in spirit; the king-servant relationship that characterizes their union throughout the year dissolves. The children sense a change in their teachers also: a feeling of relief, a lessening of the pressure that both teacher and child are subject to in the classroom.

Teachers do experience anxiety on trips because they must make certain that all the children board subways and buses safely and get off at the correct stops. But in contrast to the belligerence they experience in the classroom, they find that students on trips are willing to help and proud to show off their skill in maneuvering about the city both above and below ground. Teachers sense that if the spirit of cooperation prevailing on trips prevailed in the classroom, their jobs would be a great deal more manageable and enjoyable.

New York rarely provides bus transportation for trips. Special transportation for local excursions would make no sense. Instead, schools are allotted unlimited transportation passes, which entitle the bearer to take classes throughout the city on public transportation.

Any teacher who has taken advantage of the innumerable opportunities of trip-taking in the five boroughs has experienced the emptiness that comes with the realization, as she arrives back at the school, that at least one child is missing.

On a trip to Central Park, Mr. Worth told his class that at exactly two-fifteen they would begin to clean up and march directly to the subway station and travel back uptown to school. He made the proclamation individually and collectively at least ten times during the picnic. When the designated hour arrived, he arose, ordered all the children to clean up their respective piles of refuse, and advanced to the subway. He presented the transportation pass to the attendant, led his troops through the turnstyle, and boarded the train. Once aboard he took a head count: eight bodies short. Mr. Worth returned the seventeen faithful to the school, but he was panic-stricken over how to tell the grim news to the parents of the missing. He went upstairs to his classroom to collect his thoughts before facing the telephone. There he found the missing eight quietly awaiting his return.

Phyllis Balsette, a teacher for twenty years, boasted to her class, as she returned to school from a trip to the Museum of Natural History, that she had never had a mishap on any trip. She then counted noses and discovered that she had left three ten-year-olds on the Uptown Local.

The pilgrimage to Coney Island each spring is a must for any teacher who expects an A rating from his students. The trip is a long exhausting day that costs the parents of each child a minimum of ten dollars. The trip wears out the most hyperactive of hyperactive children. One entire class, destined for an East Side junior high school, fell asleep on the hour-long, Lexington Avenue–IRT jaunt home, and did not awaken until the train reached the Grand Concourse in the Bronx.

On an all-day trip to Rockland State Park — several buses had been chartered and over two hundred teachers and children were included — a boy named Angel Cortez was left behind. The oversight was not discovered until his mother welcomed her family home and realized that she had only four children, loudly and enthusiastically telling stories of the day's adventures, when she was entitled to five. The State Police were telephoned to determine whether or not they had located the boy. They said they had but that he had refused to give his name. Angel claimed, according to the police, that lost children were entitled to hot dogs and ice cream before they had to talk.

Theoretically, no child is to be included on a trip unless a parent has signed a Trip Permission Slip, which tells her when and where and with whom her child is traveling that day. This releases the school from any liability should some disaster befall the child while on the trip. Although most teachers religiously distribute these forms to their students well in advance of a planned outing, few slips are properly signed and returned. And although children do not often come to school with the trip slip, they always come armed with a seven-course, brown-bag lunch, blankets, towels, radios, and extra bags of potato chips. The lunch has become a surrogate permission slip.

Trips also bring children out of the woodwork. Kids who have not been in class for weeks appear on the designated day outside the classroom door laden down with all the paraphernalia, which implies they are ready to go. Few teachers have the heart to say no, and in some cases a successful trip can turn a hooky-playing child into a full-time student.

Some schools, paranoid about embarrassing and costly lawsuits, insist that permission slips be collected. They lock delinquent children in "holding areas" all day if they should overlook this responsibility. Similarly, teachers are made to understand that their responsibilities on a trip are not to be taken lightly and that all students who set out had better be returned safely. On one disastrous outing, Mr. Bloom, who lived in Brooklyn but taught in New Jersey, took his class to Broadway to see *Chorus Line*. While they were in the theater, torrential rains began falling that flooded most of New York and snarled rush-hour traffic. Mr. Bloom escorted his eighth-grade class up the West Side of Manhattan by subway to the George Washington Bridge bus terminal and deserted them there. He said goodby and switched to the downtown train toward Brooklyn. He would say later that each child knew the number of the appropriate bus, which stopped not one hundred yards from the entrance to the school, and that each had ample money to get home.

The class was somewhat taken aback by Mr. Bloom's unexpected departure but proceeded gamely upstairs to the bus terminal. A melee had broken out. Thousands of commuters stranded by the highway flooding were pushing, shoving, and fighting for the few available buses. The class was hopelessly scattered. Several little girls found themselves caught in the crowd's undertow and clung to strange men in three-piece suits.

The first of the weary travelers arrived at the school at eight o'clock. By then a lynch mob had gathered and cornered the principal in his office. The last of the class arrived home well after midnight, having walked across the George Washington Bridge in the driving rainstorm. Mr. Bloom was badgered by parents for the remainder of the year; he never did regain rapport with his students or their respect. He left voluntarily in June.

Trip-taking in New York is limitless. Museums, movies, old neighborhoods, landmarks, zoos, relics, hotels, aquariums, theaters, and parks provide teachers willing to use the opportunity with endless resources. The trick to taking great trips is to add an original twist to a visit to the most common stamping grounds. Mr. Bell's excursion to the Museum of Natural History serves as an example. He went to the museum alone on a reconnaissance mission on a Saturday and developed a list of seventy-five questions on the African and Asian animals exhibits. The list included such inquiries as these: Who donated the impala? What is the name of the small bird on the water buffalo's back? In what year was the grizzly bear given? Why are the moose fighting?

He had his students pair off and he presented each pair with the list, as if they were going on a scavenger hunt. Once inside the museum, Mr. Bell led the entire class to a large set of benches on the ground floor which he declared would serve as home base. He allowed the pairs to go off on their own, and told them only which exhibits the questions were based upon. In less than an hour pairs of children were catapulting down the stairwells, racing around the corners, and sliding into the benches at Mr. Bell's feet, screaming, "WE WON!" Although nearly every child answered nearly every question correctly, the museum guards were unimpressed. By the time the fourth excited pair arrived, the guards were calling for additional reserves and were on the telephone to what they thought was the parent school. One of Mr. Bell's children had given the guards the correct number of the school but had located the school in the wrong borough. By the time the guard was chastising a principal on the other end of the telephone for something the principal knew nothing about, the perpetrators were gathering their belongings and escaping from under his nose.

Coney Island, the Museum of Natural History, and the Bronx Zoo are "must" trips for every elementary school child every year. Any teacher who overlooks one of these three runs the risk of an unsatisfactory "she ain't no teacher" labeling at the end of the year. The Bronx Zoo seems to have discovered oil at some time in the last decade. Every year children come upon new exhibits and buildings, homes for jungle birds, habitats for aquatic birds, homes for creatures of darkness, and sky rides across the zoo. But some of the old standbys still provide the greatest attraction. Ape and monkey houses are always crowded with classes fascinated by the apparently human attributes of the creatures. Mr. Graves's class stood watching the mandrills when suddenly a shrill voice from another class raised an attention-getting cry from the other end of the building. Hundreds of children from schools in all five boroughs flowed toward the herald. A young rhesus monkey sat inches from the glass masturbating. The excitement in the crowd spurred him to a fever pitch. His denouement was welcomed by clapping and cheering from the capacity crowd. Most of the teachers were embarrassed by the performance, but unable to distract the attention of their students, they waited in the quadrangle outside the hall. When Mr. Graves's students began straggling back to his side, he asked the most innocent of his young girls what the monkey was doing. She lowered her head in embarrassment, hesitated momentarily, then said in a soft, small voice, "He was messin' with hisself."

Mr. Fox's trip to the local branch of the public library underscores the difference that a destination can make. Although the trip was only an afternoon outing, the children were as excited as if they were sailing to Europe. Their excitement was based not on the anticipation of renewing their library cards and paying their fines, but on the fact that they would be legitimately out of school. The class consisted of twenty-three boys, all handpicked for their established records of acting out in school. Mr. Fox had set the class up himself and had collected names of hard-nosed sixth graders in June of the previous year. The concept and the challenge were his own. The boys maintained a disciplined double line for two and a half blocks. But the lure of a Sabrett's vendor overcame one of their ranks. A basketball court siphoned off three more. A pizza shop attracted two others. A few more changed course and headed for home. One disappeared down a BMT entrance. Mr. Fox vainly protested the desertions but, growing annoyed, decided to march to the library and work with those children who chose to follow. When he arrived twelve blocks later, only two children remained.

After-school skating trips in Central Park attract droves of children eager to master a new sport. In one intermediate school a teacher began taking groups regularly on Friday afternoons. Soon other teachers who had dabbled in skating in their youth decided to join. Within two months, hundreds of children would gather outside the school at three o'clock, many with skates slung over their shoulders. Numbers of them had not been to school that entire week. The crowds became so great that the teachers were no longer able to get on the ice; they spent the entire time tightening skates. After skating, the horde would begin its transit back to school in the darkness of the early evening, pillaging candy and stationery stores on the way. After two weeks, the wiser shop owners began closing down early on Friday afternoons.

Finding the enthusiasm for ice skating so high, I once organized a Saturday afternoon junket to Madison Square Garden to watch the Bruins and the Rangers wage war. The aficionados of playground basketball were well out of their element. At the beginning of the second period, when the two teams returned to the ice and began their warm-ups, one little boy spun around to me and said, "You ain't tell us that this was a double-header."

One intermediate school used to take its entire student body on an annual field day to Pelham Bay Park, where a combined picnic and track meet was held. The children prepared for the great day all through the spring. But a series of mishaps finally convinced the principal to call the field day off forever.

The first year the subway fell victim to third-rail problems while underground in the Bronx. The next year the picnic was washed out by a lightning squall, which had not been forecast and did not appear until the children had arrived at their destination, spread out their blankets and buffets, tuned in WABC, and launched footballs, baseballs, and Frisbees. The following year a fight broke out on the subway platform between a teacher who was trying to hold a train door open and a transit cop who was trying to get it closed. A brawl ensued, complete with stretchers, ambulances, and paddy wagons. The fourth year the day went smoothly until the subway left the station on the trip home. Some of the kids began snatching purses from strangers on the train. The train was then ordered to go nonstop to the station nearest the school. There it was met by several hundred policemen, who escorted the children back to the school and arrested several of them.

The swan song took place at a resort town on the Hudson the following year. The principal, wary of the jinx that had consumed his predecessor at Pelham Bay Park, scheduled the trip for the upstate Hudson retreat. The outcome was no less catastrophic: several children ran away, two local preschool children were violently assaulted, and two students were arrested for harassing the train engineer. An assistant principal later griped that when his kids take a trip they have to take lunch, blankets, balls, and bail money.

On rare occasions schools corral enough money to send a group of children and their teachers out of the city to a camp for a full week during the late spring or the early summer months. The healing powers of such an experience cannot be exaggerated. Children who have been afraid to speak to one another for ten months develop lasting friendships. Housing patterns, which limit the possibilities of experiments in integration during an artificial nine-to-three school day, no longer exist. Hostilities that have developed between those who teach and those who are taught are replaced by cooperation that in school seems unlikely and impossible. A different attitude in a child, which a teacher merely glimpses on a day trip, becomes the whole child during a week of common living. A week away explores possibilities of human dynamics that school can at best only approximate.

The ethos that teachers become a part of on week-long outings and that they sense on day trips is in evidence at special moments within school life: parties. Children love parties less for the good time they know they will share than for the hours of preparation they will devote to ensuring that it is the best party ever. The collective effort that goes into creating a party usually allows teachers a glimpse of a side of their children they never knew existed. Children will throw parties for the most marginal reasons: a birthday party for each child in the class, Halloween parties, Christmas parties, Thanksgiving parties, Chanukah parties, surprise parties on the teacher's birthday, parties for the teacher's anniversary, parties for the opening of school, parties for the close of school, parties to celebrate the resignations of Ehrlichman, Haldeman, and Dean, parties to celebrate the end of the Yom Kippur War, parties for Koch's election, parties for the Yankees' victory in the World Series, parties after tests, parties on Monday to begin a new week, parties on Fridays to end an old one, parties for days.

Pretzels, potato chips, ice cream, and soda no longer cut it at a sixth-grade party. The fare in today's schools includes several hot casseroles, a gauntlet of salads, hors d'oeuvres, eclairs, pies, puddings, and cakes. All of it is homemade. When the hour of the party arrives, the children empty into the streets and dash home to their ovens and refrigerators, and bring back the delicacies to school. Parties are characterized by loud music, jealous onlookers beating unceasingly on the doors, dancing, yelling, screaming, carrying on, and acting out. Many teachers confess that they have more fun at these parties than at the staid occasions thrown by their peers. They let their hair down, jumping and dancing in awkward imitation of their charges. They forget that they are still in the school.

Trips, excursions, and parties all bring out the best in people whose lives have been locked briefly together by the hands of fate. They uncover senses of humor, laughter, and exuberance where there seemed to have been none. They offer moments of cooperation and togetherness to those whose relationships are usually marked by despair and contempt. They alter presumptions once sure and apparently unmalleable. They inspire insights and suggest possibilities.

Violence

DANNY, AGED TWELVE, is on his way to the library to get a book of Botticelli prints from which he can do tracings. He approaches the windowless, swinging fire doors. Freddy, also twelve, pursued hotly by an irate assistant principal, is racing toward the same set of doors from the opposite direction. Freddy leaps as he reaches the doors, his foot catching them three feet off the ground, whipping them open and slamming them square into Danny's face, breaking his nose.

Dawson, fourteen, hops a fence during a class trip. He finds himself alone in a yard with two four-year-old boys. He removes a wristwatch from one of them. The other screams and resists. Dawson grabs a stick and swings until the boy's jaw is broken and his left eye is out.

Geraldo, thirteen, is found hanging by a rope from his neck in the boys' bathroom. He is quickly cut down and his eyes stop popping out, and he begins to breathe again. His assailants say, "We were only playing."

Leroy, twelve, shoves a two-inch needle into Maria's buttocks as she bends over to pick up her boots in the coat closet. The teacher grabs Leroy by his shirt and slams his back up against a row of coat hooks. Leroy returns moments later with a long stick full of nails. He breaks the glass in the door, and takes several swings at his teacher before he is finally subdued.

Mrs. Deal slowly opens her desk drawer and wraps her fingers around a thirty-eight. Porkchop, fourteen, breaks the glass in the door and lets herself in, cursing all the while. Porkchop stares at Mrs. Deal and senses that there is something ominous about the quiet in the classroom. She turns and leaves. Mrs. Deal's vision of the headline in the New York *Times* passes.

Principal Simpson moves in on Lorenzo Johnson, twelve, who can't keep quiet during an assembly program. He towers over Lorenzo for an instant. A right, a left, two more rights, a left uppercut! Lorenzo is groggy at Simpson's feet.

Mike Baker, thirteen, feels he has been short-changed on a drug deal in front of the intermediate school entrance. He fires a single shot. Dead! Eighteen months for juvenile delinquency.

A lady selling lunch tickets in front of the cafeteria mistakenly accuses Sharon Bailey, eight, of stealing one of the tickets. The assistant principal jumps in to restore order. He sides with the ticket lady and tears the ticket to shreds. Sharon goes hungry.

Tyrone Mason, twelve, is on his hands and knees outside the school. An older boy holds a gun to his head and plays Russian roulette, laughing loudly in the process. Click, click, click. He decides to quit.

Sister Maria, aged sixty, a nun, is warned by one of her students that he's "goin' to tighten her motherfuckin' ass up!"

José and Phillip, both thirteen, throw bottles out the window of their sixth-floor homeroom at the children leaving the building. They exhaust their supply of bottles and grab a three-drawer file cabinet and hurl it out the window. The corner of the cabinet lands squarely on top of Nadina Rodríguez's head. The boys and their teacher are transferred to another school. Nadina undergoes four operations and wears a plate in her skull. Parents regard the event as the accident that happened, and ask, "What about all the others every day that almost happen?"

Len Taylor, thirteen, has Mr. Newton, an assistant principal, pinned down with a forty-five in the hallway outside the library. Mr. Newton is crying in fear.

Sellon and Bahi, two teachers adored by their students, are fired *over the loudspeaker*. The kids go on a rampage, racing through the halls, breaking windows, setting bulletin boards on fire, breaking furniture, and threatening their teachers. The principal returns to the loudspeaker and threatens to resign. The teachers go on a rampage.

Mr. Arch, a rotund, white substitute teacher, tells twelve-year-old Willie to stop acting like an "ignorant nigger." Willie opens up the left side of Mr. Arch's mouth with a roundhouse right.

Rodney, ten, leads the principal to Room 132, where Howard, also ten, is hiding. "If Howard can cut, then I can too," he matter-of-factly tells the principal. The principal collars Howard and starts to lead both boys back to their respective classes. Wall-eyed Fats Milner, another ten-year-old, pops his head out of the class and calls Rodney a "squealer." Rodney drops his books and pencils, sprints back down the hall, and goes nose-to-nose with Fats, hesitates, then coldcocks him with a punch that opens doors all along the hall.

Eddie, eleven, takes a lead off first. The pitch is fouled off and Eddie returns to the bag. The first baseman, twice Eddie's size, taps him on the shoulder and spits in his face.

Cheryl, nine, is trying to catch up with her class as they rush to the subway. She's too small to be effective in a crowd. A man bumps her out of the way and she's left standing on the platform, crying.

Merrick Masterson, twelve, is cornered by his irate teacher, Mr. Schaeter. Mr. Schaeter closes in and Merrick jumps from the second-floor window.

Eugene Timpson and Theresa McBride, both thirteen, are having a battle royal in the main lobby outside the principal's office. She grabs him by the coatsleeve and hurls him through the quarter-inch glass in a showcase window.

Jimmy Jones, eleven, bursts into the cafeteria with a radio cocked high over his head. He streaks across to the other side and breaks it into little pieces over Mike Malloy's skull.

The assistant principal opens the third drawer on the right-hand side of his desk and displays a cache of knives, letter openers, awls, firecrackers, and blackjacks.

James Bacon, fourteen, is caught vomiting behind a stairwell after taking a king-sized snort of cocaine. His mother is called into school from her job. She calls the principal a "scheming motherfucker" and warns him to stop picking on her son.

Scotty Peterson, eleven, goes stark raving mad in the main office. He snatches a twelve-foot window pole and starts swinging it in lethal circles. The secretaries hit the floor to avoid his swaths and the assistant principal who eventually breaks it up fractures his wrist.

Ken Ellis, twelve, unloads a blue streak of profanity at his principal. Mr. Keller sheds his cool and puts his foot straight into Ken's tail end, sending him tumbling down a flight of stairs.

Brenda Wilson, fifteen, who was expelled from school and has escaped from the Children's Shelter, fights Marion Frankel, sixteen, a high school student, in the front lobby of a junior high school, which neither of them belongs in. Mrs. Gorin from the girls' gym steps in to break it up. Brenda blasts her in the nose with a left uppercut. The police handcuff Brenda and take her away.

Mrs. Klein's feet leave the ground as an intruder of high school age lands a healthy goose.

Sixty-four-year-old, buxom Mrs. Walker stands on the corner of Pine Street and West Broadway, outfitted in her Crossing Guard uniform. A bus full of children goes by and they hang their heads out the window and scream, "Hey, you old bitch!"

Mr. Kelly won't let Wong, twelve, go to the bathroom despite the fact that he has been begging to go for hours. When he can stand it no longer, Wong unzips his fly and urinates in the desk.

Mrs. Palitz stands outside at recess watching her children play. A young stranger, twelve years old, comes up to her and asks her for the time. "Ten-thirty." "Thank you." He returns five minutes later, reveals a pistol in his trembling hand, and demands the watch. She hands it over, no questions asked.

Theresa Martin, thirteen, slips unnoticed into the intermediate school gym to steal a pair of sneakers. She is caught by Miss Norton, who orders her out. Theresa lunges at her and tears her face with her fingernails.

A fight erupts in front of the school while children are waiting for the buses to arrive. The crowd swells and moves back and forth with the action. The fighters break for the park. In pursuing them, the crowd tramples Irma, nine, so severely that she is rushed to the hospital for X rays.

Mr. Reese leaps from behind the piano to stop a fight between Vanessa Davis and Gail Forest, both thirteen. Vanessa turns on him like a raving lunatic. She breaks his glasses and hurls chairs and desks at him until help arrives. Her mother sues Mr. Reese for assault and battery.

Lorenzo Wilmott confronts a gang at the Manhattan end of the 145th Street Bridge on his way home from school. They warn him to shut up. He keeps "running his mouth," as is his custom. He is shot dead.

Carmello Penatta, thirteen, loses a dollar shooting dice with Vincent, nineteen. He runs home furious, claiming that Vincent cheated him, and returns with a Duke Snider Louisville Slugger. Vincent snatches the bat from Carmello and clobbers him over the head. Carmello goes into a coma. Three days later he is dead.

Hank Hawkins, thirteen, wants to prove to his friends that he is fearless. He drinks a full quart of wood alcohol. Four hours later he is dead.

Brian Hayford, ten, goes into the boys' room to wash up for lunch. He is slammed up against the wall. His pockets are frisked and his lunch money and house keys are taken.

Mr. Wilson escorts Pup, ten, out of his social studies class because of the disruptions Pup has caused. He leads Pup into the girls' bathroom, where he has stashed a yardstick. He wallops Pup several times before Pup is able to escape. Pup immediately reports the incident to the principal, adding, "That just proves that Mr. Wilson is a faggot. Why didn't he hide the stick in the boys' bathroom?"

Mrs. Wall calls Robin, twelve, out into the hallway. There Mrs. Wall lands a right to the chops, a left to the belly, a knee to the groin.

Mrs. Phifer forcibly removes Karen Davidson, ten, from the classroom. Karen has been disturbing the class for hours. She becomes even more defiant and lashes back with an unholy string of expletives and threats. She ends with, "I'm gonna sue you! I'm gonna have your ass on Welfare."

Glenda, twelve, is excited by the game being played in the classroom, and waves her hand frantically to be included. In her exuberance she leans a little too far backwards in her chair and crashes to the floor. She is up like a cat, embarrassed but seething, and she lands a venomous right cross on innocent Xiomara, whose misfortune was that she happened to be sitting in the adjoining seat.

Mrs. Skinner enters her classroom to discover that Eugene, eleven, has dropped his pants and is exposing himself. She shrieks to the rest of the students to stay out of the room and line up in the hallway. An eraser hits her in the middle of the back. She snatches up Orlando because he is the littlest and the nearest, and slaps him several times across the face. Back and forth. Back and forth.

During graduation rehearsal a fight that has been smoldering for months breaks out between Deborah and Regina, both fourteen. Regina bites the first joint of Deborah's index finger *clean off*. Deborah goes into her purse with her other hand and brings out a straight razor and slashes Regina across the throat. Both spend graduation in the hospital.

Inez and Carla, both thirteen, differ sharply over who is going with whom and what somebody else said about the whole thing to a third party. The two girls agree to have it out in the first-floor hallway outside the principal's office. After a few preliminary slaps, spittings, and hair-pullings, Inez runs a razor blade from the upper left-hand corner of Carla's face to the lower right, traversing her eye en route.

I once asked my sixth-grade class if they intended to go trick-ortreating on Halloween night. One third of them said they thought they were too old. One third of them said they thought they would. And one third of them said they would be out snatching other children's bags.

The New Truants

ONE RARELY HEARS TALK in 1978 of truants, truancy, and truant officers. These terms recall the fifties, a drastically different era in public education. Truants were kids with slicked-back D.A.'s, leather jackets, and motorcycles; they lived on Flatbush Avenue, grabbed headlines in gang wars, and spent their school hours in pool halls or standing outside drugstores methodically twirling key chains clockwise then counterclockwise, clockwise then counterclockwise. Truants were called J.D.'s and hoods, and terrified Central Park with gang battles between Count Dracula and the Umbrella Man. The Umbrella Man was convicted of a gang-war murder and sentenced to die in the electric chair. Asked if he cared to offer any last words for posterity, he replied, "Yeah, I want my mother to see me cook."

Hoods and J.D.'s were chased by harmless little men in gray flannel suits that didn't fit, who rivaled the Keystone Kops in their lack of efficiency. These truant officers were always a day too late, one doorway off, after the wrong child, or running down a crowded street chasing a street-wise thirteen-year-old who would duck into the subway and disappear. Spanky's pals in "The Little Rascals" were constantly ducking or booby-trapping the truant officer assigned to their case.

The concept of tracking down errant schoolchildren has undergone considerable change in the sixties and seventies. *Truant*, *truancy*, and *truant officer* have slipped quietly out of the Board of Education's lexicon. They had created enough embarrassment, and apparently the Board thought it best to let them die a quiet, unnoticed death. But the problem of children who are not attending school has prospered and multiplied. By the early seventies it had reached heroic proportions.

One New York City high school had names of nine hundred ninth graders registered for entry in September 1964. Only six hundred of them ever showed up. By June 1968, when the same class sat ready to graduate, only three hundred remained. Of the three hundred, two hundred and fifty received general certificates, a piece of paper with about as much value as yesterday's *Daily News*; fifty received diplomas. Of these fifty, three were headed for college in September.

The Board of Education now called the disaffected children dropouts and those in hot pursuit attendance officers. But the huge numbers challenged the nature of the game. A single attendance officer assigned to a junior high school was destined to failure long before he arrived for work. There were far too many children not appearing in school, most of them with incorrect addresses and disconnected telephone numbers. Attendance officers, both men and women, all have tales of frighteningly difficult moments in the course of their work. They claim that they can never be certain whether a dilapidated apartment building will house parents willing to assist them in forcing an education upon their child, or parents who will pick up anything available and back the attendance officer out of the building while threatening his life.

The Board of Education has also increased its regular army by adding school social workers, school psychologists, and whole teams called pupil personnel services. But most of these have been absorbed by the rise in chronic discipline problems and have little time for those children who fail to come to school. Dropouts are better forgotten than cared for.

The children, too, display new and confusing patterns of behavior that manifest their unhappiness and rejection. The great majority of high school dropouts hang around the schools they should be attending. Many become involved in buying and selling dope, drinking beer and cheap wine, and in learning the ins and outs of prostitution. Many of the mightiest and wealthiest pimps in New York learned their trade huddled under the archways of the public schools. Many of the dropouts congregate around the school simply because that is where their friends are, that is where the action is, that is where they feel most comfortable and secure. On occasion, groups of these children will enter the building, showing identification cards to door guards and pledging their earnest intention to go to class. Once inside they will warm themselves while walking the hallways or they will drop into the cafeteria for a bite to eat. They will never go to class. High schools abound with tales of senior teachers presented with homeroom classes of seventy-five students, none of whom ever so much as set foot in school. Many senior staff members vie for the "phantom classes."

But these children are not the true truants of the city. Those who are turn up only rarely in official reports. They bring meaning back to a word that the city would have preferred to see vanish. The real truants are the saddest, loneliest children imaginable. They are often completely homeless, and if they do have a place to call home, it is without love and compassion. They see no reason to "hang out" outside a school because they literally have no friends. They are uninterested in crime, in juvenile delinquency, in drugs, and in alcohol. They show no affection toward the devotees of such vices.

Today's truants are the city's most misunderstood children. They are also perhaps the most enlightened, aware that neither the schools nor the streets have anything to offer them. They fear both worlds.

They sense the futility of the jobs that are available even for those who do finish high school: pushing a garment wagon on Seventh Avenue, selling tokens, ushering at the Baronet Theater, hawking the *Times*, fixing hamburgers "their way," hustling, or idling away endless hours unemployed, underemployed, or on welfare.

Most of them are intelligent, sensitive children, far more accomplished in the arts of reading and mathematics than their peers who either attend the schools or lurk outside of them. These truants rarely brush with the law. Their trademark is their solitude.

Randolph Tracey is one of them. He is now (1978) sixteen but he has not been to school since the last day of fourth grade. He is poor and black. He lives with his mother and his sister Bernadette, who attends school regularly and constantly chides Randolph for his "hooky-playing." Randolph is a quiet, meek child, honest in his admission to his mother that he has not been to school in years. He was always a good student, but although he was able to read at a level several years above his grade, he had no tolerance for the continuous noise and confusion that characterized his school. Randolph is never with other children, or with other adults for that matter. He has spent the better part of the past four years in the Metropolitan Museum of Art. Although he has patronized all of the city's museums, he prefers the Met, and humbly claims that he is now familiar with each piece in the museum's standing collection. He recalls being cornered there one afternoon by a class of children he had grown up with from the school he should have attended, a class that might have been his own. He hid motionless behind a Minoan vase for twenty minutes until the danger had passed. Randolph paints and draws on his own, but derives far more pleasure from seeing and studying art in the museums.

Danny Hartman is another dropout. His life is consumed by drawing and tracing figures from comic books and art books, which he borrows from the public library. He can mimic perfectly the drawings of Leonardo and Michelangelo and the most intricate of Rembrandt's etchings. He stayed in school, reluctantly, until the spring of his eighth-grade year. Although lonely and unhappy within the mainstream of the school, Danny was discovered by an art teacher who encouraged him to apply for admission to the High

School of Music and Art. For three years she saw to it that he attended daily classes in English and math, and she allowed him to work in her room while cutting gym, science, typing, and social studies. He worked slowly, deliberately, and precisely. He was lauded for his talents by his fellow students and was in the eyes of his art teacher a "clear genius." His work was extraordinary. The portfolio he had amassed by Christmas of his eighth-grade year was breathtaking. A reporter from the New York *Times* who visited the school's spring festival saw the quality of the artwork of several of the children and ran a story on it in the following day's paper. The Museum of Natural History was impressed by the article and sent an emissary to the school to examine the work. As a result, the museum agreed to renovate a room and use it exclusively for a six-month exhibition of student art from that school. Seven of Danny Hartman's works hung in the exhibition.

But the High School of Music and Art did not admit Danny. His accomplishments on standardized reading and math tests were unconvincing and his cumulative grade-point average was distorted by his many class cuts and subsequent failures. Although his portfolio was outstanding, his overall application was not up to par. The day that Danny received word that he had been denied admission to Music and Art was the last day he ever spent in school. His mother claims that he now leaves the house only once or twice a week to visit the library and pick up a new volume of paintings or etchings. He has no friends, no burning ambitions, no direction. He's happiest when he is both alone and at work.

Gregory Miller is a fourteen-year-old boy who belongs in the eighth grade. In the fifth grade he was an excellent student. He had the highest reading score in a school of almost seven hundred children; he was absent only two of one hundred and eighty school days. Although without many friends, he seemed satisfied with life at school. During the summer of his fifth-grade year, his parents separated. As the only child, he went to live with his mother. He was heartbroken at the turn of events, unable to understand the reasons for what had happened, caught off guard. His mother had a new man move into the apartment with his three children, and Gregory was further distressed. He ran away twice, each time for three days, but each time he returned his mother seemed hardly to have noticed his absence. He overheard her on the telephone one afternoon urging his father to take him for a while; he heard her say that he had become a "pain in the butt" and that she didn't want him around anymore. He left his mother and moved in with his father that evening. He has not seen her since.

By the time school opened in September, he had become a different child. He fought every vestige and symbol of authority, and his daily outbursts ended in his shuttling back and forth between the classroom and the principal's office. His father, who showed great patience and understanding and who was as crushed by his wife's sudden departure as Gregory was, clung to Gregory more than Gregory clung to him. He was in the school regularly throughout the winter (he repaired potholes for a living and worked long hours in the warmer months but was off most of the winter) trying to do whatever he could to offset Gregory's rebelliousness. He spoiled him with favors and gifts, and took him to see the Ali-Frazier fight, even though Gregory had spent the morning in court. He stopped dating women for fear of making Gregory jealous. He devoted all of his free time on the weekends to his son. He loved him.

But Gregory's situation grew worse. He started playing hooky and staying away from school for weeks at a time. By the middle of his seventh-grade year, he was a truant. He no longer went to school at all and he no longer lied to his father about going. He stayed home from school and sat in the house reading books. His father claims that Gregory had at least thirty books out of the public library at any given time. All of Gregory's allowance went to the payment of fines. He rarely left the house and almost never spent any time with other children. He understood solitude. During the most recent of his trips to court for truancy (he only ends up in court because his father continues to push the issue, although he is quick to confess that he is uncertain whether or not he is doing the right thing), the judge asked Gregory what the devil he does all day in the house alone.

"I read," he replied.

"Comic books?" the judge said sarcastically.

"No," returned Gregory in earnest, "the book I am reading now is *The Rise and Fall of the Third Reich*."

The judge was stunned, not sure whether Gregory was putting him on or not.

"What do you think of Hitler?"

"Most of the time he seemed pretty smart," Gregory answered, "but I think he was stupid for breaking his nonaggression pact and invading Russia."

Gregory has been to court five times; each time the judge has threatened to send him away if he should appear in court again, and each time he exacts a promise from Gregory that he will return to school. But none of the court appearances have in any fashion altered Gregory's behavior. He continues to read voluminously; he continues to spend his days at home; he continues to face life alone.

Glen Pointer's father is a full-blooded Iroquois Indian who is now back on a reservation in upstate New York. He drinks a great deal and, when drunk, gets embroiled in barroom brawls that have left his face and his life permanently scarred. One of those scars is his twelve-year-old son Glen. Glen has been a truant since the end of his third-grade year. He is afraid of school and the impositions it makes on his life. He guards his freedom and his feelings closely. He is reluctant to acknowledge his birth date and his heritage (he is half Iroquois and half Irish, but discloses his father's existence to no one). He is as uncomfortable on the streets of New York as he is in its schools. He dreads confrontation of any sort: with the police, who badger him about why he is not in school; with groups of other truants, who invariably pester him; with people on the streets who look accusingly at him and awaken his guilt for not being in school.

Glen Pointer lives in Central Park. He claims that he knows every square foot of its terrain. He can pinpoint hovels and hiding places of woodchucks and rabbits few other New Yorkers ever even see. He says he has climbed every tree in the park and has sat high up in some of the taller ones for as long as an entire spring day, studying the people who pass below. He cherishes the solitude the park offers. His mother is aware of his way of living but incapable of altering it, though she has tried endlessly to do so. In her opinion his attraction to the taste of the wilderness that the park offers is part of his inheritance from his father. When Glen Pointer was asked by his mother to identify his best friends, he was unable to name even one.

Donna has not been to school more than twenty days in the last four years. She is a bright, expressive child with a warmth that seems incongruous with the life she has chosen to lead. Donna rarely leaves her apartment. She spends her days alternately sleeping and watching television. She knows every program on every channel every hour of the day. She can tell you the names of hosts of quiz shows, characters in cartoons, and actors in old movies. She tells time by the television, accurate to within two or three minutes. On the opening day of school in her sixth-grade year, which Donna chose to attend, she wrote the following composition on what she thought of school:

"School is no place for a girl like me to be. Most of the children come to school and jive around and be-bop and think they are slick. There are too many fights in school. The streets of New York aren't much better. Most of the buildings are in bad shape and the street-corners are crowded with bums and junkies. Children need models to copy to help them grow up, but where I live all models you see just get you in trouble. This is why I probably won't be in school too much this year or downstairs."

Like most of her compatriots, Donna was without either family or friends. Her young mother had dumped her in the lap of an aunt. Although the aunt had become Donna's legal guardian, relations between them were characterized more by tolerance than affection.

Raymond found the freedom and peace he sought in the flight of the pigeons he raised. Although of junior high school age, he was not even certain which school he was supposed to go to. His attendance in school had been irregular as early as the fourth grade; by the fifth grade he was out altogether. He lived with his mother, who was an incurable alcoholic, and his five brothers and sisters, each of whom were at different stages of dropping out of school. They lived in a battered two-bedroom apartment on the top floor of a five-story walkup. The door in the hallway opposite his apartment led to the roof. Because the building was occupied primarily by elderly people, he was the only person who ever took advantage of the roof. His brothers and sisters were too involved in the pulse of the streets to have any interest in the pigeons that consumed Raymond's life. As a nine-year-old boy he had nursed a lame orange-pink pigeon back to full health. He built her a sturdy cage of furring strips and chicken wire on the roof. Queenie, as he called her, multiplied and, with each multiplication, Raymond had expanded the pigeons' living quarters, collecting the wood from construction sites in his neighborhood and stealing nails and chicken wire from a hardware store on Flatbush Avenue. His mother claimed that she knew nothing of her son's pastime until nearly a year after it began, when he shyly confessed that he had not been disappearing to school each morning, but instead had been slipping quietly to the roof. He then proudly took her hand and led her to his hideaway. She says that there were twenty birds, each with its own spacious cage and separate dish for food and water. The roughly constructed cages were assembled into a complex "habitation" arrangement, that allowed each bird fresh air and sunlight and provided Raymond easy access to each cage door. Raymond had gone to the trouble of using a dictionary to ensure the proper spelling of each bird's name, which he had written above its respective cage.

When he released the birds, they always returned when he waved a small white handkerchief he kept in his hip pocket. At times he would release all twenty and marvel as they cut broad swaths across the late afternoon sky, circling the building as many as a dozen times, reminiscent of their kin in San Marco, and then hurl themselves in perilously close formation toward the small boy waving his white handkerchief, stopping a breathtaking second before landing on their dwelling. Raymond was so protective of his birds that he had decided long ago never to show them to his peers on the streets. Like so many others he had no real friends.

Stanley can't remember the last time he was in school. He can't remember his teacher's name or the name of the girl who sat next to him. He's not sure what floor his last classroom was on or what grade he was in. His mother insists that it was the fifth grade but is unclear about whether Stanley had been promoted or had been retained. The walls surrounding Stanley's bed are adorned with several brightly colored maps of the New York City bus and subway routes. Between the stops on each line on each map, Stanley has neatly penciled in two travel times: one for rush-hour traffic, the other for regular traffic. On the floor by his bed, he maintains a log of his daily MTA travels, with notes on which subway stations are being remodeled and the dates on which bus routes are adjusted. Stanley still goes to school one day a month but only to collect a free transportation pass. (Pupil transportation costs city, state, and federal taxpayers over $140 million a year.)

Stanley rides alone. On the subways he paces the length of the train, noting the number of cars used on different lines during different hours, the cleanliness of the cars, and the changes in the advertising displays. Stanley can name Miss Subway all the way back to 1967. He grows irritated when he speaks about the condition of the cars on certain lines; nostalgic about the disappearance of the corncob-seat cars on the FF trains. Stanley is a weary old man of thirteen. His reputation as a connoisseur of mass transit extends far and wide; his mother tells of complete strangers who knock on her apartment door to seek Stanley's advice on the quickest route to St. John's Street in Brooklyn. Although he is proud to share his knowledge, Stanley is anything but warm to outsiders and treasures the solitude that riding the trains and buses affords. School is a thing of the past for Stanley, much as dolls and cap guns are for other children.

The plight of New York's new truants stands in quiet condemnation of the rest of us.

Doin' Good

ACHIEVEMENT IS THE STITCHING that holds the fabric of the American Dream in place. The will to achieve is a unique personal expression with a largely collective impact. Achievement defies impossibility. Americans measure their successes against those of their fellow citizens — the essence of competition — and they measure their successes of today against those of yesterday — the essence of growth.

Schools are the traditional proving grounds for the achievers. They have served the function of sifting and separating the winners from the losers. Public educational institutions have been able to fulfill this function only as long as they could establish the rules of the game. If an A is awarded in first grade for outstanding productivity and achievement in, say, copying a row of capital T's, that A stands as the true measure of success only if the child thought the task important in the first place. If, on the other hand, the child couldn't have been less interested in or challenged by the job of copying a row of capital *T*'s, and was instead intent upon mastering a new overlapping grip on her pencil that *she* invented, her personal success or failure depends entirely on her mastery of the new grip. The unwritten agenda for schooling since its compulsory inception has been to make the objectives of the schools agree with those of their students. For the longest time that seemed simple and could be taken for granted. Parents sent their children to school to learn the three R's; children came to school to learn the three R's; and teachers sought employment in schools to teach the three R's. The unanimity of purpose made the measurement of success or failure a relatively reliable matter.

Schools are cast in the New York press as being miserable failures. Sixty-seven percent of New York City's 1.1 million students read below grade level. A look at equivalent figures for other urban areas suggests that New York is far from alone: Cincinnati (74 percent), Atlanta (73 percent), Baltimore (70 percent), Detroit (61 percent), and Cleveland (61 percent). In New York that translates into 737,000 children. The average New York City second grader scores .1 years below level; the average third grader, .4 years below; the average fourth grader, .7 years below; the average fifth grader, .8 years below; the average sixth grader, 1.0 years below; the average seventh grader, 1.3 years below; and the average eighth grader, 1.8 years below: a portrait that suggests that the longer the children stay in school, the farther behind they fall.

Eleven districts show at least 30 percent of their students two or more years below grade level. Of the elementary schools, 201 show at least 75 percent of their students below grade level. Of the junior high schools, 61 have fewer than 15 percent of their children reading on level. One junior high school has 2.8 percent of its pupils on grade level. In thirteen districts, not a single junior high school has more than 25 percent of the children at or above grade level. Of the 116 junior high schools in Manhattan, the Bronx, and Brooklyn, 79 show more than 75 percent of their students below grade level. None of these figures include the truants and hall-walkers who are not around to take the tests.

What the papers assume, and in their defense they must assume it, is that all those of the school community are of common purpose. If this assumption were accurate, then the use of grade-equivalent reading scores on standardized reading tests might be accurate measures of the success or failure of individual children and individual schools.

An art teacher who is devoting two months to helping a class produce an hour-long, sixteen-millimeter movie is only marginally, if at all, concerned with reading scores. She would never measure her success or failure in terms of her students' success in reading. Similarly, a student starring in that movie will cherish his performance on the screen far more than his performance on a multiple-choice answer grid.

What lies at the very heart of the matter of success or failure is an estimation of each individual's ego. A child discouraged by difficulty in learning to read, write, and add columns of fractions with different denominators will intuitively seek out another path by which he can pass his time in school, achieve some success, and not diminish his ego by failure to "do good" according to the norms the school chooses to espouse. Children redefine the issue into one of alternative value structures. Teachers, too, place their egos on the line and make considerable compromises in the quality and quantity of their daily objectives in order to retain an image of themselves as competent, as growing, as achieving, and as succeeding. Principals, paraprofessionals, guidance counselors, and door guards also have altered their day-to-day ambitions in order to ensure some measure of success in their own minds. The tragedy of the public schools is not that they are not rampant with tales of success, they are; but that the nature and purpose of their ambitions have been so greatly compromised.

Tales of "success" in school, in fact, abound. Barbara Hoffman, a seventh grader, not the kind of child about whom teachers would say "Oh isn't she cute," measures her success by the grades that *end up* on her report card. She strives for a straight-A average at each marking period. Most of the time she is able to get those grades through diligence and hard work, but when her best efforts fall short, she says "the fun really begins." Both her parents are willing to come to school on a moment's notice to "get those B's and C's corrected to A's." They badger the teachers and the principal; they will muckrake their personal lives if need be; they have gone so far as to threaten suits on "due process" and procedure. Barbara's idea of the best day she ever had in school was when her parents had three grades changed to A's in a single afternoon and reduced both the cooking and physical education teachers to tears. (If you've ever spent any time among girls' gym teachers you know that was no mean feat.) Barbara has never once missed the straight-A honor roll.

James Data, a blond, blue-eyed, bright-looking little fifth grader, whose teachers might well have said "Oh isn't he cute" (until he opened his mouth), measures success by the expletives he calls his teachers and gets away with. Although suspended from school several times, and often sent home early to his distressed mother, he remembers the day he threw a screaming and cursing fit in math class, was dragged through a gauntlet of open-mouthed fellow students directly to the *principal*'s office, where he called the principal a "cunt-face" (that should perhaps be spelled as one word — I've never seen it in print), and his mother never heard a word of the entire incident.

Lois Paulson, a veteran of twelve years of teaching, measures the success of any given year by the amount of work — preparing lessons, keeping records, and correcting papers — that she is forced to do at home. In a great year, and she confesses that she has had a few, she is home in front of the soap operas by three-fifteen every single day and does not do one lick of preparation for the entire year.

John Blau, a slow fifth grader, is happy just to remember his locker combination from one day to the next. (It is interesting to note that it has now become highly unfashionable to talk about "dumb" kids. Anyone who broaches the subject is branded a racist, an anti-Semite, or both. Unfortunately, the quarantine on discussion of such children has done little to decrease the numbers in the average school.)

Mrs. Weistonary, a diminutive fifth-grade teacher at a volatile uptown school, measures her successes not by what happens in the course of a day, but by what could have happened and did not. On a fair day she will be cussed at in only two or three of her six teaching periods, walk the halls uneventfully, and even have a small but measurable percentage of her students paying attention to her lessons. On a good day she will not suffer a single word of abuse, she will command the attention of most of her students, and one of the secretaries in the main office will pronounce her name correctly. On a great day, in addition to all of the above, some child will bring in his homework. "Teaching," she says, "is like being in love. It's either all the way up, or all the way down."

To Melissa McDuff, a junior high school student, success means getting to school and to each of her classes on time. "It's only happened once this year," she laments, "but when it happens, it sure makes you feel proud."

Principal James Harold defines "doin' good" as keeping parents away from his school and out of his office. His experience with parents, as is true of most principals, is that when things are going well with their children, they'll stay away. But when their axes need grinding, they come in droves. Being well enough acquainted with individual parents to know whose backs to scratch over the telephone, and those who need to be roughly intimidated, is part of his personal strategy in keeping his office empty and in achieving his own personal form of success.

Keith Erickson's idea of success is to have his dog follow him to school and slip unnoticed into the building. Invariably "Duke" throws classes and entire corridors into a blissful panic and Keith ends up paged to the principal's office *over the public-address system* and being instructed to leave school and take the dog home immediately. Keith's achievement is twofold: first in attracting all that attention — he thrives on it — and second in getting permission to be out of school for what usually amounts to at least an hour (he takes in a few unscheduled stops along the way). The greatest of those great days included being stopped and queried by the law and being able to produce a written pass excusing his mission, one endorsed by none other than the principal himself.

Sheila, a fifth grader, goes to school primarily to steal. On even her most inauspicious days she snatches an extra dessert or a chocolate milk from a neighbor's tray as he turns his head for a fraction of a second. A successful day nets her at least a set of keys, a driver's license, and once, her teacher's paycheck. On a great day a well-planned ruse will pan out: like the time she told all the girls in her class to bring ten dollars to school for cheerleading suits and went home with eighty dollars in cold cash. On another day she heard that thirty dollars was nestling in the coat pocket of an unidentified fellow student (whose intention was to buy a new pair of shoes after school), and started dipping into her classmates' coat pockets during gym period. She hit the thirty dollars on the first dip. Part of Sheila's success is due to her mother, who comes to school to back her daughter to the hilt no matter how weighty the evidence against Sheila may be. "Did you *see* her take it?" she hollers. The principal is convinced that Sheila is only her mother's agent, which would mean that Sheila's idea of "doin' good" meshes neatly with her mother's.

Mr. Williamson, a school custodian, measures the success of a day according to the number of clogged toilets he is called upon to unclog, a perfectly inverse relationship. He dreads the flu season.

Chucky Rodríguez, a twelve-year-old, whose idea of success in school revolves around being the center of his peers' attention, recalls his finest hour. During the five minutes between seventh and eighth periods he slipped into the boys' room, and slipped out of his clothes — all of them. He "streaked" the length of the cor-ridor and down a back staircase, where he hurriedly got dressed (he had carried his clothing in his arm à la O. J. Simpson). He slipped out the back door, raced around to another entrance at the far extremity of the large building, and rapped on the door to his wood-shop class. He apologized to Mr. Baker for his tardiness (school people never say "lateness") and explained that he had dropped into his guidance counselor's office momentarily to pick up a high school handbook. By the time the assistant principal caught up with Chucky's caper, Chucky was hard at work sanding the rough edges of his bookends. The audacity of Chucky's act cannot be over-stated. Whereas high school and college "streakers" are usually ad-vertising their bodies, Chucky was barely through the initial stages

of puberty. Chucky claimed that, being new to the school and needing desperately to establish a reputation, he had no other alternative. When notified by the school of his son's daring, Mr. Rodríguez
lamented, "Oh my God, my oldest boy Roger did the same thing in
high school yesterday."

Success to Robin Callas means talking and acting big and bad
when he knows he is outweighed and will have to rely on his fleet-
ness of foot, which is considerable. One of his fondest memories is of
a fall afternoon in front of the Museum of Modern Art during a class
trip. Believing that a hot-pretzel vendor had shortchanged him,
Robert and his sidekick Angus, each of whom weighed all of sixty
pounds, unloaded on the man.

"Fuck him up, Angus! Tip over his fuckin' wagon! Kick his butt!
Mister, I should tighten your cheap-ass motherfuckin' self up good!"
And then in a moment of apparent mercy, "But this time I'm gonna
let you slide."

Robin claims that this kind of performance, which he knows the
class delights in and is confident that the teacher will break up, is
what "doin' good" in school is all about.

Cheryl claims that the best thing about school is not going. She
confesses correctly that she hasn't been in the building for more
than two years. And although she dreads the inevitable court scenes
and her father's frequent beatings, she treasures the solitude she
finds in being home alone. Cheryl recalls a day when the school
social worker came to her apartment and she unleashed her German
shepherd in his direction; another, when she spotted her father
coming home early and she slipped into the basement and hid. Ten
minutes later, books under each arm, she rang the doorbell and
began telling her father about her day at school.

To Connie, succeeding in school means writing "Connie 132 as
The Fox" in chartreuse Magic Marker in every conceivable place,
and not getting caught: on the subway walls, along the halls, inside
her desk, all over the walls of the girls' room, and perhaps even
boldly on the counter in the main office.

To nurse Mrs. T., a good day at school implies that some of the
children who appeared for treatment actually needed it.

Shirley Larou, a buxom and vivacious school secretary, who turns the main office into a warehouse for "hot" clothes whenever the boss is at a meeting downtown, measures her days by the pairs of shoes she sells or by the orders for dresses and jewelry she records on what she refers to as "Shirley Originals."

Jimmy Richardson weighs the measure of a day by the number of classes he is able to cut without repercussion. On a good day he misses six of eight; on a great one he ducks them all without ever leaving the building.

To a boy named Kid "doin' good" in school means showing up for gym class every Tuesday at one-thirty and pouring in forty points in the next ninety minutes. The rest of the "junk at school," he says, "ain't worth my time."

For Joe Anville a successful day at school means lurking in the boys' bathroom by the cafeteria at lunchtime and shaking down scared little boys for nickels and dimes. On a good day Joe will gross six or seven dollars and not get ripped off in return.

For "Champ" a good day in school will net twenty bucks from sales of tiny bags of pot, pills, and a white powder he advertises as cocaine but says "is really only chalk dust. I'm only playin' with 'em."

To Samson Sorruellas success in school is measured by the fights he is able to generate and those he is able to win. In a good year — fourth grade he remembers as his best — he was involved in at least one fight a day. Aggravating and cussing out teachers, he adds, is a close second in terms of good clean fun. To the great dismay of his teachers, Samson's attendance is nearly perfect.

Victor Oster, eleven years old, is not satisfied unless he smokes at least a half pack of cigarettes a day. He accomplishes his aim in the few minutes between classes, after lunch, and any other time he can squeeze a smoke in.

Mrs. Perry is pleased when half the class does half the work. The teacher across the hall is only happy with the same children when all of them do all of their work.

To Mark Margolis the greatest moments in school are those spent "squeezing titties" and "patting behinds." "Squeezing some big titties on a Monday," claims Mark, "can make you feel good for the rest of the week." Fortunately for Mark, and others like him, plenty of girls go to school exclusively to get their "behinds" patted and their "titties" squeezed.

Learning the three R's, scoring well on standardized reading tests, and bringing home excellent report cards continue to motivate some children and most teachers. But for far too many children these are no longer primary concerns: not one of the R's is mastered; the answer grids on the reading tests are filled in while the seal on the textual part of the exam remains unbroken; and report cards never make it all the way home. But this means not that many students are not "doin' good," but that in the eyes of the children the schools are measuring the wrong commodities. Success is a largely personal phenomenon, combining the concerns of id, ego, and superego in a delicate balance that the bigness and blindness of the public schools are unable to understand, incorporate, or amend. How long schools can continue to function at cross purposes with so many of their clients is open to speculation.

Acting Out

I SPENT THE PAST decade studying, teaching in, and administering urban schools. Like so many others, many of whom contributed far more time and effort than I did, I tried to leave my mark. I did take part in a great deal of learning — but too much of that learning was my own.

Of my original thirty-two sixth-grade homeroom children, three are now in college, two have been murdered and one has committed murder, two are imprisoned on Riker's Island, at least one is a prostitute. Fewer than half finished high school; four never even showed up to start high school. Most of them have low-paying, low-skilled jobs; two have moved back down South; five are mothers and three of these are on welfare; the rest are either on the streets or have disappeared.

I no longer work in the New York public schools. I am studying law at Columbia. I left public education worn out, exasperated from trying to cope with an institution at odds with its own clients. I had

251

begun to regard the tremendous energy, vitality, and chaos in the schools as insurmountable obstacles. I had begun to see discipline, decorum, and order as ends in themselves — and I had begun to despair. The plight of the schools seemed drearier, less amusing, less hopeful, more desperate.

But I find I miss the New York schools — less for what they could be but for what they actually are. I miss chasing Samson Sorruellas out of the hallways; I miss lamenting over Jeffrey Atherton's ravaged scrapbook. I miss sending Richard Licker packing. I miss watching children climb all over each other to catch a glimpse of a snowflake or avoid a dog or escape a fart. I miss hearing people say "O-O-O-O-O *sit!*" and complain of "bein' abuuuused."

I miss the hallway confrontations and the parlays in the Teachers' Room. I miss the tenure struggles and holding the hands of rookie teachers. I miss reading notes about flying grapes, donuts, and dictionaries. I miss the flamboyance of educational politics and even the irritations of the public-address system. I miss Dobson Bradley, and Lord knows I miss Three-fingered Theotis Davis.

I wonder what has happened to Gregory and Stanley and Raymond and Glen and Danny and Randolph and the thousands of others like them in the hundreds of schools around the city. I wonder who is looking after Donna, whose aunt never really cared for her. I wonder whether Mr. Caldwell has had to grapple with a successor to the Mad Crapper.

I miss the public schools. And it is the very chaos and vitality that wore me out that I miss the most.

Belinda Davis, who set K. B. Wilson on fire the first day I ever spent in the public schools, turned out to be a success. She is now a junior at Smith College. Her competitiveness and ferocity touched all she did. But there are too few successes in the New York public schools. I miss Belinda Davis but I also miss Hank Hawkins, who died after drinking a quart of wood alcohol. He simply refused to *believe* that he couldn't meet that challenge, that he couldn't drink that quart and come on bigger and badder than ever. He was no less proud of himself than Belinda Davis will ever be of herself.

I understand what Principal Holtzman meant when he scorned

that proposal on his desk. He *did* have too many acting-out children in his school. If the children in the New York public schools were ever given grounds to believe that education is a challenge worth taking on, I would love to have a part in the acting-out that would take place then.